Threats, Disinformation, and Regulations in the European Digital Environment

Threats, Disinformation, and Regulations in the European Digital Environment

The Inseparable Issues

Edited by
Kateřina Turková and Veronika Macková

BLOOMSBURY ACADEMIC
NEW YORK • LONDON • OXFORD • NEW DELHI • SYDNEY

BLOOMSBURY ACADEMIC
Bloomsbury Publishing Inc, 1359 Broadway, New York, NY 10018, USA
Bloomsbury Publishing Plc, 50 Bedford Square, London, WC1B 3DP, UK
Bloomsbury Publishing Ireland, 29 Earlsfort Terrace, Dublin 2, D02 AY28, Ireland

BLOOMSBURY, BLOOMSBURY ACADEMIC and the Diana logo are trademarks of Bloomsbury Publishing Plc

First published in the United States of America 2026

A catalog record for this book is available from the Library of Congress

ISBN: HB: 978-1-6669-7208-5
ePDF: 979-8-216-26526-9
eBook: 978-1-9787-5969-5

Typeset by Newgen KnowledgeWorks Pvt. Ltd., Chennai, India

For product safety related questions contact productsafety@bloomsbury.com.

To find out more about our authors and books visit www.bloomsbury.com
and sign up for our newsletters.

Contents

Acknowledgments

This book was supported by Resilient Media for Democracy in the Digital Age (ReMeD), an international multidisciplinary project supported by the European Union's Horizon Europe Research and Innovation Programme, HORIZON-CL2-2022-DEMOCRACY-01-06: "Media for Democracy—Democratic Media," under grant agreement no. 101094742.

Research in Chapters 1, 2, 3, 4, 9, and 10 has been funded by the European Union. Views and opinions expressed are, however, those of the author(s) only and do not necessarily reflect those of the European Union or the granting authorities named in each chapter. Neither the European Union nor the granting authorities can be held responsible for such views and opinions.

Conflict of Interest Statement: No potential conflict of interest was reported by any of the authors.

Preface

Kateřina Turková

This book is dedicated to the current threats, disinformation, and regulations in the European digital environment. As past research shows, these phenomena are inseparable, and it is then effective to understand them in the broader context (Datzer and Lonardo 2022; Nannini et al. 2024; Shattock 2021), which is exactly what this publication—dedicated to the Resilient Media for Democracy in the Digital Age (ReMeD), an international multidisciplinary project supported by the European Union's Horizon Europe Research and Innovation Programme—seeks to offer.

Despite the ongoing initiatives and efforts to harmonize the European digital environment, geographical, historical, and cultural differences still prevail (Humprecht et al., 2022). Due to that, the body of research covering the aforementioned issues needs to be further expanded. This edited volume not only covers the general state in Europe and/or the European Union but also provides regional or country-specific insights into the legislature or concrete cases. Where possible, the cases are illustrated by examples.

This book is thematically divided into four parts that cover the threats, disinformation, and regulations predominantly in the European digital environment, while the parts, respectively the chapters, appropriately complement each other. The first part, entitled "Mapping the Threats and Trust in Disinformation in the European Digital Environment," aims to document the threats and trust in disinformation in the European digital environment based on evidence from European countries. Because the COVID-19 pandemic and the vaccination were accompanied by various disinformation and, in a certain sense, also paved the way for further initiatives (Bajwa 2021), the first chapter[1] uses the example of COVID-19 vaccination for illustration of the trust in information sources in two post-communist countries with common past, Czechia and Slovakia.

While this region is particularly vulnerable to disinformation, fake messages, and alternative truth (Gregor and Mlejnková 2021), the third chapter[2] tackles the concrete narratives related to COVID-19 and war in Ukraine spread on

Czech disinformation websites. The second chapter[3] focuses on disinformation and hate speech against migrants, both from the legal and practical sides; hence, it has become a highly actual topic of discussion along with multiculturalism and cosmopolitanism (Johansson 2022).

However, this book seeks not only to sum up or even criticize the current situation but also offers or contributes to finding solutions. The second part of the edited volume, called "Approaches to Threats and Combatting Disinformation in the European Digital Environment: Examples of Good Practices," summarizes the efforts given to the threats' prevention and tackling disinformation in different countries. The chapter entitled "Attempting to Fight Disinformation without Jeopardizing Media and Speech Freedom: A Comparative Analysis of Eight European Countries"[4] compares the approaches used in Austria, Belgium, Czechia, Germany, Ireland, Norway, Spain, and the UK. The subsequent chapters then describe the fight against disinformation in Croatia,[5] respectively public policy support in Romania.[6] Thanks to that, the examples of good practices can be identified and possibly implemented in the whole European digital environment in the future.

With the attempts to combat disinformation and fake news in the digital sphere, regulatory initiatives appeared, and the new legislature has slowly but surely come into force (Marsden et al. 2020; Tenove 2020). The third part of this edited volume, entitled "Regulations in the European Digital Environment in Relation to Disinformation," then begins with a chapter debating the legal aspects of disinformation[7] while explaining the relationship between disinformation and freedom of expression at the European level as defined by the most important human rights document—the European Convention on Human Rights (van Dijk and van Hoof 2023). The European Union's attempts to fight and prevent disinformation are outlined in the subsequent chapter.[8] Nevertheless, the country-specific legislation and legislature have also evolved under these circumstances, as the final chapter in this part devoted to the new Spanish law on journalism and media[9] confirms.

Although the progress that has been made both in prevention and in interventions is non-negotiable, new threats related to the aforementioned issues appear. The fourth and final part of this book—"Current Challenges of the European Digital Environment in Relation to Disinformation"—disputes two among many of them. The first chapter of this part[10] aims at hate speech and hate crime in the European digital environment while touching on the problems, documented effects, and coping mechanisms. The final chapter of the edited volume[11] covers the topic of potentially misleading visual content in the context of military conflicts and wars, while the questions related to ethics are raised by the authors.

As previously stated, this publication can offer an overview of both the current state and in-depth insights into country-specific issues or concrete cases within the European digital environment. It presents the results of the analyses and outlines the possible solutions. While taking that into account, the book can be useful not only for academics but also for media practitioners and the general public.

Notes

1 See Chapter 1, this volume.
2 See Chapter 3, this volume.
3 See Chapter 2, this volume.
4 See Chapter 4, this volume.
5 See Chapter 5, this volume.
6 See Chapter 6, this volume.
7 See Chapter 7, this volume.
8 See Chapter 8, this volume.
9 See Chapter 9, this volume.
10 See Chapter 10, this volume.
11 See Chapter 11, this volume.

References

Bajwa, Aman. 2021. "Information disorder, the Triumvirate, and COVID-19: How media outlets, foreign state intrusion, and the far-right diaspora drive the COVID-19 anti-vaccination movement." *Journal of Intelligence, Conflict, and Warfare* 4 (2): 16–45. https://doi.org/10.21810/jicw.v4i2.3067.

Datzer, Veronika, and Luigi Lonardo. 2022. "Genesis and evolution of EU anti disinformation policy: Entrepreneurship and political opportunism in the regulation of digital technology." *Journal of European Integration* 45 (5): 751–66. https://doi.org/10.1080/07036337.2022.2150842.

Gregor, Miloš, and Petra Mlejnková. 2021. "Facing disinformation: Narratives and manipulative techniques deployed in the Czech Republic." *Politics in Central Europe Sciendo* 17 (3): 541–64. https://doi.org/10.2478/pce-2021-0023.

Humprecht, Edda, Laia Castro Herrero, Sina Blassnig, Michael Brüggemann, and Sven Engesser. 2022. "Media systems in the digital age: An empirical comparison of 30 countries." *Journal of Communication* 72 (2): 145–64. https://doi.org/10.1093/joc/jqab054.

Johansson, Thomas Roland. 2022. "In defence of multiculturalism: Theoretical challenges." *International Review of Sociology* 34 (1): 75–89. https://doi.org/10.1080/03906701.2022.2045141.

Marsden, Chris, Trisha Meyer, and Ian Brown. 2020. "Platform values and democratic elections: How can the law regulate digital disinformation?" *Computer Law & Security Review* 36: 105373. https://doi.org/10.1016/j.clsr.2019.105373.

Nannini, Luca, Eleonora Bonel, Davide Bassi, and Michele Joshua Maggini. 2024. "Beyond phase-in: Assessing impacts on disinformation of the EU Digital Services Act." *AI and Ethics*. https://doi.org/10.1007/s43681-024-00467-w.

Shattock, Ethan. 2021. "Self-regulation 2:0? A critical reflection of the European fight against disinformation." *Harvard Kennedy School Misinformation Review* 2 (3). https://doi.org/10.37016/mr-2020-73.

Tenove, Chris. 2020. "Protecting democracy from disinformation: Normative threats and policy responses." *International Journal of Press/Politics* 25 (3): 517–37. https://doi.org/10.1177/1940161220918740.

van Dijk, Pieter, and Godefridus J. H. van Hoof. 2023. *Theory and practice of the European Convention on Human Rights*. Martinus Nijhoff.

Part 1

Mapping the Threats and Trust in Disinformation in the European Digital Environment

1

Trust in Information Sources in Czechia and Slovakia Using the Example of COVID-19 Vaccination

Kateřina Turková, Ľuboš Greguš, Jana Radošinská, and Veronika Macková

Eroding Trust in Czechia and Slovakia

Contemporary European society deals with a plethora of serious issues. Almost all of them are becoming increasingly urgent due to one persistent problem: the ways we perceive information (or rather underestimate disinformation and fake news). However, the core issue does not lie in the nature of the (dis)information itself but rather in our careless and indifferent attitudes toward it. Our willingness to acknowledge that fake news and disinformation pose a serious threat to democracy, citizenship, and political stability is, therefore, the most important first step to take. Moreover, people's information literacy is the key to evaluating whether information is true or false, even though our personal opinions on specific topics and political views may differ. Without precise information, we are unable to make informed and competent decisions as citizens, parents, or members of any other societal group we identify with. If we cannot find out whether the information is correct or incorrect in its nature, we usually evaluate it based on its source. In this context, we need to talk about the credibility of news and news media, especially about our trust in the media.

In this confusing, ever-changing world, our need to stay well-informed is only growing stronger, but given the information chaos around us, which includes a whirlwind of contradictory media messages and a wide spectrum of controversy, it is literally impossible to verify everything (Škarba and Višňovský 2022). The number of news sources is practically unlimited, mainly in the online environment, and not all of them are produced and maintained by professionals who respect ethical or professional standards and values. Therefore, we find it crucial to know which information sources are trustworthy in the recipients' eyes and why and how often they are willing to search for them again to obtain news items they perceive as having quality.

Academic research focusing on trust in news media is anything but new; however, this line of inquiry still retains its timeless importance. Based on what we experienced during the COVID-19 pandemic and in terms of the ongoing war in Ukraine, we may claim that production of fake news and disinformation has been strongly connected to international hybrid threats and global security risks. To predict the future processes shaping democratic societies, it is necessary to expand research focused on disinformation campaigns and hybrid intelligence operations occurring globally. The latest findings show that in Central and Eastern European countries, trust in the media has hit an all-time historical low. Only in four countries, including Czechia, more than 50 percent of people trust the media. In contrast, Slovak citizens express their long-term distrust in information disseminated by the media. Surprisingly, the public opinion on media freedom is rather positive. For example, in Czechia only 53 percent of people trust the media, but 72 percent of Czechs consider them as rather or completely free. In Slovakia, 64 percent of citizens regard the media as rather or completely free, but just 37 percent of Slovaks trust them. Such a trend can also be seen in the rest of the Visegrad Four (Hajdu et al. 2023).

The question is whether it is even possible to measure people's trust in something or someone only by simply asking them to articulate their opinions. In the recipient's mind, the word trust might possess a meaning that is quite different from the term's scholarly definition. Trust in media can be manifested, for example, by regular consumption of content offered by a specific media outlet or by the recipient's will to verify information obtained from a different source by confronting it with information stated by their preferred provider. That is why we center our attention on this semantic level in our research, focusing on two specifics connected to media trust: (1) which media the Czech and Slovak audiences use as their trusted information sources and thus repeatedly, and (2) to which media they turn to verify information encountered elsewhere.

In the empirical part of our chapter, we present the results of this representative research focused on Czechia and Slovakia. These two countries significantly differ in terms of their political development and cultural environment even though they share a considerable part of their cultural history and had the same "starting point" as independent countries. Both were founded on the same day due to the peaceful dissolution of Czechoslovakia in 1993; both are Member States of the European Union and NATO. They also share the cultural and sociological roots of common democratic and also totalitarian history during the twentieth century. However, their current media environments are diametrically different. Our goal is to define the main differences in Czech and Slovak audiences' habits in light of the trust parameters described above and to provide a clearer picture of their media preferences. To obtain more complex data we focus not only on information and verification sources in general, but especially on issues connected with the COVID-19 pandemic as one of the most significant global events of the century with an impact on the perception of information and COVID-19 vaccination.

Literature Review

Trust in Media and Other Information Sources

Scholarly discussions concerning the term *trust* are interdisciplinary in their nature because the topic is associated with a wider spectrum of sociological phenomena. In sociology, debates on trust represent a strong tradition claiming that collective life is stable only if we cross the boundaries of self-interest. Therefore, the element of trust is an essential part of social life (Scott 2014). Giddens (1990) claims that what we perceive as trust is our confidence that a person or system is reliable. Our current understanding of the term is, however, quite complicated. The so-called post-truth era limits our ability and willingness to trust anyone and anything. Moreover, the characteristic traits of the post-truth world weaken the effectiveness of educational systems (Peters 2017). While discussing the consequences of the post-truth era in terms of journalism and media production, we need to emphasize that today ideologies tend to undermine or even replace facts (van Bavel and Pereira 2018), limiting the audience's trust in information disseminated by the media. In a post-trust era, the general distrust in mediated content has become an unwelcome yet inevitable dimension of the journalist–audience relationship (Aharoni et al. 2022).

Multiple published studies also confirm that trust heavily influences the ways information is selected, received, and evaluated (e.g., Tsfati and Cappella 2003). Journalism studies have also addressed this issue and related phenomena quite extensively. Media trust is an extremely volatile communication phenomenon in its nature. Boosting trust in news media is reliant on the audience's willingness to share content online and personal relationships involving recipients and producers alike (Molitorisz 2020). We may also mention Quandt's (2012) contribution to the critical discussion on trust in terms of societal communication or extensive comparative analysis of public trust in the press conducted by Hanitzsch et al. (2018). Usher (2018) claims that rethinking what it means to trust in the news is necessary. According to the author, research into trust in journalism is critically flawed, because trust is usually measured as news consumption while the relational nature of trust (that includes journalists, audiences, sources, and other social actors) is mostly overlooked. This issue is particularly tempting in post-authoritarian and post-totalitarian countries (Němcová Tejkalová et al. 2017), thus also in Czechia and Slovakia. Political cynicism of journalists—which explicitly implies that all politicians are in fact greedy and selfish, seeing the public service as a means to fulfill their own business and personal interests—has inevitable society-wide consequences. Journalists' distrust in public institutions is strongly associated with questions of media freedom, corruption, and ownership (Hanitzsch and Berganza 2012).

Even though the rise of nonmainstream (and specifically conspiracy) media is a complex problem, media skepticism, that is, the audience's lack of trust in the (traditional) media and their credibility, is positively associated with seeking nonmainstream information sources and negatively associated with mainstream news exposure (Tsfati and Cappella 2003). Moreover, Kyriakidou et al. (2023) argue that many people are concerned with a much broader spectrum of pathological communication phenomena than just fake news and disinformation, mentioning their daily encounters with biased news, political spin, or manipulated information. While evaluating the credibility of journalistic information, the audiences naturally consider not only the message itself and its source but also the way the information is presented (Carr et al. 2014).

As noted by Peifer and Meisinger (2021), media transparency is often seen as a factor strengthening the credibility of news content in the eyes of the audience. Transparency is perceived as the media outlet's willingness to publicly disclose and communicate how their editorial processes work, how and why news items are selected and processed in the first place, who owns and finances that organization, and so on. However, the authors' study highlights the limitations of transparency in terms of increasing or at least maintaining news trust and engagement. What seems to be more significant, however, is people's ideological and political orientation (Blom 2021).

Previous studies (e.g., Wawrzyński 2022) confirm that ideological proximity contributes to the polarization of society (and its influence on media trust). Conservatives generally manifest lower trust in (mainstream) media, and they generally express higher belief in conspiracy theories (van der Linden et al. 2020). According to Reinemann et al. (2022), during the initial phase of the first lockdown in Germany, the perception of the severity of COVID-19, another heavily politicized topic, was influenced by several factors, including "the use of different information sources, the trust in these sources and the right-wing political attitudes" (2022, 134). A sizeable segment of the German population was not willing to acknowledge the risks of the pandemic, voicing their skeptical attitudes or even denial, and questioning the scientific consensus on which mitigating measures were based. These people's political views were strongly associated with right-wing populist attitudes and with low degrees of trust in traditional media, politics, and science as information sources (Reinemann et al. 2022).

The research undertaken by Ihlebæk and Holter (2021) confirms that certain groups of ideologically nonmainstream-oriented people feel strong fear, which constitutes their anger expressed toward mainstream news media. The ways mainstream news items are constructed do not match their everyday experience, and thus they consider those as highly provocative and inaccurate. In Slovakia, this phenomenon has led to the increased popularity of far-right political parties such as Republika (The Republic) represented by Milan Uhrík and Milan Mazurek. A similar strategy is applied by the Czech politician Tomio Okamura and his party SPD—*Svoboda a přímá demokracie* (Freedom and Direct Democracy Party) (Charvát et al. 2022).

Trust and Spread of Disinformation Narratives in Czechia and Slovakia

In terms of Slovakia and Czechia, recent studies and data tell us more about local and regional particularities related to trust in the media, as well as about universal traits possessed by Czech and Slovak media audiences that can be observed on a global scale. For example, Brník and Kapec (2021) focus on the ways in which Slovak radio listeners were impacted by the COVID-19 pandemic. The global pandemic is also addressed by Gálik and Gáliková Tolnaiová (2022), who discuss its consequences in terms of shaping media coverage of prominent societal topics. Quantitative analyses and data are available in Krajčovič's (2022) study on viewing figures and interactions achieved by Slovak elite media, tabloids, and conspiracy outlets present on Facebook during the COVID-19 outbreak. Chlebcová Hečková and Smith (2023) see the Slovak media scene as quite turbulent, like the current political situation in the country. Slovakia has recently witnessed continued attacks on journalists by politicians, incidents resulting from professional and ethical misconduct of journalists, and even cases of espionage. Trust of the Slovak people in news is very low (27 percent), which is the inevitable result of decades marked by business and political leaders interfering with the healthy and independent development of the country's media environment. The public broadcaster RTVS (Radio and Television of Slovakia)[1] still enjoys relatively high levels of trust, despite the organization's struggles to offer critical political reporting and fulfill its duty related to producing impartial news on the domestic political climate.

Lipka (2021) argues that many people in Slovakia tend to seek conspiracy theories to find simple answers to questions that are not easy to understand. Living in an ever-changing world full of complex phenomena, they need new certainties, maybe a new meaning of life. Irrational belief in disinformation provides these people with a feeling of exceptionality; they feel like they belong to a "chosen" group aware of the real truth, and a feeling of being threatened by others also persists. Slovak people feel threatened by many, including the West, the United States, migrants, and ethnic and sexual minorities. People in Slovakia are afraid of losing their imaginary identity based on traditional values; most of them believe Slovakia has always been oppressed and has never been able to determine its own path and fate. Such a perception of the world is related to the distorted historical context (that the nation was always oppressed by an external force, for example, the Hungarians prior to 1918, or by the Germans during the Second World War). This means that Slovaks are, in their nature, more distrustful and prone to look for "alternative" explanations hiding behind the experienced events.

In Czechia, the situation has recently worsened as well. According to Štětka (2023), overall trust of Czech people in the news has reached a historical low (30 percent—it is, however, notable that this number is still higher than in Slovakia). The possible reasons for this decline in news trust include the cost-of-living crisis and the ongoing war in Ukraine. The presidential election campaign in January 2023 needs to be mentioned as well, since this political event was marked by polarization and spreading of disinformation across the country. Czech public service broadcasters, although they enjoy their rather stable position as the most trustful Czech media outlets, remain exposed to potential political pressure due to the way they are financed and operated. Further information can be found in Plevák (2023) who did an interview with the Czech security expert Syrovátka. The expert claims that in the context of Czechia, it is more appropriate to use the term disinformation narrative instead of disinformation campaign. Specific fake news always reacts to current affairs, following up on long-term, stable disinformation narratives—immigration, COVID-19 (and vaccines related to it), and global politics, especially in relation to the armed conflict in Ukraine. However, while considering the Slovak scenario, that is, the successful Russian disinformation campaign in Slovakia, Syrovátka claims that Czechia is not so easy a target, because Slovak people's distrust in the public authorities is much deeper and more serious due to the country's political instability and socioeconomic problems. Addressing the issue of selective news exposure and (political and ideological) polarization in Czechia, Hungary, Poland, and Serbia, Tóth et al. (2023) reveal significant cross-country differences—the more selective news repertoires seem to be more prominent in countries characterized by higher levels of polarization.

Both Czech and Slovak people are quite aware of the existence of fake news and disinformation. When asked for their opinion about being exposed to fake news and disinformation (i.e., how often do they think such encounters happen on a weekly basis), 13 percent of Czech audiences claim that they encounter fake news very often, and 16 percent often. However, 32 percent of the surveyed sample report that these situations happen only occasionally (European Parliament 2022a). Reacting to the same questions, 15 percent of Slovak respondents think their media consumption involves fake news and disinformation very often and 21 percent often, while 26 percent of the sample perceive their exposure to fake news and disinformation as occasional (European Parliament 2022b). This data suggests that the answers of both Czech and Slovak citizens significantly differ from the EU27 averages (throughout the whole of EU, only 10 percent of citizens think they encounter fake news very often, 18 percent often, and 33 percent occasionally). What is particularly interesting is the fact that 62 percent of all EU citizens (including Czechs and Slovaks) are quite confident, maybe overconfident, that they can recognize fake news and disinformation when they encounter it (European Parliament 2022c).

Methodology

The aim of this chapter is to detect what sources the Czechs and Slovaks use for gaining and verifying information about COVID-19 vaccination and what positions they hold in terms of COVID-19 vaccination and related issues. While considering the differences and similarities between those two countries, both of which used to be a federation (Elster 1995), the essay has the ambition to answer the following research questions:

- RQ1: What are the common sources of gaining and verifying information about COVID-19 vaccination within Czech and Slovak society?
- RQ2: What are the opinions of Czechs and Slovaks on the COVID-19 vaccination?
- RQ3: Are there any differences in opinions on the COVID-19 vaccination of specific target groups, for example, (possibly) pregnant women or children?

Regarding the method, a questionnaire survey method allowed us to conduct research on a representative sample of the population with the option of presence of certain subgroups of interest, whose responses could be then analyzed separately (Roy 2019). The CAWI (computer-assisted web interview) method of collecting responses was applied because of time and accuracy requirements (Bryman 2016). Moreover, questionnaire surveys were previously successfully used for research on similar topics in other European countries (e.g., Raftopulos et al. 2021; Reznik et al. 2021).

The surveys in both countries were conducted using a sample representative of the internet-using population (18+) using the CAWI method. Quota sampling (age, education, municipality size, standard of living) was used. The respondents were recruited through the Czech National Panel, and data were collected by the STEM/MARK research agency, with long-term members of the Association of Market and Opinion Research Agencies (SIMAR) guaranteeing conduction and objective interpretation of high-quality research (SIMAR 2023). The data collection period lasted from June 1 to June 12, 2022, in Czechia and from June 1 to June 17, 2022, in Slovakia. Representative samples were collected both in Czechia (N = 1,002) and in Slovakia (N = 1,013). The survey consisted of a combination of various types of closed and open-ended questions (Banerjee 2019; Bryman 2016). The language of the questionnaire corresponded with the respondents' national language, and the average time taken to complete the questionnaire was, in both mutations, around ten minutes, which was proven to be still efficient enough in terms of interest and response rate (Galesic et al. 2009; Guo 2016).

The conducted research complies with the ethical principles of voluntary participation, confidentiality, and anonymity. All the participants filled in the research voluntarily and had a chance to opt out at any point in time. Their personal data was also anonymized, and individual respondents could not be recognized in the data corpus (Banerjee 2019). The data was further processed using Microsoft Excel and IBM SPSS software, both of which are commonly used programs for data processing in the field of social sciences (Abbot 2016; Acton et al. 2009).

Results

Sources of Gaining and Verifying Information about COVID-19 Vaccination within Czech and Slovak Society

More than half of the Czech respondents gain information in general from news websites (67 percent), public television (59 percent), friends (52 percent), and family (52 percent). When respondents verify information, the most popular sources are friends (37 percent), family (36 percent), and news websites (35 percent). The situation in Slovakia is similar, with the most used source of information being news websites, at 50 percent. These are followed by public TV (48 percent), family (44 percent), and friends (43 percent).

The national public TV channel Česká televize (ČT) is the main source of information for Czech respondents who use audiovisual media for news. To verify information, these respondents often watch ČT (28 percent) or the private channel FTV Prima (21 percent). Czechs prefer audiovisual media (TV channels) to purely audio (radio stations) for gaining and verifying information. The most popular newspapers and magazines for gaining and verifying information in Czechia are the broadsheet daily newspapers *MF Dnes*, *Deník*, and *Lidové noviny*. *MF Dnes*, *Lidové noviny*, and *Metro* (free daily) are operated by the MAFRA group, which was previously owned by Agrofert Holding and directed by former Czech prime minister Andrej Babiš, who transferred ownership to two private trust funds to comply with conflict-of-interest laws (Giereło-Klimaszewska 2020).

Although the structure of the Slovak mediascape differs from that of the Czech, the primary TV channel Jednotka, operated by national public TV and radio broadcaster RTVS, is also the main source of information for Slovaks who use audiovisual media for news (54 percent). For news verification, the research participants often watch Jednotka (26 percent) or the private television channel Markíza (26 percent). Slovaks prefer audiovisual media (TV channels) to audio sources (radio stations) to gain and verify information. The most popular Slovak newspapers for gaining and verifying information are elite daily newspapers *Denník N*, *SME*, and *Pravda*. The most popular tabloid in terms of gaining and verifying information is the daily newspaper *Nový čas*. Besides daily newspapers, the respondents frequently mentioned additional sources for gaining or verifying information, such as *Zdravie*, *Plus 7 dní*, and *Život* magazines.

Czech respondents using news websites for gaining and verifying information rely most on easy-to-access platforms. Almost two-thirds (63 percent) of respondents gain their information from the news platform Seznam zprávy, closely followed by 60 percent who gain information from the Novinky server. If Czech respondents gain or verify information on social media, they do so most often on Facebook (obtaining 75 percent, verifying 23 percent). For verification, YouTube (27 percent) is even more commonly used, and is second as a social media source of information (54 percent of respondents gain information from this source).

The most used source for gaining and verifying information in Slovakia is the private news website Aktuality.sk (78 percent), which gained popularity after the shocking murder of its journalist Ján Kuciak and his fiancée in 2018 (Urbániková and Haniková 2021). Slovaks often gain or verify information on Facebook (obtaining 70 percent, verifying 27 percent). While talking about verification, YouTube is the second most popular social media source of information (54 percent of respondents gain information from it), whereas the percentage of Slovak respondents using this social networking site for verification is slightly higher than in the Czech case (30 percent).

Regarding the sources of gaining and verifying information about COVID-19 vaccination, the most common source among the Czech population is ČT. The national public TV is used for this purpose by 68 percent of respondents, who use it for gaining or verifying information in general. Information about COVID-19 vaccination is also commonly verified by family or friends (32 percent of respondents gain or verify information with their relatives).

Similarly, the most common sources of gaining information about COVID-19 vaccination among the Slovak population are TV channels of RTVS, which are used for this purpose by 59 percent of respondents who use public TV for gaining or verifying information in general. Regarding options on the best source to verify information on COVID-19 vaccination, Slovaks favor family or friends (35 percent of respondents use them for gaining or verifying all the information).

Opinions of Czechs and Slovaks on COVID-19 Vaccination

Seven Czech respondents out of ten (70 percent) state that they received a COVID-19 vaccination, whereas six people out of ten in Slovak sample (63 percent) claim they were vaccinated against COVID-19. In Czechia, more than half the respondents (51 percent) completely or somewhat support COVID-19 vaccination. On the other hand, 28 percent of the sample is composed of determined opponents of COVID-19 vaccination. The same opinion is held by another 15 percent of Czechs, who stated their position less strongly. In their attitude to COVID-19 vaccination, women are more reserved than men. We also identify a higher percentage of women (42 percent) than men (15 percent) who completely disagree with the statement. More than six respondents out of ten in the 30–44 age group do not support COVID-19 vaccination (somewhat or completely). Czechs living in bigger cities (with more inhabitants) tend to support COVID-19 vaccination, while respondents from small-sized municipalities are more reserved. The acceptance of COVID-19 vaccination also declines with the fall in the standard of living. More than one-third of respondents with a very high standard of living somewhat or fully support vaccination, whereas only 16 percent of people with a very low living standard state the same.

Slovak respondents in general are slightly more reserved regarding COVID-19 vaccination than Czechs, but the tendencies follow a similar direction. Less than half of the Slovak sample (47 percent) completely or somewhat support COVID-19 vaccination. Moreover, 31 percent of the sample consists of determined opponents of COVID-19 vaccination. Similarly, this opinion is also shared by another 10 percent of the participants who did not express their disagreement as strongly. In terms of their attitude to COVID-19 vaccination, men are generally more supportive of vaccination—52 percent of them completely or somewhat agree with it. Contrarily, women do not seem to possess any clear attitude toward this issue, since 44 percent of them support vaccination and 44 percent do not. In general, the strongest supporters of vaccination belong to the oldest age group (60+ years of age—56 percent). More than four out of ten in the 30–59 age group do not support COVID-19 vaccination. Slovaks living in cities with more inhabitants tend to support COVID-19 vaccination, while respondents residing in small-sized municipalities are more reserved on this issue.

For the Czech respondents, the type of vaccine matters. Only 28 percent think (somewhat or completely) that COVID-19 vaccination should be given to the population without considering the type of vaccine. More than one-third of people (35 percent) completely disagree with the statement that people should be vaccinated against COVID-19, no matter what type of vaccine. Another one-quarter of the sample share the same opinion, but do not express it that confidently (somewhat agree). Czech women place greater importance on the type of vaccine than Czech men. Only 24 percent of women agree with the statement. In the case of male respondents, the percentage is higher (32 percent). There is also a higher ratio of strong supporters among men. The most effective vaccine according to Czechs is the Pfizer/BioNTech vaccine (considered somewhat or very effective by 50 percent of the sample). Pfizer/BioNTech is followed by Moderna and AstraZeneca, but more than four out of ten respondents are not sure about the effectiveness of those vaccines. Also, one-fifth to one-quarter of Czech respondents do not think those vaccines have any effect at all. Over two-thirds of Czechs (69 percent) would not get vaccinated if the only possible vaccination type available were Sputnik. The possible acceptance of the Sputnik vaccine is quite low (13 percent). Greater possibility of acceptance of Sputnik is among the oldest generation (respondents aged 60 and above)—one out of five in this age group (22 percent) somewhat or completely disagree with the statement. Gender, level of education, municipality size, and standard of living do not play a substantial role in the respondents' decision-making.

Slovaks also favor Pfizer/BioNTech as the most effective vaccine (seen as somewhat or very effective by 43 percent of respondents). This is followed by Moderna and AstraZeneca. More than three in ten respondents are uncertain about the effectiveness of any vaccine other than Pfizer/BioNTech. Similarly to the Czech results, the vaccine type they considered to be most ineffective is Sputnik—42 percent of respondents find it somewhat or completely ineffective. As for the effectiveness of vaccines, the Pfizer-made vaccine is seen as the best, based on sociodemographic factors with dominance in all segments. It is considered effective by more than half of university-educated respondents

(55 percent) or residents of large cities with over 100,000 inhabitants (52 percent). Five out of ten people with a good standard of living (52 percent) and six out of ten people with a very good standard of living (62 percent) are convinced of the effectiveness of this vaccine.

Opinions on COVID-19 Vaccination of (Possibly) Pregnant Women and Children

Slightly less than one-third of the Czech sample (30 percent) somewhat or completely agree that COVID-19 vaccination can complicate pregnancy. In contrast, 24 percent disagree with this statement. A relatively high percentage of respondents (45 percent) do not express an opinion on this issue. This may be due to a lack of specialized medical education and a reluctance to share unfounded opinions. There has been a lot of disinformation in the Czech media about the adverse effects of vaccines on pregnant women; hence such disinformation has been refuted by the WHO. In line with Czech results, around one-third of Slovak respondents (31 percent) somewhat or completely reject the statement that COVID-19 vaccination can complicate pregnancy. On the contrary, almost the same number of respondents agree with this statement (30 percent), and a relatively high percentage of participants (38 percent) do not wish to express their opinion on this issue.

Regarding COVID-19 vaccination of children, Czech respondents approach the topic more skeptically than they do in general. Only 12 percent of respondents completely agree that they support COVID-19 vaccination of children, and further 19 percent of respondents somewhat agree. On the other hand, more than half of the sample (54 percent) do not support COVID-19 vaccination of children, and 37 percent of that percentage are completely sure in their opinion. Women support COVID-19 vaccination of children even less. Hence 58 percent of them did not support it (somewhat or completely). Only 49 percent of men expressed a negative opinion. The reserved attitude of Czechs toward COVID-19 vaccination of children is also evident from an unwillingness to vaccinate their own children. Only 22 percent of people agree with the statement, "I would like to vaccinate (or have already vaccinated) my child/children against COVID-19." Four out of ten respondents completely disagree. Men are slightly more open than women to COVID-19 vaccination of children (25 percent men versus 20 percent women agree; 48 percent men versus 55 percent women disagree). The middle generation (30–44 years old) disagrees the most intensely with

COVID-19 vaccination of their children (66 percent somewhat or completely disagree with the statement).

In Slovakia, the vaccination of children against COVID-19 has also significantly less supporters than vaccination in general. Only 11 percent of respondents completely agree that they support COVID-19 vaccination of children, and further 21 percent of participants somewhat agree with the statement. In contrast, more than half of the sample (54 percent) do not support COVID-19 vaccination of children, while 40 percent of them are completely against such a measure. Women support COVID-19 vaccination of children less often than men. Based on the results, 59 percent of women do not support it, while 44 percent are completely against it. Only 49 percent of men express negative opinions on this issue. A lower level of willingness to have a child vaccinated is apparent when the respondent's own child/children are involved. More than half of respondents (51 percent) would not have their child/children vaccinated, and only 27 percent of people would prefer to have their children vaccinated. Compared to the previous results on favoring vaccination of children, we can see an increase in the number of people who did not want or were unable to answer (21 percent).

The Perception on COVID-19 Vaccination in Czechia and Slovakia in Light of the Shared Past

This chapter deals with media trust in two countries— Czechia and Slovakia— with a shared past but different political development and cultural environment. The trust in information sources, including media, was empirically tested by a representative survey aimed at the perception of issues and factors connected with COVID-19 vaccination.

The research addresses three main research questions:

- RQ1: What are the common sources of gaining and verifying information about COVID-19 vaccination within Czech and Slovak society?
- RQ2: What are the opinions of Czechs and Slovaks on COVID-19 vaccination?
- RQ3: Are there any differences in opinions on COVID-19 vaccination of specific target groups, for example (possibly) pregnant women or children?

Regarding the common sources of gaining and verifying information about COVID-19 vaccination, the most favored source among the Czech population is

ČT. The national public TV is used for this purpose by more than two-thirds of respondents who use it for gaining or verifying information in general. Information about COVID-19 vaccination is also frequently verified by family or friends. The situation in Slovakia is quite similar, while the most common sources of gaining information about COVID-19 vaccination among the Slovak population are TV stations operated by RTVS. Regarding options on the best source to verify information on COVID-19 vaccination, more than one-third of Slovaks favor their family or friends. These results confirm the claims about the relative trust in public media in Czechia and Slovakia accented by previously published studies and reports (e.g., Chlebcová Hečková and Smith 2023; Štětka 2023).

While talking about the opinions of Czechs and Slovaks on COVID-19 vaccination, it is important to mention that 70 percent of Czech respondents declare that they have had a COVID-19 vaccination, whereas 63 percent of the Slovak sample stated they were vaccinated against COVID-19. In Czechia, more than half of respondents support COVID-19 vaccination. In contrast, more than one-quarter of the sample is composed of determined opponents of COVID-19 vaccination. Less than half of Slovaks (47 percent) support vaccination against COVID-19, and 41 percent of respondents are against it. Considering the types of vaccine and their predicted effectivity, both Czech and Slovaks favor Pfizer/BioNTech, followed by Moderna and AstraZeneca. Sputnik is not very trustworthy for our respondents.

The differences in opinions on COVID-19 vaccination of specific target groups, concretely (possibly) pregnant women or children, were recorded in both countries under research. Slightly less than one-third of the Czech and Slovak sample (30 percent) somewhat or completely agree that COVID-19 vaccination can complicate pregnancy. The Czech and Slovak respondents also approach COVID-19 vaccination of children more skeptically than they do in general. Only 12 percent of Czech and 11 percent of Slovak respondents completely agree that they support COVID-19 vaccination of children, and a further one-fifth of participants in both countries agree. Women support COVID-19 vaccination of children even less. The reserved attitude of Czechs toward COVID-19 vaccination of children is also evident from an unwillingness to vaccinate their own children. Only 22 percent of Czechs and 27 percent of Slovaks agree with the statement, "I would like to vaccinate (or have already vaccinated) my child/children against COVID-19."

Overall, this research confirms that the shared past of Czechia and Slovakia still plays a significant role and shapes the way of gaining and verifying information, as our results prove. Despite the declared use of media, especially public mass media, for gaining and verifying information, this essay demonstrates that the declining media trust in the countries of Visegrad Four detected by past research (Hajdu et al. 2023) is still significant and empirically declarable. Due to that, the crucial question in the next few years may not be "How much do we trust the media?" but "What do we really believe?"

Acknowledgment

The research was supported by the Central European Digital Media Observatory (CEDMO), an international multidisciplinary project supported by the European Commission under the call CEF-TC-2020-2 (European Digital Media Observatory), Reference 2020-EU-IA-0267.

Conflict of Interest Statement

No potential conflict of interest was reported by the authors.

Note

1 The chapter uses the name and information about the structure and financing of the organization valid in the period of the research. From July 1, 2024, the RTVS was replaced by STVR (Slovak Television and Radio) through a new law. The critics of this law claim that the content of the broadcasting may be influenced by the government and politicians, and the media's independence can be threatened (ČTK 2024).

References

Abbott, Martin Lee. 2016. *Using statistics in the social and health sciences with SPSS and Excel.* John Wiley & Sons.

Acton, Ciaran, Robert L. Miller, Deirdre Fullerton, and John Maltby. 2009. *SPSS for social scientists.* Palgrave Macmillan.

Aharoni, Tali, Keren Tenenboim-Weinblatt, Christian Baden, and Maximilian Overbeck. 2022. "Dynamics of (dis)trust between the news media and their audience: The case of the April 2019 Israeli exit polls." *Journalism* 23 (2): 337–53. https://doi.org/10.1177/1464884920978105.

Banerjee, Tanmoyee. 2019. "Designing a primary survey-based research." In *Research methodology for social sciences*, edited by Rajat Acharyya and Nandan Bhattacharya. Routledge.

Blom, Robin. 2021. "Believing false political headlines and discrediting truthful political headlines: The interaction between news source trust and news content expectancy." *Journalism* 22 (3): 821–37. https://doi.org/10.1177/1464884918765316.

Brník, Andrej, and Miroslav Kapec. 2021. "Impact of the first and second waves of coronavirus on Slovak radio audiences." *Media Literacy and Academic Research* 4 (2): 166–86. https://cejsh.icm.edu.pl/cejsh/element/bwmeta1.element.desklight-ca42b1a4-bc6c-492f-aad7-5c9fcab7936c.

Bryman, Alan. 2016. *Social research methods* (5th ed.). Oxford University Press.

Carr, D. Jasun, Matthew Barnidge, Byung Gu Lee, and Stephanie Jean Tsang. 2014. "Cynics and skeptics: Evaluating the credibility of mainstream and citizen journalism." *Journalism & Mass Communication Quarterly* 91 (3): 452–70. https://doi.org/10.1177/1077699014538828.

Charvát, Jakub, Denisa Charvátova, and Eva Niklesová. 2022. "Populism as a communication strategy: A case study of the Freedom and Direct Democracy Party and Tomio Okamura." *Communication Today* 13 (2): 106–20. https://communicationtoday.sk/wp-content/uploads/07_CHARVAT-et-al_CT-2-2022.pdf.

Chlebcová Hečková, Andrea, and Simon Smith. 2023. "Digital news report: Slovakia." *Reuters Institute for the Study of Journalism*. https://reutersinstitute.politics.ox.ac.uk/digital-news-report/2023/slovakia.

ČTK. 2024. "Pavel: Financování veřejnoprávních médií z rozpočtu by mohlo vést k ovlivňování." *České noviny*. www.ceskenoviny.cz/zpravy/pavel-financovani-verejnopravnich-medii-z-rozpoctu-by-mohlo-vest-k-ovlivnovani/2539680.

Elster, Jon. 1995. "Transition, constitution-making and separation in Czechoslovakia." *European Journal of Sociology/Archives Européennes de Sociologie* 36 (1): 105–34. www.jstor.org/stable/23999435.

European Parliament. 2022a. "Media & news survey 2022: Country factsheets Czechia—cs." *Eurobarometer*. https://europa.eu/eurobarometer/api/deliverable/download/file?deliverableId=82797.

European Parliament. 2022b. "Media & news survey 2022: Country factsheets Slovakia—sk." *Eurobarometer*. https://europa.eu/eurobarometer/api/deliverable/download/file?deliverableId=82819.

European Parliament. 2022c. "Standard Eurobarometer 96: Winter 2021–2022—Media use in the European Union." *Eurobarometer*. https://europa.eu/eurobarometer/surveys/detail/2553.

Galesic, Mirta, and Michael Bosnjak. 2009. "Effects of questionnaire length on participation and indicators of response quality in a web survey." *Public Opinion Quarterly* 73 (2): 349–60. https://doi.org/10.1093/poq/nfp031.

Gálik, Slavomír, and Sabína Gáliková Tolnaiová. 2022. "Media coverage and its determinants in the context of the COVID-19 pandemic." *Communication Today* 13 (1): 46–58. https://communicationtoday.sk/wp-content/uploads/04_GALIK_GALIKOVA-TOLNAIOVA_CT-1-2022.pdf.

Giddens, Anthony. 1990. *The consequences of modernity*. Stanford University Press.

Giereło-Klimaszewska, Katarzyna. 2020. "Oligarchizacja mediów w Czechach na przykładzie koncernu Mafra Andreja Babiša (Oligarchization of the Czech media in the Czech Republic as illustrated by the example Andrej Babiš' Mafra Company)." *Studia Politologica* 324 (24): 183–200. http://cejsh.icm.edu.pl/cejsh/element/bwmeta1.element.desklight-9ccaa7f4-eba6-42c8-b83e-aa9dc634503d.

Guo, Yimeng, Jacek A. Kopec, Jolanda Cibere, Linda C. Li, and Charles H. Goldsmith. 2016. "Population survey features and response rates: A randomized experiment." *American Journal of Public Health* 106 (8): 1422–6. www.ncbi.nlm.nih.gov/pmc/articles/PMC4940641/.

Hajdu, Dominika, Jana Kazaz, Katarína Klingová, Patrik Szicherle, and Viktoria Musilová. 2023. "Globsec trends 2023: United we (still) stand." *Globsec*. www.globsec.org/what-we-do/publications/globsec-trends-2023-united-we-still-stand.

Hanitzsch, Thomas, and Rosa Berganza. 2012. "Explaining journalists' trust in public institutions across 20 countries: Media freedom, corruption, and ownership matter most." *Journal of Communication* 62 (5): 794–814. https://doi.org/10.1111/j.1460-2466.2012.01663.x.

Hanitzsch, Thomas, Arjen Van Dalen, and Nina Steindl. 2018. "Caught in the nexus: A comparative and longitudinal analysis of public trust in the press." *International Journal of Press/Politics* 23 (1): 3–23. https://doi.org/10.1177/1940161217740695.

Ihlebæk, Karoline Andrea, and Carina Riborg Holter. 2021. "Hostile emotions: An exploratory study of far-right online commenters and their emotional connection to traditional and alternative news media." *Journalism* 22 (5): 1207–22. https://doi.org/10.1177/1464884920985726.

Krajčovič, Peter. 2022. "The media in times of the pandemic: Comparing viewing figures and interactions of serious, tabloid and conspiracy media on Facebook during the COVID-19 pandemic." *Media Literacy and Academic Research* 5 (2): 212–24. www.ceeol.com/search/article-detail?id=1083429.

Kyriakidou, Maria, Marina Morani, Stephen Cushion, and Ceri Hughes. 2023. "Audience understandings of disinformation: Navigating news media through a prism of pragmatic scepticism." *Journalism* 24 (11): 2379–96. https://doi.org/10.1177/14648849221114244.

Lipka, Roman. 2021. "Slováci veria hoaxom viac ako iné národy. Prečo je to tak? (Slovak people tend to believe in hoaxes more than different nations. Why is that?)." *CTVI*.

https://vedanadosah.cvtisr.sk/ludia/sociologia/slovaci-veria-hoaxom-viac-ako-ine-narody-preco-je-to-tak/.

Molitorisz, Sacha. 2020. "More top-down than peer-to-peer: Talking to Australians about their ideal news source." *Media International Australia* 175 (1): 109–23. https://doi.org/10.1177/1329878X19891586.

Němcová Tejkalová, Alice, Arnold S. de Beer, Rosa Berganza, Yusuf Kalyango Jr., Adriana Amado, Liga Ozolina, Filip Láb, Rawshon Akhter, and Sonia Virginia Moreira. 2017. "In media we trust: Journalists and institutional trust perceptions in post-authoritarian and post-totalitarian countries." *Journalism Studies* 18 (5): 629–44. https://doi.org/10.1080/1461670X.2017.1279026.

Peifer, Jason T., and Jared Meisinger. 2021. "The value of explaining the process: How journalistic transparency and perceptions of news media importance can (sometimes) foster message credibility and engagement intentions." *Journalism & Mass Communication Quarterly* 98 (3): 828–53. https://doi.org/10.1177/1077699021 1012953.

Peters, Michael A. 2017. "Education in a post-truth world." *Educational Philosophy and Theory* 49 (6): 563–6. https://doi.org/10.1080/00131857.2016.1264114.

Plevák, Ondřej. 2023. "Český expert na dezinformácie: Slovenský dezinformačný scenár nám nehrozí (Czech expert on disinformation: Slovak disinformation scenario will not happen here)." *Euractiv*. https://euractiv.sk/section/kultura-a-media/interview/cesky-expert-na-dezinformacie-slovensky-dezinformacny-scenar-nam-nehrozi/.

Quandt, Thorsten. 2012. "What's left of trust in a network society? An evolutionary model and critical discussion of trust and societal communication." *European Journal of Communication* 27 (1): 7–21. https://doi.org/10.1177/0267323111434452.

Raftopoulos, Vasilios, Stelios Iordanou, Angeliki Katsapi, Xanthi Dedoukou, and Helena C. Maltezou. 2021. "A comparative online survey on the intention to get COVID-19 vaccine between Greek and Cypriot healthcare personnel: Is the country a predictor?" *Human Vaccines & Immunotherapeutics* 17 (8): 2397–404. https://doi.org/10.1080/21645515.2021.1896907.

Reinemann, Carsten, Alexander Haas, and Diana Rieger. 2022. "'I don't care, 'cause I don't trust them!' The impact of information sources, institutional trust and populist attitudes on the perception of the COVID-19 pandemic during the first lockdown in Germany." *Studies in Communication and Media* 11 (1): 132–68. https://epub.ub.uni-muenchen.de/92823/.

Reznik, Alexander, Valentina Gritsenko, Vsevolod Konstantinov, Natallia Khamenka, and Richard Isralowitz. 2021. "COVID-19 fear in Eastern Europe: Validation of the fear of COVID-19 scale." *International Journal of Mental Health and Addiction* 19: 1903–8. https://doi.org/10.1007/s11469-020-00283-3.

Roy, Malabika. 2019. "Sampling methods: A survey." In *Research methodology for social sciences*, edited by Rajat Acharyya and Nandan Bhattacharya. Routledge.

Scott, John. 2014. *Oxford dictionary of sociology*. Oxford University Press.

SIMAR. 2023. "Agentury." https://simar.cz/agentury/.

Škarba, Tomáš, and Ján Višňovský. 2022. "Deliberative communication in the context of authoritarian sentimentalism and disinformation chaos." *Communication Today* 13 (1): 4–16. https://communicationtoday.sk/wp-content/uploads/01_SKARBA_VISNOVSKY_CT-1-2022.pdf.

Štětka, Václav. 2023. "Digital news report: Czech Republic." *Reuters Institute for the Study of Journalism*. https://reutersinstitute.politics.ox.ac.uk/digital-news-report/2023/czech-republic.

Tóth, Fanni, Sabina Mihelj, Václav Štětka, and Katherine Kondor. 2023. "A media repertoires approach to selective exposure: News consumption and political polarization in Eastern Europe." *International Journal of Press/Politics* 28 (4): 884–908. https://doi.org/10.1177/19401612211072552.

Tsfati, Yariv, and Joseph N. Cappella. 2003. "Do people watch what they do not trust? Exploring the association between news media skepticism and exposure." *Communication Research* 30 (5): 504–29. https://doi.org/10.1177/0093650203253371.

Urbániková, Marína, and Haniková, Lenka. 2021. "Coping with the murder: The impact of Ján Kuciak's assassination on Slovak investigative journalists." *Journalism Practice* 16 (9): 1927–47. https://doi.org/10.1080/17512786.2021.1877179.

Usher, Nikki. 2018. "Re-thinking trust in the news: A material approach through 'objects of journalism.'" *Journalism Studies* 19 (4): 564–78. https://doi.org/10.1080/1461670X.2017.1375391.

van Bavel, Jay J., and Andrea Pereira. 2018. "The partisan brain: An identity-based model of political belief." *Trends in Cognitive Sciences* 22 (3): 213–24. https://doi.org/10.1016/j.tics.2018.01.004.

van der Linden, Sander, Costas Panagopoulos, and Jon Roozenbeek. 2020. "You are fake news: Political bias in perceptions of fake news." *Media, Culture & Society* 42 (3): 460–70. https://doi.org/10.1177/0163443720906992.

Wawrzyński, Patryk. 2022. "Pride and compassion: How emotional strategies target audiences in political communication?" *Central European Journal of Communication* 15 (32): 416–33. https://doi.org/10.51480/1899-5101.15.3(32).5.

2

Disinformation About Migrants: Fueling Hate Speech

Ana Azurmendi and María Fernanda Novoa-Jaso

Current State: Migrants and Hate Speech

European countries are seeing an increasing presence of migrants in their populations. According to the latest Eurostat report (European Commission 2023), in 2022, 8 percent of people living in EU countries were non-national. A total of 3 percent were citizens from other EU countries, while 5 percent were from non-EU countries. When analyzing the percentages by country, Germany emerged in 2021 as the nation with the highest projected immigration intake outside the EU (439,000 persons or 19 percent of all immigrants from non-EU countries), followed by Spain (421,000 or 19 percent). Migrants in both Italy and France each represent 11 percent (Italy 248,000, France 238,000). The absolute number of immigrants in Europe in 2021 was projected to be 2.3 million, according to the Eurostat report (European Commission 2023). The citizens of these countries, aware of the changes in the population, are easily targeted by negative news on the subject. People also have feelings of insecurity about whether the country can integrate this immigrants. Economic news, such as reports on unemployment, and other news related to cultural and social change observed in a particular community, can contribute to these feelings. (Culloty et al. 2022, 10).

This unsettling perception can be used—in fact it is—by some politicians (Sibrian Díaz et al. 2023, 20), also by xenophobic activists (Wardle 2017, cited by Sibrian Díaz et al. 2023, 20), to generate rejectionist emotions against migrants. It is within this context that the relationship between disinformation and hate speech flourishes, forming a highly effective combination.

This is something that has been shown in tragic events such as that of Southport, UK, in July 2024. When a British teenager, the son of Rwandan refugees, broke into a dance class killing three children and seriously injuring eight others, fake news on social media, which went viral on X and Telegram thanks to the intervention of some influencers, fueled xenophobic violence on the streets of Southport, London, Hartlepool, Manchester, and Aldershot (Casciani and BBC Verify 2024). They insisted that the assassin was an illegal immigrant and a radical Islamist. So much so that Pat de Brún, deputy director of Amnesty Tech,[1] said:

> The racist violence spilling across the streets follows a period of intense scapegoating of refugees and migrants by politicians and others, through dangerous rhetoric and policies. In this context, social media algorithms have actively amplified and escalated xenophobic discourse.
>
> These toxic algorithms are deliberately designed to prioritize engagement and act as incendiaries that fuel division, disinformation, and hate.

The aim of this chapter is, first, to present the main arguments about the conflict between freedom of expression and respect for the rights of others, such as the right to reputation and the right to inclusion in society—rights that are present in these hostile discourse scenarios. A second objective is to analyze the types of disinformation about migrants present in both social media and the media (legacy and online media), their characteristics, effects, and main actors. A third objective is to study the relationship between disinformation and hate speech related to migrants. The fourth is to propose actions to combat both the false narratives and the harmful rhetoric directed at them.

The methodology employed involved a comprehensive review of existing literature on these issues, complemented by a detailed examination of the European Court of Human Rights' resolutions referred to the freedom of expression and an in-depth analysis of international and state-level measures in this domain.

Journalists and Users' Freedom of Expression According to the European Regulations and the European Court of Human Rights

The European Treaty of Fundamental Rights (2012) and the European Convention on Human Rights (1950), for instance, recognize the indispensable role of freedom of expression, particularly as exercised by journalists and the press, in maintaining the political health of democracies. Every European country has incorporated this principle into their constitutional or primary legislation, thereby accepting the associated obligation. As the European Court of Human Rights has observed:

> "The press plays an essential role in a democratic society. Although it must not overstep certain bounds, in particular in respect of the reputation and rights of others, its duty is nevertheless to impart—in a manner consistent with its obligations and responsibilities—information and ideas on all matters of public interest," says the European Court of Human Rights in many of its Resolutions on Freedom of Expression. (*Bédat v. Switzerland* 2016, §50; *Rusu v. Romania* 2016, §23, and *Couderc and Hachette Filipacchi Associés v. France* 2015, §89)

Conversely, individuals perceive freedom of expression to be one of their most fundamental rights, particularly accessible using social media. Nevertheless, in contrast to the press, they typically do not perceive a sense of accountability for their occasionally abusive statements on social media. This has the effect of increasing the potential for the dissemination of misinformation and offensive content directed at particular individuals or even groups. In such circumstances, a lack of equilibrium existed between the various rights in question, most notably the right to freedom of expression and the right to reputation.

In the view of the European Court of Human Rights, there is a distinction to be drawn between the responsibility of a journalist and that of an ordinary citizen in relation to the freedom of expression.

> The protection of the right of journalists to impart information on issues of general interest is subject to the proviso that they are acting in good faith and on an accurate factual basis and provide "reliable and precise" information in accordance with the ethics of journalism. (*NIT S.R.L. v. The Republic of Moldova*, 2022 §180)

Consequently, there are particular stipulations referring to the freedom of expression when journalists are engaged in their professional duties. Such conditions are not present in the current citizens' use of social media. Meanwhile, journalists are obliged to work on the basis of an "accurate factual basis" and "reliable and precise information," in accordance with their professional standards. This is not a requirement for the general public.

In the context of disinformation surrounding migrants, the responsibility of the press in reporting on this issue is greater than that of individual users. In light of their obligation, under both the human rights and constitutional mandates, journalists bear a particular responsibility to seek out and disseminate accurate information about current affairs. Even when a particular news is negative, provocative, and annoying (as evidenced by the European Court of Human Rights' 2018 *Stomakhin v. Russia resolution*, §88).

Examples such as the Hutchins Commission (1947) and the McBride Report (1980) underscore the critical role of the media in not only ensuring accuracy but also fostering a public discourse that strengthens social cohesion. This becomes particularly significant in addressing the challenge of inflammatory rhetoric that reinforces prejudice and undermines democratic values.

What Do We Mean by Misinformation and Hate Speech?

As many authors and institutions agree, disinformation can be defined as the intentional dissemination of false information through social media or other means, with the aim of deceiving large numbers of citizens. Such disinformation is frequently linked to "strategies for manipulating public opinion and eroding the stability of states and institutions" (Serrano-Puche et al. 2023; Ministerio de Asuntos Exteriores, Gobierno de España 2023). Nevertheless, different aims can be addressed in relation to specific groups of population, economic sectors, and so forth. For example, the objective may be to deter the mobility of individuals or entities toward a particular region or country, to damage the reputation of a specific product or service, or to achieve other similar outcomes (Olivares-Delgado et al. 2023, 544). Deception is the fundamental aspect of disinformation, as emphasized by Narváez-Linares and Pérez-Rufi (2022, 841). The act of deceiving involves misleading others by presenting false information in a seemingly authentic manner, many times with the intention of attracting visitors and monetizing the resulting traffic.

In its communication "Tackling Online Disinformation," the EU, and in particular the European Commission, has shifted the focus toward the term "disinformation," which is defined as "all forms of false, inaccurate, or misleading information designed, presented and promoted to intentionally cause public harm or for profit" (European Commission 2018). This definition also differs from the term "misinformation," which is understood as false, confusing, and deceptive information that has been caused by error. This implies the absence of any intention to deceive or mislead (Culloty et al. 2022, 3).

In the context of the term "hate speech," a majority of authors concur that hate speech is designed to inflict harm upon the dignity of an individual or group, taking into account a number of defining characteristics, both inherited and acquired. Hate speech can be defined as a form of expression that openly promotes, justifies, and disseminates the disparagement and exclusion of certain social groups based on ethnicity, nationality, religion, sexual orientation, gender, disability, and other characteristics (Amores et al. 2020). Controversial topics such as immigration often serve as fertile ground for such expressions, where immigrants are stigmatized as economic, cultural, or security threats, perpetuating harmful stereotypes and deepening social tensions.

To What Extent Does Disinformation about Migrants Endanger Democratic Processes?

The proliferation of disinformation on the internet, largely facilitated by digital platforms, represents a significant challenge to democratic societies. The EU has implemented a series of measures to address the issue of disinformation (Moreno-Castro et al. 2023, 4), which it perceives as a threat to the democratic stability of its member states. These measures are focused on three key areas: preventing the manipulation of citizens, limiting the influence of third countries on domestic affairs within the EU, and addressing the phenomenon of political radicalization.

In this context, the dissemination of disinformation about migrants has the specific effect of fostering social rejection toward this group of individuals (Alonso González 2019, 32; Narváez-Linares and Pérez Rufi 2022, 841). It can be argued that the dissemination of false information with the intention of inciting hatred and discrimination against migrants constitutes a form of hate speech (Narváez-Linares and Pérez Rufi 2022, 842). As Humprecht et. al. (2020, 496) points out, "As more people turn to social media as a primary news source, online disinformation could become a major challenge to political communication in advanced democracies."

Culloty et al. (2022, 4) insist that one additional consequence of disinformation about migrants is the perpetuation of a negative narrative that has become a commonplace phenomenon. Consequently, those engaged in communication, along with politicians and citizens, are unable to discern the traces of public discourse that, in fact, adhere to the parameters of disinformation. In a gradual yet persistent manner, they demonstrate a lack of sensitivity to this fact, which ultimately leads to the incitement of hatred and discrimination against migrants. Furthermore, they also provide a justification for anti-migration policies (Culloty et al. 2022, 4). Ultimately, this gives rise to a democratic crisis characterized by social polarization, whereby opposing groups are driven by mutual repulsion. In such an atmosphere, it becomes challenging to engage in constructive dialogue and collaboration between political parties and social groups (Culloty et al. 2022, 7; Narváez-Linares and Pérez Rufi 2022, 841).

One direct consequence of the creation of this climate of confrontation is the utilization of arguments and slogans by both individual politicians and political parties with the objective of mobilizing their supporters or, in some cases, discrediting their opponents. In some political narratives, the core arguments for this confrontation is misinformation about migrants (Culloty et al. 2022, 10; Sibrian Díaz et al. 2023, 5–8). This phenomenon has been evidenced in the context of the campaign for the regional elections in Germany in August 2024. Indeed, the far-right, anti-immigration party Alternative for Germany (AfD) won in two regions and was on the verge of winning in a third. In the French elections held in July 2024, the RN Rally National (the political party led by Marie Le Pen) concentrated its communication efforts on the topic of migration policies. The repeated assertion made throughout this campaign, namely the introduction of a legal regime of "national preference" that would afford French citizens priority access to housing and employment while simultaneously limiting the scope of welfare benefits available to non-French nationals (Millar 2024), is indicative of a clear discriminatory stance and the propagation of hatred toward migrants. This strategy was also employed by the Italian electoral campaign of September 2022, which was led by the party of Giorgia Meloni, Fratelli d'Italia.

In conclusion, disinformation about migrants has ramifications that extend beyond the migrants themselves. It also has significant implications for the health and stability of democratic systems. This is due to the fact that disinformation has the potential to erode confidence, promote polarization, and manipulate public opinion (Narváez-Llinares and Pérez-Rufi 2022, 853).

Disinformation about Migrants, Social Media, and Media: An Efficient Combination

One of the earliest cases of crisis related to disinformation in the context of social media was the so-called "migrant crisis" of 2015. As a consequence of the conflict in Syria and Iraq, hundreds of thousands of refugees fled to Italy and Greece via the Mediterranean, seeking asylum from the war and persecution they had fled from. They also sought refuge in Germany, traveling through Austria and Hungary (UNHCR 2015). As Biškup Mašanović (2021, 188) notes, the arrival of a significant number of refugees, particularly in Germany, in conjunction with the portrayal of this phenomenon by the country's principal media outlets, contributed to the formation of a negative image of migrants. The argumentation of this narrative was based on the pressure exerted on the EU's borders and the influx of individuals from diverse cultural and religious backgrounds. Consequently, a feeling of fear toward Muslims[2] was instilled. Meanwhile, there was a concomitant increase in political polarization and subsequent radicalization.

Rebollo Díaz (2021, 21) identifies Twitter (now known as X) as a primary medium for the dissemination of misinformation and polarizing narratives surrounding the refugee crisis. These narratives, characterized by a lack of empathy and a tendency to stereotype, are often accompanied by negative discourses that perpetuate hatred and racism, as well as anti-Islam sentiments. These tweets exhibited a commonality in their emotional component, which manifested through the use of metaphors, catastrophism, indignation, and exaggeration. This resulted in a perception of chaos and the consolidation of fear. Additionally, a significant characteristic of the content on Twitter was that the majority of these discourses were either anonymous or lacked sufficient information (Rebollo Díaz 2021, 23).

This perception of danger and chaos was reinforced by a series of isolated incidents, including allegations of sexual assault against young immigrants during New Year celebrations in 2016 in Cologne, Hamburg, and other German cities. These facts were also overlooked by the international press. In this occasion, social media acted as a channel for the dissemination of misinformation and sensationalist content, which contributed to a climate of fear and confusion. It is of considerable interest to examine the analysis presented by Jermi Brenner and Katrine Ohlendorf in the 2016 report about these criminal actions: "Time for Facts. What Do We Know about Cologne Four Months Later?" (Brenner and Ohlendorf 2016).

In examining the main German newspapers, it becomes evident that the conventional portrayal of German jihadists "as German citizens of Muslim descent who participated in the war in Syria" and the persistent emphasis on the perceived threat of terrorism, often linked to Muslims, contribute to the construction of migrants as a disruptive force within German society (Biškup Mašanović 2021, 188).

On the other hand, the Council of Europe report of 2017, entitled "Media Coverage of the 'Refugee Crisis,'" undertook a content analysis of the press in eight European countries (Czech Republic, France, Germany, Greece, Hungary, Ireland, Serbia, UK) as well as the two main Arabic-language newspapers *Al-Hayat* and *Al-Araby Al-Jadeed*. The study identified two deficiencies in media coverage that contribute to an increase in hostility toward refugees:

- "Temporal trends: The narratives of the coverage changed across Europe during 2015. The sympathetic and empathetic response of a large proportion of the European press in the summer and especially early autumn of 2015 was gradually replaced by suspicion and, in some cases, hostility towards refugees and migrants" (Georgiou and Zaborowski 2017, 3).
- "Media trends: Press coverage that promoted hate speech and hostility towards migrants and refugees was systematic and persistent in a proportion of the press. This was especially the case in some parts of Eastern Europe (esp. Hungary), throughout 'the crisis' and in a significant section of some countries' right-leaning press in the East and West Europe alike" (Georgiou and Zaborowski 2017, 3).

With the exception of media outlets that deliberately incited hatred toward migrants, the majority of media coverage contributed to a climate of suspicion and hostility toward refugees. Nevertheless, this occurred primarily through neglecting and erratic journalistic work, which did not intentionally aim to mislead or incite hatred (Georgiou and Zaborowski 2017, 3).

A decade later, many of these narrative aspects remain prevalent in social media and mainstream media.

Forms of Disinformation about Migrants

There are numerous methods through which disinformation about migrants can be created. This perception is reinforced when misinformation is regarded as a distinct category of disinformation. Nevertheless, a series of common patterns can be identified across the variety of forms of disinformation, both in social media and in traditional media. In the opinion of Narváez-Linares and Pérez-Rufi (2022, 843) and Sibrian Díaz et al. (2023, 20), one of the patterns is the

Table 2.1 Types of Problematic Content in Media Ecosystem.

Type of content	Description	Intentionality
Satire or parody	Without any intention of damaging, but with the potential to cheat	Low
False connection	Headlines, images, footnotes are no consistent with content	Low
Misleading content	Misleading use of information for incriminating	Medium
False context	Authentic content shared out of context	Medium
Impostor content	Authentic sources supplanted	Medium
Manipulated content	Manipulation of authentic information and images	High
Fabricated content	Content 100 percent false, designed to mislead	High

Source: Sibrian Díaz et al. (2023, 20) who refer to Wardle in this regard.

repetition of negative stereotypes, such as "invaders," "subvention recipients," and "delinquents." The aforementioned authors present a classification of misleading content based on the strength of the intention to deceive.

From a different perspective, Lawlor and Tolley (2017, 976)[3] present a classification of forms of disinformation based on the news frames of media coverage of migration.

The proposed models demonstrate how framing reinforces specific positions and significantly shapes public opinion. Both the intent behind the frames and the narratives employed are critical to understanding these phenomena.

Some Aspects of Disinformation Directly Related to Hate Speech against Migrants

What are the mechanisms through which disinformation is employed to engender sentiments of rejection, hostility, and even hatred toward migrants? It would be useful to identify whether there is a specific type of narrative that is closely linked to harmful rhetoric directed at migrants. A recurring theme in the history of disinformation campaigns is their use in times of war or inter-war periods. One illustrative example is the rhetoric of scapegoating (Vergani et al. 2022). In the present era, it has become a common practice to ascribe most societal issues to migrants, thereby perpetuating a cyclical pattern (Essalhi-Rakrak and Pinedo-González 2023). Concurrently, as evidenced by some of

Table 2.2 Categorical Dictionary Frames and Examples.

Frame	Description	Example from text
Economy	Economic impact of admitting immigrants/refugees	"No other aspect of the temporary foreign worker program carries that benefit for low-skill-jobs."
Ethnicity	The ethno-racial, national or religious background of immigrants/refugees	"The Tories have already moved against false refugee claims, by making it easier to remove those whose claims aren't valid and by penalizing mass arrivals such as the boatloads of Sri Lankans who showed up in 2009 and 2010."
Rights	Dialogue around individual rights afforded to immigrants/refugees	"The government refused and she twice appealed the decision, arguing that her rights to life, liberty and security of the person under the Charter of Rights and Freedoms had been violated."
Security	Possible threats to security on account of the admission of immigrants/refugees	"The department's priority at the time was to target unsuccessful refugee claimants who were on the run rather than criminals, because that way the deportation numbers were higher."
Services	Access to and use of state services by immigrants/refugees	"In 2009, about 2,000 investor immigrants and their families were accepted from China, most of them private citizens drawn by the promise of a better environment, education system and health care."
Validity	Discussion around the validity, legitimacy, or deservedness of immigrants/refugees	"The new legislation aims to speed up the determination process, making it easier both to grant asylum to those who deserve it, and to reject and remove those who don't."

Source: Lawlor and Tolley (2017).

the tragic events referenced in the first section, there are instances where the criminalization of migrants is intensified in the aftermath of a tragedy that has a significant impact on public opinion. In such circumstances, social media platforms have facilitated the dissemination of xenophobic fakes. However, the press has played a significant role in the proliferation of this disinformation, amplifying the circulation of such fake news.

The FAD (Friends of Africa Development) foundation (2022) has recently pointed out the relevance of five mechanisms through which the "fabrication of hate" can be carried out (Essalhi-Rakrak and Pinedo-González 2023):

- the creation or exaggeration of fear toward a group without justified evidence;

- the pointing out of supposed culprits who, in fact, have nothing to do with wrongdoing;
- the creation of unjustified fear and its amplification until it becomes a great threat;
- the prediction of the appearance of a great leader who will "save" us; and
- the acting against the "enemy" without any scruples.

On the other hand, Fernández et al. (2023, 15–18) have identified three main factors that contribute to the polarization against migrants in particular:

- social conflict;
- the divisive line between legal and illegal migrants;
- the perception of migrants as a taskforce, with a disregard for their status as human beings.

In this view, social media is seen to offer an incomplete and biased representation of migration, which they regard as redundant in this dialectical context. These symbolic constructions serve to reinforce the tendency toward a comprehension of migration that is characterized by negative narratives. For example, it is relatively simple to locate false content published by anonymous users on X (previously Twitter), which is designed to amplify their ideas with a propagandistic objective. Such messages are designed to prompt a reaction from other users, often manifesting as emotional messages of hostility, anger, and rejection directed at migrants. This ultimately contributes to the normalization of offensive discourse against migrants on social media. This kind of "cyberhate" has a direct impact on the growth of crimes against the groups toward which this hate is directed (Hanzelka and Schmidt 2017, 45–153).

Among the aforementioned contents, images are particularly effective in conveying a sense of veracity. Qi et al. (2020, 143) discuss the prevalence of misleading images, particularly in the context of fake news. Such images are typically derived from artistic works or outdated images that have been published in conjunction with early events. It is relatively simple to present images without their original context and, consequently, their original meaning. Furthermore, in our society, which is inundated with information, the use of image is an efficient method to capture the attention of the user. In fact, tweets containing images received 18 percent more clicks, 89 percent more likes, and 150 percent more retweets than those without images (Qi et al. 2020). In the view of Culloty et al. (2022, 78), decontextualized images represent a significant category of disinformation pertaining to migration issues. In their study, which covered nearly 1 million tweets during the US–Mexico border crisis, they identified decontextualized images as the most prevalent form of disinformation.

Narváez-Linares and Pérez-Rufi (2022, 843–5), together with Essalhi-Rakrak and Pinedo González (2023), Sibrian Díaz et al. (2023, 19 and 20), and Radue (2019, 72), reiterate the perpetuation of negative and racist stereotypes about migrants. Such representation presents migrants as "invaders" and "delinquents," which in turn fuels xenophobic attitudes. Gonzáles (2023, 267) highlights the use of anonymized environments on social media platforms, in which "immigrants are typically a less accepted group" in terms of "hostile citizens of a host country."

In addition, in times of economic crisis or social instability, disinformation about the rights and specific benefits applied to migrants creates the perception that migrants receive disproportionate privileges in comparison to native citizens (Sibrian Díaz et al. 2023, 20).

Which Actors Are Primarily Responsible for Disinformation Regarding Migrants?

Some authors have drawn attention to the fact that politicians and institutions are engaged in the dissemination of fakes about migrants. This is particularly striking given that they are expected to be especially responsible in this decisive matter for social cohesion. Sibrian Díaz et al. (2023) insist that a considerable proportion of disinformation originates from political parties, which frequently utilize deceptive narratives to advance anti-migrant agendas. It is asserted that governments and other institutions are, on occasion, the source of the fakes. This represents a significant influence on how the general public perceives migrants and migratory policies. The aim is to discourage human mobility by employing falsehood as a strategic tool (Sibrian Díaz et al. 2023, 21–22). In this context, the authors reiterate that the frames and discursive axes of documented disinformation are aligned with the exploitation of migration as a problem. This represents a strategy of informational disorder. And it constitutes an agenda-setting strategy that includes a diagnostic and a solution, wherein immigrants are positioned as the scapegoats for systemic and economic crises.

For example, in relation to the economic impact of migration, the idea of immigrants lowering salaries or taking jobs from native workers is a common ground of most discourses, among other rhetorical elements. This happens in the European "migrant crisis" of 2015, the "Rohingya crisis" in Myanmar of 2017, and in the ongoing "Mexico-US border crisis" (Komendantova, Erokhin and Albano 2023, 5). These discourses usually fear low-skilled workers, but as is the case in Germany (Hayo and Roth 2024, 3) with regard to cross-border commuters from the Czech Republic to Germany, there are other variables to consider, such as the fears of mature workers who feel they can be replaced by younger ones.

In addition to politicians, governments, and other institutional actors, media outlets and other entities also contribute to disinformation and negative stereotypes about migrants (Rebollo Díaz 2021, 21; Culloty et al. 2022, 7), to the extent that "the use of fear as a framing device results in a perpetual flow of 'bad news' about migrant crime, public unrest and violence" (Culloty et al. 2022, 10). This phenomenon was observed in the news coverage of the refugee crisis in Europe in 2015 and has since been repeated in the context of migration from North Africa (Culloty et al. 2022, 10).

Other influential actors involved in the dissemination of disinformation and the promotion of hatred toward migrants are those identified by Culloty et al. (2022, 3) as "bad actors." The term "bad actors" is used to describe individuals or entities that intentionally create and disseminate disinformation. Such actors may be states, corporations, social movements, or individuals, and their motivations encompass a range of political, ideological, and financial interests. Furthermore, there is considerable variation in terms of the audiences they target and the level of coordination involved. Subsequently, there are those who may be considered "amplifiers" of disinformation: "The media pundits, politicians, celebrities and online influencers who contribute to the proliferation of disinformation, whether intentionally or otherwise, by disseminating it among their extensive networks" (Culloty et al. 2022, 3).

Nevertheless, in conjunction with media outlets that discriminate against migrants indirectly, as mentioned above, there exists a phenomenon known as "hyperpartisan media." These ideological outlets frequently amplify disinformation (Culloty et al. 2022, 17). This phenomenon has been observed in the United States (Culloty et al. 2022, 17), Chile (Sibrian Díaz et al. 2023), Spain (Narváez-Linares and Pérez-Rufí 2022), South-East Asia (Radue 2019), the Czech Republic (Hanzelka and Schmidt 2017), and Germany (Hanzelka and Schmidt 2017).

Building Resilience to Disinformation about Migrants

One of the most pressing concerns for international and domestic institutions alike is the question of how to effectively combat disinformation, with a particular focus on the impact of such disinformation on migrants.

The EU has launched a range of initiatives, including the incorporation of hate speech crimes into national criminal codes, the implementation of media literacy action plans, and the initiation of educational campaigns. Examples of the diversity of European measures include the publication of laws such as the Digital Services Act (Regulation (EU) 2022/2065) in November 2022. This act provides incentives for the control of activities related to disinformation and hate speech through digital platforms. European campaigns, such as the 2018 "Action Plan against Disinformation" by the European Commission, seek to address this threat in a coordinated manner, in a plan comprising four pillars (Cocchini 2021, 102):

- enhancing the capacity of the EU to detect, analyze, and expose disinformation;
- strengthening the coordination of responses to disinformation;
- mobilizing the private sector (primarily social media platforms) to combat disinformation; and
- increasing societal awareness and responsiveness.

A further initiative of the EU in the context of efforts to combat disinformation is the Digital Media Observatory (EDMO), which has a presence in numerous European countries.

Nevertheless, the creation of a defensive frame against disinformation about migrants requires long-term projects. In order to combat the increase in polarization, immediate measures must be taken in conjunction with long-term strategies (Carlson and Terry 2023, 260; Cullotti et al. 2022, 15). These strategies should be designed to detect and counter disinformation campaigns. Therefore, policymakers, technology platforms, NGOs, media outlets, and researchers should be engaged in both long- and short-term measures.

Among them, the implementation of hate speech legislation would prohibit offensive discourse and incitement of violence. Such legislation can be employed to combat disinformation targeting specific groups, including migrants.

It is also imperative that media and platform regulation be implemented to prevent false information and harmful rhetoric directed at migrants. The promotion of transparency in the dissemination of information may prove beneficial. Furthermore, there is a need to monitor the presence of disinformation in their content.

However, in light of the recent surge in hate campaigns targeting migrants on social media, it becomes evident that these regulations are insufficient in the absence of the involvement of digital platforms.

In line with these considerations, a number of regulatory proposals have been put forth with a view to holding platforms accountable for the content they disseminate. One such proposal is the EU's "The Strengthened Code of Practice on Disinformation," which was adopted in June 2022. The code calls for greater transparency regarding online advertising, with the objective of demonetizing disinformation. Furthermore, the establishment of a consensus regarding the definition of "impermissible manipulative behavior" and the adoption of measures requiring greater effort to detect disinformation and empower users to protect themselves from it are essential (European Commission 2022).

In a preliminary manner, Fernández et al. (2023, 16) put forth a proposition for public awareness initiatives. These would aim to provide information about the reality of migration while also discrediting prevalent myths. Such initiatives may assist in the refutation of negative narratives and stereotypes. In collaboration with experts on migration and civil society organizations, reliable information based on evidence from migrants can be created and disseminated. Moreover, Narváez-Llinares and Pérez-Rufí (2022, 850) and Culloty et al. (2022, 8) emphasize the necessity for journalists to receive training and for resources to be made available to enable them to report responsibly on migration. From the latter's point of view, "contemporary newsrooms are under-resourced, and journalists often lack the time and money to provide in-depth, contextual coverage." Additionally, some journalists may lack the requisite training to achieve this goal, while others are constrained by the influence of political and financial interests, which can lead to a culture of self-censorship within newsrooms. As a result, a considerable proportion of media reporting on migration is characterized by a lack of contextual depth and a tendency toward superficiality, simplistic analysis, and misinformation. Furthermore, there is often discernible political bias in such reporting. Even in countries with high levels of media freedom, news coverage tends to reflect the priorities and concerns of the government in power (Narváez-Llinares and Pérez-Rufí 2022, 843).

All of the aforementioned authors consider media literacy campaigns to be an indispensable measure for assisting users—and society as a whole—in countering disinformation about migrants. This entails providing the public with the tools to critically evaluate information, identify hate speech, and comprehend the impact of discriminatory language. Such measures can assist in combating the proliferation of harmful narratives targeting migrants (Culloty et al. 2022, 13). Fernández et al. (2023) and Essalhi-Rakra and Pinedo-González (2023, 17) propose the promotion of positive narratives about migrants in the media, with the aim of counteracting the negative representations of them that incite hatred.

Following Dragomir et al. (2024) and Humprecht et al. (2020, 513), resilience in the face of disinformation can be understood as a structural context in which disinformation does not reach a significant number of citizens. This implies the existence of a system that provides a safeguard for society against false narratives and propaganda.

In summary, the principal measures employed to combat disinformation against migrants can be grouped into four categories.

In regard to digital platforms and social media:

- Conducting research and data analysis to gain a deeper understanding of the mechanisms through which hate speech is disseminated on these platforms and to identify the most effective ways to combat it.
- The implementation of verifying tools, which could be facilitated by agreements with registered fact-checkers.
- The development of more effective content moderation systems, which can identify instances of disinformation and hate speech.
- The provision of accessible and straightforward claims systems for users.

These measures are in accordance with the provisions of the UE Digital Services Act, 2022 (Azurmendi 2023, 287–301).

In regard to governments and educational institutions:

- The promotion of media literacy. It is also of the utmost importance to pay special attention to the knowledge of digital rights, in addition to the availability of reporting resources for disinformation and hate speech.

- The promotion of collaboration with human rights organizations.
- The promotion of collaboration with media outlets and journalists, with the objective of providing more resources for the dissemination of accurate information about migrants.

The measures in question are mentioned by Narváez-Linares and Pérez-Rufí (2022), Dragomir, Rúas-Araújo, and Horowitz (2024), Humprecht, Esser, and Van-Aelst (2020), Culloty et al. (2022), and Sibrian Díaz, Colmenares Mejías and Nuñez Silva (2023).

Discussion

Disinformation and hate speech against migrants are usually studied separately, as they represent different phenomena. Authors such as Fernández et al. (2023, 15–18) insist on the factors that contribute to the polarization against this population group, in particular social conflict, the divisive line between legal and illegal migrants, and the perception of migrants as a task force, without mentioning disinformation. They consider the existence of negative news as a fact that influences attitudes toward migrants, but fakes are not part of this narrative. From a different perspective, Amores et al. (2020) focus on the problem of hostile rhetoric on controversial topics that facilitates harmful stereotypes. Disinformation is an existing phenomenon, but apart from those narratives that promote hostility.

Nevertheless, Culloty et al. (2022, 4) insist on the definitive role of disinformation in the spread of rejectionist emotions toward these citizens. Often, it is not a deliberate campaign of fakes, but a permanent presence of misleading traces about migration in media and social media. And this ultimately has the consequence of a "commonplace phenomenon" of insensitivity toward the stereotyping and depiction of this issue on public opinion (Culloty et al. 2022, 4). According to Sibrian Díaz et al. (2023, 20), politicians with rejectionist ideas, as well as xenophobic activists build their arguments and campaign strategies based on this arena. There are some cases, such as the European refugee crisis, among others, that confirm this idea (Georgiou and Zaborowski 2017, 3).

Beyond these reflections, Alonso González (2019, 32) and Narváez-Linares and Pérez Rufi (2022, 841) emphasize the reality of intentional disinformation about migrants. As they confirm, it has the specific effect of fostering social rejection toward this group. Therefore, it can be argued that the dissemination of false information with the intention of inciting hatred and discrimination against migrants constitutes a form of hate speech (Narváez-Linares and Pérez Rufí 2022, 842).

Conclusions

Disinformation is an effective way to generate sentiments of rejection against migrants; therefore, one line of fighting hate speech against this population group it to combat disinformation.

As a consequence of the persistent negative narrative about migrants, journalists, politicians, and citizens become in many cases unable to perceive the disinformation present in a range of aspects of public opinion referring to this issue (Culloty et al. 2022, 4). This is particularly relevant because the position on immigration becomes an essential element of the identity of political parties (Narváez-Linares and Pérez Rufi, 2022, 841).

Cases like the so-called European "migrant crisis" of 2015 or, more recently, the Southport riots of 2024, or even the recent electoral campaigns in Germany (2024), France (2024), and Italy (2022) show that immigration is at the center of the polarization phenomena, promoted by social media (Sibrian Díaz 2023, 8).

The creation of a defensive framework against disinformation about migrants requires a long-term project involving different actors and fields of action. For example, in this regard, countries must have adequate laws in place to both discourage hate speech and require digital platforms to remove it from their services. Journalists should receive more resources and training to report on migration in order to avoid fostering negative feelings toward migrants in a particular community. At the same time, citizens should become more media literate to identify disinformation on this issue.

Acknowledgment

The research was supported by Resilient Media for Democracy in the Digital Age (ReMeD), an international multidisciplinary project supported by the EU's Horizon Europe Research and Innovation Programme,

HORIZON-CL2-2022-DEMOCRACY-01-06: "Media for Democracy—Democratic Media," under grant agreement no. 101094742.

Conflict of Interest Statement

No potential conflict of interest was reported by the authors.

Notes

1 Amnesty Tech is part of Amnesty International, see www.amnesty.org/en/tech/; statements in this section taken from www.amnistia.org/es/noticias/2024/08/reino-unido-las-grandes-plataformas-tecnologicas-desempenan-un-papel-activo/

2 The European Commission report *Media Coverage of the "Refugee Crisis": A Cross-European Perspective* (2017) uses both terms alternatively—Europe's "refugee crisis" and Europe's "migration crisis." Authors of the report explain their use of "refugee/migration crisis," conscious that the refugee identity is a specific case of migrants. Nevertheless, there are authors like Amores, Arcila-Calderón, Carlos, and Blanco-Herrero (2020) who consider different communication frames for each group.

3 Andrea Lawlor and Erin Tolley (2017) make this classification after an analysis of Canadian press of the decade 2005–14.

References

Alonso González, María. 2019. "Fake news: desinformación en la era de la sociedad de la información." *Ámbitos Revista de Comunicación* 45: 29–52. http://dx.doi.org/10.12795/Ambitos.2019.i45.03.

Amores, Javier, Carlos Arcila-Calderón, and David Blanco-Herrero. 2020. "Evolution of negative visual frames of immigrants and refugees in the main media of Southern Europe." *Profesional de la Información* 29 (6). https://doi.org/10.3145/epi.2020.nov.24.

Azurmendi, Ana. 2023. *Derecho de la comunicación*. Eunsa.

Biškup Mašanović, Ljiljana. 2021. "The mythologisation of the migrant issue in the Federal Republic of Germany as a result of the 2015 European migrant crisis and its effect on changes in German migration policy." *Migracijske i etničke teme* 37 (2): 177–209. https://doi.org/10.11567/met.37.2.3.

Brenner, Jermi, and Katrin Ohlendorf. 2016. "Time for facts. What do we know about Cologne four months later." *The Correspondent*, May 2. https://thecorrespondent.com/4401/time-for-the-facts-what-do-we-know-about-cologne-four-months-later/1073698080444-e20ada1b.
Carlson, Caitlin Ring, and Christopher Terry. 2023. "The devil's in the details: How countries' defamation laws can (and can't) combat hate speech." *Journalism Practice* 18 (2): 242–64. https://doi.org/10.1080/17512786.2023.2251976.
Casciani, Dominic, and BBC Verify. 2024. "Violent Southport protests reveal organising tactics of the far-right." *BBC*, August 2. www.bbc.com/news/articles/cl4y0453nv5o.
Cocchini, Andrea. 2021. "Desinformación y noticias falsas (las Fake News): Medidas Internacionales y Europeas para combatirlas." In *Tratado de Derecho Digital*, edited by E. Valpuesta Gastaminza and Juan Carlos Hernández Peña. Wolters Kluwer.
Culloty, Eileen, Jane Suiter, Itay Iriri, and Sara Creta. 2022. *Disinformation about migration: An age-old issue with new tech dimension. World migration report.* International Organization for Migration. https://publications.iom.int/books/world-migration-report-2022-chapter-8
Dragomir, Marius, José Rúas-Araújo, and Minna Horowitz. 2024. "Beyond online disinformation: Assessing national information resilience in four European countries." *Humanities and Social Sciences Communications* 11 (101). https://doi.org/10.1057/s41599-024-02605-5.
Essalhi-Rakrak, Abdellah, and Ruth Pinedo-González. 2023. "#EspañaInvadida. Disinformation and hate speech towards refugees on Twitter: A challenge for critical thinking." *Profesional de la información* 32 (3). https://doi.org/10.3145/epi.2023.may.10.
European Commission. 2018. *Tackling online disinformation*. COM/2018/236 final. https://eur-lex.europa.eu/legal-content/EN/TXT/?uri=CELEX%3A52018DC0236.
European Commission. 2022. *The strengthened code of practice on disinformation*. https://disinfocode.eu/wp-content/uploads/2023/01/The-Strengthened-Code-of-Practice-on-Disinformation-2022.pdf.
European Commission. 2023. *Eurostat report. 2023. Migration and asylum in Europe*. https://ec.europa.eu/eurostat/web/interactive-publications/migration-2023.
European Court of Human Rights. 2022. Case of NIT S.R.L. v. The Republic of Moldova. HUDOC Database https://hudoc.echr.coe.int/#{%22fulltext%22:[%22NIT%20S.R.L.%20v.%20The%20Republic%20of%20Moldova,%202022%22],%22documentcollectionid2%22:[%22GRANDCHAMBER%22,%22CHAMBER%22],%22itemid%22:[%22001-216872%22]}
Fernández, Ángel, Lucía Andaluz Antón, Javier Pérez Sánchez, and Almudena Revilla Guijarro. 2023. "Desinformación, manipulación visual y representación de la migración en Twitter: análisis del Caso Aquarius." *ASRI. Arte y Sociedad. Revista de Investigación en Artes y Humanidades Digitales* 24: 15–31. https://doi.org/10.33732/ASRI.6356.

FAD (Friends of Africa Development) Foundation. 2022. Discurso de odio en redes. https://fad.es

Georgiou, Myria, and Rafal Zaborowski. 2017. *Media coverage of the "refugee crisis": A cross-European perspective.* Council of Europe. DG1(2017)03. https://rm.coe.int/1680706b00.

Hanzelka, Jan, and Ina Schmidt. 2017. "Dynamics of cyber hate in social media: A comparative analysis of anti-Muslim movements in the Czech Republic and Germany." *International Journal of Cyber Criminology* 11 (1): 143–60. www.cybercrimejournal.com/pdf/Hanzelka&Schmidtvol11issue1IJCC2017.pdf.

Hayo, Bernd, and Duncan H. W. Roth. 2024. "The perceived impact of immigration on native workers' labour market outcomes." *European Journal of Political Economy* 85: 102610. https://doi.org/10.1016/j.ejpoleco.2024.102610.

Humprecht, Edda, Frank Esser, and Peter Van-Aelst. 2020. "Resilience to online disinformation: A framework for cross-national comparative research." *International Journal of Press/Politics* 25 (3): 493–516. https://doi.org/10.1177/1940161219900126.

Komendantova, Nadejda, Dmitry Erokhin, and Teresa Albano. 2023. "Misinformation and its impact on contested policy issues: The example of migration discourses." *Societies* 13 (7): 168. https://doi.org/10.3390/soc13070168.

Lawlor, Andrea, and Erin Tolley. 2017. "News media framing of immigrants and refugees." *International Journal of Communication* 11: 967–91. https://ijoc.org/index.php/ijoc/article/view/6273/1946.

Millar, Paul. 2024. "How France's far right changed the debate on immigration." *France 24*, June 20. www.france24.com/en/france/20240620-how-france-s-far-right-changed-the-debate-on-immigration.

Ministerio de Asuntos Exteriores, Gobierno de España. 2023. *La lucha contra la desinformación.* www.exteriores.gob.es/es/PoliticaExterior/Paginas/LaLuchaContraLaDesinformacion.aspx.

Moreno-Castro, Carolina, Vania Baldi, Ana Azurmendi, Miguel Paisana, María Iranzo-Cabrera, Dafne Calvo, Miguel Crespo, Yolanda Cabrera, Germán Llorca-Abad, Gustavo Cardoso, Pablo Hernández and Ramón Salaverría. 2023. *Report on political and legal aspects of disinformation in Portugal and Spain.* Iberian Digital Media Observatory. https://doi.org/10.15581/026.004.

Narváez-Linares, Ángel, and José P. Pérez-Rufí. 2022. "Fake news y desinformación sobre migración en España: prácticas del discurso xenófobo en redes sociales y medios online según la plataforma Maldita Migración." *Estudios sobre el Mensaje Periodístico* 28 (4): 841–54. https://doi.org/10.5209/esmp.82845.

Olivares-Delgado, Fernando, Mayte Benlloch-Osuna, Daniel Rodríguez-Valero and Eva Breva-Franch. 2023 "Corporate disinformation: Concept and typology of forms of corporate disinformation". In *Advances in design and digital communication III. DIGICOM 2022. Springer series in design and innovation*, edited by N. Martins and Daniel Brandão. Springer. https://doi.org/10.1007/978-3-031-20364-0_46.

Qi, Peng, Juan Cao, Tianyun Yang, Junbo Guo and Jintao Li. . 2020. "Exploring the role of visual content in fake news detection." In *Disinformation, misinformation, and fake news in social media: Emerging research challenges and opportunities*, edited by K. Shu, Wang Suhan, D. Lee, and Liu Huan. Springer. https://arxiv.org/pdf/1908.04472.pdf.

Radue, Melanie. 2019. "Harmful disinformation in Southeast Asia: 'Negative campaigning', 'information operations' and 'racist propaganda'—Three forms of manipulative political communication in Malaysia, Myanmar, and Thailand." *Journal of Contemporary Eastern Asia* 18 (2): 68–89. https://doi.org/10.17477/JCEA.2019.18.2.068.

Rebollo Díaz, Carolina. 2021. "Tuiteando sobre refugiados: una comparación internacional de discursos, imaginarios y representaciones sociales." PhD diss., University of Huelva. https://rabida.uhu.es/dspace/handle/10272/20113.

Serrano-Puche, Javier, Natalia Rodríguez-Salcedo, and Pilar Martínez-Costa. 2023. "Trust, disinformation, and digital media: Perceptions and expectations about news in a polarized environment." *Profesional de la información* 32 (5). https://doi.org/10.3145/epi.2023.sep.18.

Sibrian Díaz, Nairbis Desirée, Neida Josefina Colmenares Mejías, Juan Carlos, and Núñez Silva. 2023. "Estrategias desinformativas sobre migración en Chile: encuadre de noticias falsas respecto a la movilidad humana." *Migraciones* 59: 1–27. https://doi.org/10.14422/mig.2023.021.

UNHCR. 2015. *El año de la crisis de refugiados en Europa.* www.acnur.org/noticias/stories/2015-el-ano-de-la-crisis-de-refugiados-en-europa.

Vergani, Matteo, Bárbara Perry, Joshua Freilich, Steven Chermak, Ryan Scrivens, Rouven Link, Daniel Kleinsman, John Betts, and Muhammad Iqbal. 2022. "Protocol: Mapping the scientific knowledge and approaches to defining and measuring hate crime, hate speech, and hate incidents." *Campbell Systematic Reviews* 18 (2): e1228. https://doi.org/10.100Serran/cl2.1228.

Wardle, Claire. 2017. Noticias falsas. Es complicado. First Draft. https://firstdraftnews.org/articles/noticias-falsas-es-complicado/

3

New Topics but Still the Same Narratives: COVID-19 and War in Ukraine on the Czech-Language Disinformation Websites (Case Studies)

Alice Němcová Tejkalová, Veronika Macková, and Victoria Nainová

In contemporary society, social media have become powerful tools for disseminating both information and disinformation that certain people and groups share. The primary aims of creating and distributing disinformation are economic gain and misleading the public (European Commission 2018). Disinformation can also exacerbate societal polarization and evoke fear, anxiety, and uncertainty, leading to significant public reactions. It creates the basis of the so-called hybrid war. This form of conflict uses disinformation, cyber-attacks, or economic pressure to destabilize enemy states and prepare the conditions for achieving strategic goals (Khorram-Manesh et al. 2023).

As Juhász (2024, 1076) argues: "While disinformation campaigns are not used exclusively by authoritarian states against democracies, democracies are more vulnerable targets due to their openness and fundamental values." For this research, we use Weedon et al.'s definition of disinformation:

> Inaccurate or manipulated information/content that is spread intentionally. This can include false news, or involve more subtle methods such as false flag operations, feeding inaccurate quotes or stories to innocent intermediaries, or knowingly amplifying biased or misleading information. (Weedon et al. in Zerback et al. 2021, 1081)

Even though disinformation topics have changed during the time periods, being regularly updated to continue causing societal disturbance, the narratives and patterns stay the same.

As the Czech Republic has been, since the end of the Second World War, perceived by the USSR and later Russia as its sphere of influence, especially after the Russian annexation of Crimea in 2014, there have been many disinformation actors operating with more or less tight ties to the Russian state itself, ranging from the Czech version of *Sputnik News* to websites founded by Czech citizens but distributing pro-Russian content, for example, Aeronet News or ProtiProud (in English counter-stream), which was one of the analyzed websites in our case studies introduced later in this chapter (more about the Central European sociopolitical context regarding the disinformation scene can be found in Němcová Tejkalová 2023 or Wenzel et al. 2024). On the other hand, it is no longer a unique Central European experience with Russian-made disinformation content influencing the internal political situation of a state. It has been a cause of all European states and, more broadly, the western part of the world—when the troll factories have topics that they want to use to create society's disintegration, they use them. Bennett and Livingston (2018) mention evidence of this kind of activity from the United States, the UK, Germany, Sweden, Norway, and the Netherlands.

On a global level, Russian political leaders actively seek to influence the media and spread their propaganda through various communication channels to manipulate public opinion and maintain control over information to destabilize the political scene in other countries (Krajčovič 2022). Since 2014, anti-American rhetoric in the Russian media has started to increase. The Russian government even invested 450 million dollars in broadcasting this information abroad and spreading it worldwide (Gerber and Zavisca 2016). In addition to television broadcasting, online propaganda has also become a tool of modern warfare (Scott 2022). Anti-Americanism took hold in Russia, which was also manifested during the COVID-19 pandemic.

With social media flourishing, they are typical environments for spreading these types of information and are suitable for use for all the possible campaigns. The (dis)information spreads quickly there, with some of the social media companies trying to do their best with fact-checking (Garz and Szucs 2023), being logically disadvantaged here because they are always only reacting. Enders et al. (2023) found that those who frequently use social media are likely to believe conspiracy theories and disinformation. For our case studies, we focused on disinformation spread on Facebook because it is, according to the AMI Digital Index (2024), the second most popular social medium in the Czech Republic with 89 percent users, particularly for GenX and boomers, conquered only by YouTube with 90 percent. Far fewer Czechs fancy Instagram (63 percent), TikTok (34 percent), or X (27 percent), even though Instagram and TikTok have been growing quickly in recent years (AMI Digital 2024). As Turková and Macková (2024) realized from their quantitative survey, Czech citizens most often—in 75 percent of cases—gained and—in 23 percent of cases —verified the information directly from Facebook.

In the first case study, we focused on the typical schemes and patterns around which the content of two Facebook pages of Czech disinformation websites—ProtiProud and Otevři svou mysl (in English: Open Your Mind), later followed by Otevři svou duši (Open Your Soul)—has been built. We compared the situation in 2020 and 2021 (when the topic of disinformation was mainly COVID-19, especially vaccination against it) with that in 2024.

The second case study tackles the situation directly preceding the war in Ukraine. Even though our primary research goal was to understand better how disinformation content had been spread among the Facebook accounts of individual users in the case of COVID-19 and how the filter bubbles algorithms have been working, we realized that the troll factories had been already preparing the floor for the Russian invasion of Ukraine by framing the opposition against vaccination and anti-COVID-19 measures as a fight from freedom, connecting it with the "liberating activities" of Russian president Putin. According to Geissler et al. (2023), after the start of the invasion, pro-Russian messages were spread on Twitter using bots.

Establishing Fear as a Tool of Persuasion on Czech Disinformation Websites

The first case study identifies the basic parameters exhibited by disinformation websites that appear on social media. Facebook pages of two Czech disinformation websites, ProtiProud (2024) and Otevři svou mysl (2024), were selected for analysis. These websites exploit topics relevant to Czechia and spread disinformation and negative posts to position themselves in opposition to mainstream opinion. One part of this qualitative content analysis focusing on spreading information about COVID-19 (a research period starting from December 1, 2020, and ending March 20, 2021) was conducted for the Czech educational project Infomore.cz (Němcová Tejkalová et al. 2021). For this essay, we added the analysis of data from June 1, 2024, to July 31, 2024, to incorporate current information and to show how the disinformation-spreading patterns stay the same.

To briefly introduce both outlets, we start with ProtiProud. Its editor-in-chief is Petr Hájek, a former journalist and press spokesperson for former Czech president Václav Klaus. The author of Otevři svou mysl is (unless otherwise stated) David Formánek, who translates and publishes foreign-language videos and contributions. Both disinformation sites use social media such as Facebook to disseminate their content. The Facebook pages share the same names as their respective websites. Both of these Facebook pages have a relatively high number of followers. As of July 26, 2024, ProtiProud had approximately 20,000 page likes and 22,000 followers, while Otevři svou mysl had approximately 5,800 page likes and 25,000 followers. Both pages are highly active, posting several times a week, and have well-defined target audiences. Since May 2022 (according to the date of the first post), Otevři svou mysl has launched a side project called Otevři svou duši, which has both a website and a Facebook page. This project focuses on topics such as spirituality, extraterrestrial civilizations, and human history (Otevři svou duši 2024).

Disinformation content has been proliferating on social media for several years, although social media such as Facebook have been attempting to suppress such content (de-Lima-Santos and Ceron 2024) by marking some posts as containing false information or deleting pages. However, administrators of these disinformation sites tend to find ways of circumventing these measures. Otevři svou mysl's Facebook page has been removed from the platform several times but has always returned to continue its activities. The administrator of Otevři svou mysl's Facebook page also publishes content on other platforms, modifying the names of these platforms in the posts to avoid detection and erasure by Facebook moderators. In fact, this tactic implicitly acknowledges the publication of false and disinformation content, but it is framed as the "heroic" fight of the administrator against an "evil" social medium.

Findings

The findings of the case study indicate that both ProtiProud and Otevři svou mysl use topics such as the COVID-19 pandemic, vaccination, and migration linked to armed conflicts, most recently war in Ukraine, alongside strategic tools to spread disinformation. Through qualitative content analysis, three factors that assist in recognizing disinformation pages similar to the analyzed ones on Facebook were identified: (1) the content format of posts on social media, (2) the use of ideological propaganda, and (3) follower profiles.

During the observed periods, posts on ProtiProud and Otevři svou mysl contained multimodal elements—both textual and visual components. According to Heley et al. (2022), spreading disinformation through a multimodal approach that combines textual and visual content such as photos, collages, and videos is very effective because these forms of content can be easily shared across various channels. Visual content particularly plays a role in strengthening disinformation. As Hameleers et al. (2020) and Hameleers (2024) point out, readers are more likely to perceive a message as trustworthy if it includes visual elements that enhance the sense of reality (Sundar 2008).

Messages containing visual content on the social media also tend to attract more attention and are consequently shared more frequently (Brennen et al. 2021). This level of increased dissemination can be particularly dangerous in fields such as health and medicine, where disinformation may lack expert references or be removed from context (Southwell et al. 2022). This is what both analyzed websites exploit in connection to previously mentioned controversial topics. However, they differ in their approach to formality. The posts on ProtiProud are visually misleading, incorporating collages and containing negative or intimidating elements.

Posts contain simpler elements, and the visual and language styles are more formal. These posts do not contain any vulgarisms or slang expressions. Instead, they use a more formal presentation, typically featuring only photos of people in the background and the post's title in the foreground, lending a veneer of scientific credibility to the content that largely comprises conspiracy theories (Figure 3.1). For example, a post related to vaccination included a video of a woman living in Israel describing the treatment of vaccinated and unvaccinated individuals. The post generated more than 1,300 comments and 5,400 reactions. Commenters expressed concern about the situation in Czechia and the restrictions imposed on people who refuse vaccination.

Posts on the Otevři svou mysl's Facebook page frequently include disinformation that is able to give readers the impression of a trustworthy source on account of claimed professional expertise or reputation, thereby increasing the likelihood that the content will be trusted. An example of such a post concerns an alleged link between the COVID-19 vaccine and infertility. The post aims to instill fear or a sense of threat in readers, and its credibility is supposedly reinforced by an informant from a pharmaceutical company. However, another

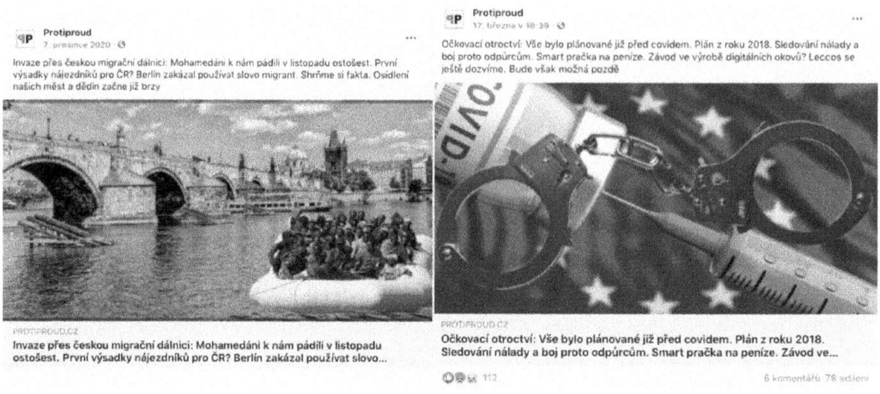

Figure 3.1 Examples of posts with manipulative graphic elements published by ProtiProud.

example of a video post by Paul Joseph Watson, a British right-wing YouTuber and conspiracy theorist, about a public survey in Germany related to migration lacks any citation of a source. The translated video similarly omits information about the source or even the name of the survey or its initiator.

The second important identified aspect of these disinformation outlets was the use of ideological propaganda. On their Facebook page, ProtiProud publishes radical material and disinformation that promote an anti-Western ideology, align it with official Russian policies, and convey negative sentiments toward minorities. Their ideological propaganda resembles that of the Nazi (using even the same font for their messages) and Communist (by spreading conspiracy theories based on the presupposition that the world is ruled by a secret order of enormously rich capitalists) regimes of the twentieth century. Accompanied by misleading collages, these posts support the thematic agenda of conspiracies and foster a sense of threat and insecurity among readers.

ProtiProud's Facebook page features conspiracy-laden posts, such as claims that the COVID pandemic is part of a vaccine-assisted conspiracy against humanity, or accusations against Bill Gates and his child vaccination scheme (Figure 3.1 and 3.2). The founders of these disinformation sites position themselves as saviors attempting to "awaken" the population, which reflects the sectarian nature of such communities.

Similarly, Otevři svou mysl includes posts referencing conspiracy theories about Bill Gates and a cabal of powerful individuals who control the world, unbeknown to "ordinary" people. This narrative is presented in a more

Figure 3.2 A post concerning Bill Gates's child vaccination scheme, dated July 25, 2024.

sophisticated form as a series of documentaries in which journalist Janet Ossebaard claims that Bill Gates is behind the COVID-19 virus. According to Newton Media, a European media-monitoring and analytics company, this theory is the second most common disinformation circulated in the Czech media in connection with speculation about the origins of COVID-19 (Vodochodský 2021). Otevři svou mysl's Facebook page also contains posts about the so-called "Great Reset" conspiracy, explained by American YouTuber JP Sears as a secret government program purportedly designed to simulate future events based on data collected about the population.

Followers of ProtiProud's and Otevři svou mysl's Facebook pages share a worldview that portrays the West as depraved and corrupt, drawing on the traditions of totalitarian regimes such as Nazi Germany and promoting anti-immigration ideologies.

Examining the profiles of these followers reveals common characteristics: they often lack personal profile photos, opting instead for images of animals, animated characters, or similar nonpersonal visuals. Some profiles feature images intended to convey well-being, starkly contrasting with the hateful and radical content shared by these followers. In addition to sharing stereotyped personal images (e.g., for women—cute animals, flowers, or culinary creations; for men—motorbikes, cars, military themes), these profiles frequently include content directly reposted from or ideologically aligned with the monitored platforms.

To sum up, the Facebook pages of ProtiProud and Otevři svou mysl disseminate false and misleading posts designed to evoke fear and intimidation, fostering the impression of an insidious global conspiracy of powerful elites against which there is no defense except to follow these disinformation platforms. These platforms present themselves as purveyors of "the truth" and claim to enlighten the public. However, the styles of these pages differ significantly. Otevři svou mysl is a monothematically focused Facebook page that employs formal language and visuals. In contrast, ProtiProud adopts an "old-school" disinformation style, initially having spread anti-EU and anti-migration content before shifting focus to the COVID pandemic and later to the war in Ukraine. This older model also corresponds to a noticeably less credible manner of expression, both linguistically and visually.

Radical Discourse and Polarization on Facebook: Sharing Posts against Vaccination and Pandemic Measures as Perceived Anti-Western Rebellion

The second case study, conducted also for the Czech educational project Infomore.cz (Němcová Tejkalová et al. 2022), focuses on the Facebook profiles of people who spread information about the demonstrations against vaccination and anti-pandemic measures, radically polarizing the society on the eve of the start of the Russian war in Ukraine. The research interest was on how these people commented on these media texts and what else they publicly posted on their Facebook pages. The three most shared posts regarding anti-vaccination demonstrations and anti-pandemic government measures on the Facebook page of one of the most-read Czech news servers—iDNES.cz—and on ProtiProud have been selected and then tracked on the users' Facebook profiles for the research period from November 17, 2021, to January 31, 2022. Quantitative content analysis was used to map the number and manner of sharing as well as sentiment of the comments (whether they supported or opposed demonstrations). Qualitative content analysis was applied on the content of shared texts, commented topics, and other content on sharing profiles. A total of 1,793 comments on six posts and public content across 505 sharing profiles were analyzed.

The analysis showed that this type of news is spread exclusively by people who share false and manipulative news on various other topics, such as Russian–Ukrainian relations, migration, or the status of women in society, regardless of whether these were neutral pieces of news published on iDNES.cz, or biased ones published on ProtiProud.cz. The sharers and commentators were not ashamed of their attitudes and spoke of themselves as “free people.” This social group attacked citizens who followed the rules and labeled them as Western (mainly American) agents or a herd of sheep and ridiculed them. These people also downplayed the entire situation, including health impacts or measures against the spread of this virus as, for example, Calvillo et al. (2020) described in their research focused on the situation in the United States. With regard to the intense frequency of their publication (e.g., a post published almost every single minute, every day, exclusively shared anti-establishment content, nothing original), we can speculate that some of these profiles are in fact robotic, products of troll factories (as observed in other cases by Zerback et al. 2021 and Hunter 2023).

Findings

Despite our previous assumptions that posts on iDNES.cz about the anti-government demonstrations would be shared by a broader audience, not only by people supporting them, the most shared post on iDNES.cz’s Facebook profile was shared exclusively by the citizens who also shared other disinformation content. The article titled “Demonstrations rock European cities. Yellow stars were carried in Vienna, cars were on fire in The Hague” was written by Daniela Pešková and Czech News Agency. The post was published on iDNES.cz’s Facebook page on November 21, 2021, and had 3,117 reactions, 865 comments, and 730 shares (until February 9, 2022 2:07 p.m.). It turned out that people also shared stories similar to this one from other problematic sources spreading conspiracies, such as AC24, CZ24, Raptor TV, SputnikNews, Zivot.org, or Aeronet.

The remaining two investigated posts on iDNES.cz were also found to be shared by profiles that published other disinformation content. The second most shared post in the monitored branch was a post with an article written also by Daniela Pešková, with the headline “Tens of thousands of opponents of lockdown and mandatory vaccination met in Vienna.” This post generated 1,256 reactions,

368 comments, and 91 shares (until February 4, 2022, 3:39 p.m.), and the third most shared post was an article from November 22, 2021: "Demonstrators riot in Prague again. Hundreds of them gathered at the Castle," authored by Rémy Vlachos. Considering that iDNES.cz is one of the most-read websites in the Czech Republic and over 279,000 people follow the Facebook page of this medium, even the third post in the sample generated substantial engagement. Under this article appeared 1,357 reactions, 589 comments, and 88 shares (until February 4, 2022 3:36 p.m.). Regarding the tone of comments, out of a total of 1,822 comments in all three posts, 34 percent were supportive toward the people at demonstrations, 28 percent were negative, and in 38 percent of cases it was not possible to evaluate the tone of a comment.

Many users who shared content on their profiles often expressed disapproval of the political actions of the governments of the Czech Republic and Slovakia, especially with response to the COVID-19 pandemic (Figure 3.3). Criticism of government measures often included skepticism about vaccinations, concerns about restrictions on personal freedoms, and mistrust of official information. The Czech government was criticized for its handling of the pandemic, while Slovak president Zuzana Čaputová faced criticism for, say, the decision to allow the presence of US military troops in the context of rising tensions between Russia and Ukraine. Users often shared posts that opposed Western politics and highlighted positions that did not align with official statements.

More personal content could also be found on the profiles, such as photos of animals or tips on strengthening health and immunity. Men frequently shared pictures of attractive women, cars, and favorite music performers. Both sexes then often posted motivational quotes and simple jokes on various topics. At

Figure 3.3 A sample of other content from profiles that shared posts about demonstrations against the government's anti-COVID 19 measures.

the same time, it was noticeable that users were expressing their opinions on the pandemic, vaccination against COVID-19, and related government measures. Motivations to reject official information about the pandemic could be found in conspiracy theories and fake news that Facebook and other platforms labeled as disinformation and which the users spread. However, some of these posts have been removed by Facebook after verification.

This mix of personal and political themes suggests that people are connecting their everyday experiences with global events, showing how easily political polarization and disinformation can become part of everyday communication. The COVID-19 pandemic has exacerbated this trend, with people often looking for quick explanations and thus becoming more susceptible to manipulation and disinformation campaigns. Even though, in response to this content, social media have introduced fact-checking and started tagging fake posts, disinformation remains a significant part of online debates. All this shows that the issue of trust in official sources and the degree of influence of disinformation are strongly connected with political attitudes, education, and trust in authorities.

It was the COVID-19 pandemic that has created many opportunities for Russia to attack its adversaries and take advantage of the chaos and uncertainty created during the pandemic (Moy and Gradon 2020). As with one of the most widely read media in the Czech Republic (iDNES.cz), also with the disinformation website ProtiProud, people spread information about demonstrations and anti-government measures not only from these Facebook pages but also from other disinformation websites. All three examined articles from the ProtiProud website had several features in common. They were characterized, for example, by long titles referring to recognized professions such as doctors, paramedics, firefighters, policemen, or a large group of people such as students. Furthermore, other countries have already appeared in the title to show that things are happening also worldwide and to support the Czech demonstrations' legitimacy.

The most shared post was one linked to the article titled "The rebellion is gaining momentum: In Brussels, in Prague and overseas. The convoy of freedom has already reached 70 kilometers. Theo Fleury: Give us back our freedom! Fiala's government is flat-out lying. The vaccination decree is still valid. Are we inspiring Canadians to uprising?" The author was Pavel Kopecký, and the post was published on January 29, 2022. This post had 411 reactions, 28 comments, and 92 shares (until February 13, 2022, 6:54 p.m.). Creators of alternative content do not have the same reach as the national medium iDNES.cz, which is also why their content was not read as much. The second article—entitled "The Unyielding has spoken again: Is the 'pot revolution' coming? Prague is in turmoil—just like Vienna and other European cities. Thousands of protesters gather in front of the Babiš's and Vojtěch's Straka Academy. Now, the police and firemen have also joined"—was liked by 375 people, had 86 shares, and 67 comments (until February 14, 2022, 6:31 p.m.). ProtiProud published the third most shared post on this topic on January 8, 2022, on their Facebook profile. Radek Pokorný wrote the article "Doctors, paramedics, policeman, firefighters, and students send a message to the government: We won't be forced into vaccination! At Šeberák, the unyielding called on their colleagues to show courage. Nurse: It was all about money. COVID was just a prelude. The main event is yet to come." This post had 191 likes, 22 comments, and 80 shares. Out of a total of 117 comments in all the posts, 55 percent were supportive toward the editorial content, 19 percent negative and in 26 percent cases we were not able to evaluate the tone.

According to Soares et al. (2023), conservatives who frequently share political views on social media were more susceptible to pro-Kremlin disinformation. The content of the articles on ProtiProud.cz often takes the side of the protesters, who are repeatedly presented as defenders of freedom and democracy. In the texts, they are referred to by the term "disobedience," which, although it normally evokes negative connotations associated with noncompliance, is presented in a positive light. The sharers of this page, in addition to their strong opposition to vaccination, hold anti-Western and pro-Russian positions. They widely share disinformation, including accusations of the former Slovak president Zuzana Čaputová having ties to the United States, which is often accompanied by offensive photo montages aimed at Czech political leaders, especially Markéta Pekarová Adamová. These users often spread content that is quickly labeled as false by social media, especially Facebook. Politically, they gravitate toward personalities publicly supporting Russian stances, as well as Czech political parties with a right-wing orientation, known for their conservative and nationalist positions that have strong anti-European Union stances and strong opinion about its immigration policy. They proudly refer to themselves as "anti-vaxxers," emphasizing their opposition to government health regulations and vaccination campaigns.

Russian president Vladimir Putin is referred to as the defender of freedom in numerous collages and texts. An example of ideological misuse of the message is posts sharing quotes by Karel Kryl (e.g., from 1969), one of the main faces of the Czech resistance against the Soviet occupation in 1968, in support for anti-vaccination positions among the multitude of pro-Russian materials. Those who share ProtiProud.cz's posts very often also share homophobic, nationalist, or chauvinistic content. In marked contrast to hateful comments toward other people or groups of people, there is affection for animals.

Information about demonstrations was used for propaganda purposes by both disinformation websites and their followers, who, in addition to the content of these sites, also shared news from the mainstream media on this topic. One of the distinguishing features of disinformation campaigns is their focus on emotionally charged events that polarize society and create divisions between individual social groups (European Parliament 2019). Most of the people who shared posts about demonstrations had militant posts directed against vaccination and its supporters appearing on their profiles, as well as other disinformation, especially about human rights issues and the geopolitical situation. Sharers very often emphasized the beauty of nature or traditional family values in a flood of aggressive opinions, but at the same time avoided publishing larger details from their privacy. They created an image of a mass of uncompromising fighters for the right cause, using common sense, with their hearts in the right place.

In the comments on articles on the Facebook pages of iDNES.cz and ProtiProud, there was a minimum of constructive discussion; on the contrary, insults, humiliation, and mockery through irony are significantly represented. The discussion was more supportive toward anti-system movement on ProtiProud's webpage. The difference in the supportive tone (34 percent at the posts published on the mainstream medium iDNES.cz page and 55 percent at the posts published on the disinformation ProtiProud page) can be explained by the diversity of readers at the mainstream medium and ideological homogeneity of ProtiProud's audience. Some of the comments and published information in shared content can even be considered as astroturfing, which Zerback et al. (2021) witnessed in the case of online discussions in Germany—a strategy where social bots and fake accounts are involved to highlight particular opinion and make the impression that it is widely shared.

Conclusion

In our chapter, we tried to document how the current Czech disinformation websites use their social media pages to share the content and how they are probably used also by the troll factories to extend the pro-Russian propaganda and give it a more significant impact than would typically have through astroturfing. We described the strategies used by disinformation social media pages to avoid being tagged by social media companies or even being banned. We also described how they use the old conspiracy narratives about the hidden elites ruling the world, partially even using the collages resembling both Nazi and Communist propaganda.

While Hunter (2023) warns against the possibility of (mainly authoritarian but not exclusively) governments spreading disinformation to discredit the opposition, we witnessed a different trend with anti-establishment movements leaning toward the East and their supporters sharing disinformation about the democratic leaders and blaming them for being gay or American sagents, trying to prove that they are weak and rotten as the whole Western liberal civilization. With the Russian invasion of Ukraine coming closer in early 2022, the presentation of Vladimir Putin as a freedom fighter intensified in the shared content on the analyzed users' profiles, as well as the diminishing of Czech and Slovak democratic leaders, documenting that hybrid war started before the physical war.

When we could come up with some recommendations, we believe it is worth supporting the news audience to more critically interpret the disinformation content by issue-specific inoculation message before the audience encounters this type of "real-life" content (as Zerback et al. (2021) proved by their experiment). With the repeating narratives of disinformation websites, it is possible to create inoculation messages that can work, and they can be spread before the predictable events the disinformation actors attempt to influence, for example, the elections.

Acknowledgment

The research was supported by Resilient Media for Democracy in the Digital Age (ReMeD), an international multidisciplinary project supported by the EU's Horizon Europe Research and Innovation Programme, HORIZON-CL2-2022-DEMOCRACY-01-06: "Media for Democracy—Democratic Media," under grant agreement no. 101094742.

Conflict of Interest Statement

No potential conflict of interest was reported by the authors.

References

AMI Digital. 2024. "Index 2024—Tahák" (Index 2024—Cheat Sheet). https://amidigital.cz/wp-content/uploads/2024/05/tahak24.pdf.

Bennett, Lance W., and Steven Livingston. 2018. "The disinformation order: Disruptive communication and the decline of democratic institutions." *European Journal of Communication* 33 (2): 122–39. https://doi.org/10.1177/0267323118760317.

Brennen, Scott J., Felix M. Simon, and Rasmus Kleis Nielsen. 2021. "Beyond (mis) representation: Visuals in COVID-19 misinformation." *International Journal of Press/Politics* 26 (1): 277–99. https://doi.org/10.1177/1940161220964780.

Calvillo, P. Dustin, Bryan J. Ross, Ryan J. B. Garcia, Thomas J. Smelter, and Abraham M. Rutchick. 2020. "Political ideology predicts perceptions of the threat of COVID-19 (and susceptibility to fake news about it)." *Social Psychological and Personality Science* 11 (8): 1119–28. https://doi.org/10.1177/1948550620940539.

De-Lima-Santos, Mathias-Felipe, and Wilson Ceron. 2024. "Mind the gap: Facebook's measures against information disorder do not go far enough." *Media, Culture & Society* 46 (5): 1075–90. https://doi.org/10.1177/01634437241237936.

Enders, Adam M., Joseph E. Uscinski, Michelle I. Seelig, Casey A. Klofstad, Stefan Wuchty, John R. Funchion, Manohar N. Murthi, Kamal Premaratne, and Justin Stoler. 2023. "The relationship between social media use and beliefs in conspiracy theories and misinformation." *Political Behavior* 45 (2): 781–804. https://doi.org/10.1007/s11109-021-09734-6.

European Commission. 2018. *Tackling online disinformation: A European approach.* European Commission. https://eur-lex.europa.eu/legal-content/EN/TXT/PDF/?uri=CELEX:52018DC0236&qid=1583456906698&from=EN.

European Parliament. 2019. "Disinformation and propaganda: Impact on the functioning of the rule of law in the EU and its member states." www.europarl.europa.eu/RegData/etudes/STUD/2019/608864/IPOL_STU(2019)608864_EN.pdf.

Garz, Marcel, and Ferenc Szucs. 2023. "Algorithmic selection and supply of political news on Facebook." *Information Economics and Policy* 62 (2023). https://doi.org/10.1016/j.infoecopol.2023.101020.

Geissler, Dominique, Dominik Bär, Nicolas Pröllochs, and Stefen Feurriegel. 2023. "Russian propaganda on social media during the 2022 invasion of Ukraine." *EPJ Data Science* 12 (35). https://doi.org/10.1140/epjds/s13688-023-00414-5.

Gerber, Theodore P., and Jane Zavisca. 2016. "Does Russian propaganda work?" *Washington Quarterly* 39 (2): 79–98. https://doi.org/10.1080/0163660X.2016.1204398.

Hameleers, Michael. 2024. "The nature of visual disinformation online: A qualitative content analysis of alternative and social media in the Netherlands." *Political Communication* 42 (1): 108–26. https://doi.org/10.1080/10584609.2024.2354389.

Hameleers, Michael, Thomas E. Powell, Toni G. L. A. Van Der Meer, and Lieke Bos. 2020. "A picture paints a thousand lies? The effects and mechanisms of multimodal disinformation and rebuttals disseminated via social media." *Political Communication* 37 (2): 281–301. https://doi.org/10.1080/10584609.2019.1674979.

Heley, Kathryn, Anna Gaysynsky, and Andy J. King. 2022. "Missing the bigger picture: The need for more research on visual health misinformation." *Science Communication* 44(4): 514–27. https://doi.org/10.1177/10755470221113833.

Hunter, Lance Y. 2023. "Social media, disinformation, and democracy: How different types of social media usage affect democracy cross-nationally." *Democratization* 30 (6): 1040–72. https://doi.org/10.1080/13510347.2023.2208355.

Juhász, Krisztina. 2024. "European Union defensive democracy's responses to disinformation." *Journal of Contemporary European Studies* 32 (4): 1075–94. https://doi.org/10.1080/14782804.2024.2317275.

Khorram-Manesh, Amir, Krzysztof Goniewicz, and Frederick M. Burkle Jr. 2023. "Social and healthcare impacts of the Russian-led hybrid war in Ukraine: A conflict with unique global consequences." *Disaster Medicine and Public Health Preparedness* 17: e432. https://doi.org/10.1017/dmp.2023.91.

Krajčovič, Peter. 2022. "The risks and opportunities associated with social media during the COVID-19 pandemic and the war in Ukraine." In *Social media: Opportunities and risks*, edited by Shafizan Mohamed and Shazleen Mohamed. IntechOpen. www.intechopen.com/chapters/84531

Moy, Wesley, and Kacper Gradon. 2020. "COVID-19 effects and Russian disinformation." *Homeland Security Affairs* 16 (8). www.hsaj.org/articles/16533.

Němcová Tejkalová, Alice. 2023. "The battle against disinformation and Russian propaganda in Central and Eastern Europe." *European Journalism Observatory*, June 1. https://en.ejo.ch/media-politics/the-battle-against-disinformation-and-russian-propaganda-in-central-and-eastern-europe.

Němcová Tejkalová, Alice, Veronika Macková, and Victoria Nainová. 2021. "Na vlně strachu, negativity a dezinformací" (On the wave of disinformation, fear and negativity). *Infomore*, April 6. www.infomore.cz/news-detail/cs/38-vlna-strach-negativita-dezinformace-koronavirus.

Němcová Tejkalová, Alice, Victoria Nainová, and Veronika Macková. 2022. "Antivaxeři (a)nebo nepodvolení? Šíření příspěvků o demonstracích proti očkování a opatřením na Facebooku" (Anti-vaxxers (and) or disobedient? Spreading posts about anti-vaccination demonstrations and measures on Facebook). *Infomore*, February 25. www.infomore.cz/res/file/analyzy/20220225-antivaxeri/20220225-antivaxeri.pdf

Otevři svou mysl (Open Your Mind). 2024. www.facebook.com/otevrisvoumysl.

Otevři svou duši (Open Your Soul). 2024. www.facebook.com/otevrisvoudusi.

ProtiProud (Counter Stream). 2024. www.facebook.com/ProtiProud.cz.

Scott, Rachel Bailey. 2022. *"Russia Interferes with Their Brain": Understanding Russian Foreign Propaganda Strategies, 1980–2022*. Princeton University Press.

Soares, Felipe B., Anatoliy Gruzd, and Philip Mai. 2023. "Falling for Russian propaganda: Understanding the factors contributing to belief in pro-Kremlin disinformation on social media." *Social Media + Society* 9 (4). https://doi.org/10.1177/20563051231220330.

Southwell, Brian G., J. Scott Babwah Brennen, Ryan Paquin, Vanessa Boudewyns, and Jing Zeng. 2022. "Defining and measuring scientific misinformation." *Annals of the American Academy of Political and Social Science* 700 (1): 98–111. https://doi.org/10.1177/00027162221084709.

Sundar, S. Shyam. 2008. "The MAIN model: A heuristic approach to understanding technology effects on credibility." In *Digital media, youth, and credibility*, edited by Miriam J. Metzger and Andrew J. Flanagin. The John D. and Catherine T. MacArthur Foundation Series on Digital Media and Learning. MIT Press. https://doi.org/10.1162/dmal.9780262562324.073.

Turková, Kateřina, and Veronika Macková. 2024. "The effects and structure of individual forms of disinformation on the population in connection with the COVID-19 pandemic in the Czech Republic." In *CEDMO reports on disinformation 2021–2024*, compiled by Karina Stasiuk-Krajewska. Newsline.

Vodochodský, Ivan. 2021. "Mýty spojované s COVID-19." *Infomore*, March 8. www.infomore.cz/news-detail/cs/31-koronavirus-myty-klasicka-media.

Wenzel, Michal, Karina Stasiuk-Krajewska, Veronika Macková, and Kateřina Turková. 2024. "The penetration of Russian disinformation related to the war in Ukraine: Evidence from Poland, the Czech Republic and Slovakia." *International Political Science Review* 45 (2): 192–208. https://doi.org/10.1177/0192512123 1205259.

Zerback, Thomas, Florian Töppfl, and Maria Knöpfle. 2021. "The disconcerting potential of online disinformation: Persuasive effects of astroturfing comments and three strategies for inoculation against them." *New Media & Society* 23 (5): 1080–98. https://doi.org/10.1177/1461444820908530.

Part 2

Approaches to Threats and Combating Disinformation in the European Digital Environment: Examples of Good Practices

4

Attempting to Fight Disinformation Without Jeopardizing Media and Speech Freedom: A Comparative Analysis of Eight European Countries

Alice Němcová Tejkalová, Anna Shavit, Kateřina Turková, Veronika Macková, and Nicole Stremlau

Disinformation[1] has been a part of hybrid wars and impacts both communication and social order (Bennett and Livingston 2018). In Europe, it became a topic after the Russian annexation of Crimea in 2014 when Russian troll factories started intervening through online content in politics in various countries, creating communication disorder; this situation even deepened after the migration crisis in 2015–16 (Humprecht 2018) and following each major crisis, namely the COVID-19 pandemic and the war in Ukraine.

Frequent ways to approach disinformation in communication research have been content analyses of legacy or social media. This chapter focuses on this topic from a different perspective. Based on a comparative research of the situation in eight European countries (Austria, Belgium, Czechia, Germany, Ireland, Norway, Spain, and the UK) for the Horizon Europe project ReMeD (Resilient Media for Democracy in the Digital Age), we analyzed media legislation and governmental responses to disinformation (and possible security threats) spread in the online environment connected particularly to the COVID-19 pandemic and the war in Ukraine. We were particularly interested in whether any legislature or institution focused specifically on disinformation and potential hybrid threats and how it had (or had not) been involved in combating the disinformation connected to the two crises mentioned above.

First, we describe the situation with disinformation in the European media environment and then introduce the legal framework for EU regulation of digital media and freedom of speech with a focus on national legislation. Furthermore, we set the governmental responses into a broader context of freedom of speech and remind the importance of fact-checking organizations in Europe as a frontline response to disinformation.

Disinformation in the European Media Environment

Disinformation has been a threat to democratic societies and institutional trust for many decades. However, the current situation is arguably different and more serious given, as Bennett and Livingston (2018) remind us, today's information flow is less easily controlled by traditional media with their information verification processes and gatekeeping strategies. With the rapid development of social media, the cost of production of disinformation has become almost trivial. Generative AI has further accelerated this trend, enabling people to create deep fakes of such quality that their earliest versions, which fascinated the world several years ago, seem just like childish attempts at reality counterfeiting. As disinformation is one of the most common weapons of foreign interference (Juhász 2024) in a hybrid war, European societies have been ideal targets for disinformation actors whose primary goal is to seed unrest, discomfort, and mistrust by their campaigns that frequently take place during periods around important societal events, for example, migration crisis, elections, or Brexit, depending on the respective society's most pressing trigger point.

What came massively into politics within first term of American president Donald Trump was the use of the words "fake news" for any piece of news he did not particularly like, mainly published by the legacy media. He even launched the Fake News Awards to "reward" the media he disagreed with, including CNN, the *New York Times*, and *Washington Post* (Bennett and Livingston 2018). This mistrust, publicly and longitudinally expressed by one of the most powerful people in the world, was accompanied with a heavy toll:

> The distracting attacks on the mainstream press, paired with supportive but spurious storylines in the alt-right media liberated large numbers of people from the constraints of evidence and reason and fueled public discourses driven by anger, hate, prejudice and lies. (Bennett and Livingston 2018, 125)

For many populist (not only right- but also left-wing) leaders in the world, including those in Europe, Trump served as an example for increasing the level of their social media communication. In the past, they would not be able to deliver these messages to their audience through the gatekeepers, and it would be impossible for them to fight the media in such a way, but with their own communication channels and disinformation media platforms eager to transmit the information, everything is possible. Bennett and Livingston (2018) further warn that it is essential to broaden the perspective and

> to resist easy efforts to make the problem go away by fact-checking initiatives and educating citizens about the perils of fake news. Many citizens actively seek such information in order to support identities and political activities that stem from emotional and material dislocations from the modern national and global institutional orders. (2018, 135)

According to Brogi and De Gregorio (2024), the COVID-19 pandemic and the Russian invasion of Ukraine brought the European institutions to the point where it was impossible not to pursue further immediate actions: "The policy tackling the dissemination of disinformation was also deemed as essential for safeguarding fundamental rights like freedom of expression, whilst ensuring that online discourse does not undermine democratic values and societal cohesion" (Brogi and De Gregorio 2024, 3). As mentioned before and will be developed further in this chapter in greater detail, the understanding of freedom of speech differs in European countries from the US perspective because the EU emphasizes "the protection of democratic values and public integrity over the absolute freedom and discretion of online platforms" (Brogi and De Gregorio 2024, 2). Tenove (2020, 517) further highlights the necessity to protect by these measures "three important normative goods of democratic systems: self-determination, accountable representation, and public deliberation."

Legal Framework for EU Regulation of Digital Media and Freedom of Speech and Implementation of EU Media Regulations in the Countries under Study

EU-wide approach and concrete regulation related to the digital sphere have been widely criticized, because their connection with economic integration, which is the original main purpose of the EU foundation, is not direct. Moreover, the attempts to apply legal instruments against disinformation shared online were perceived as a threat to the political stability of the Union by some European authorities, experts, and entities (Bayer 2024). On the other hand, other organizations support them and cooperate on their implementation (European Commission 2024a).

Likewise, it is evident that social media nowadays undisputedly allows spreading of fake messages; hence controlling these processes is almost impossible (Bayer 2024). Due to the possible harm to fundamental human rights caused by the dissemination of disinformation, the need for legal EU-wide rules related to digital media has intensified (Rowbottom 2024; Turillazzi et al. 2023), and actions in the digital sphere even become one of the EU's visions for the upcoming decade (European Commission 2024a).

One of the essential parts of the EU-wide legal framework related to digital media is the Digital Services Act (DSA), which was introduced at the end of 2020 as part of a regulatory package along with the Digital Markets Act (DMA). This package reacted to the high level of fragmentation of the European digital sphere, which became problematic, among others, by lowering productivity and creation of additional costs (Husovec 2023; Turillazzi et al. 2023). The DSA, effective from November 2022, addresses the various ethical, legal, and social challenges caused by the activities of digital access providers, hosting providers, and search engines (Kosters and Gstrein 2024). Through this initiative, the EU imposed responsibility on online platforms in the established digital single market and took back sovereignty and control from the platforms that are often based outside the EU (Schlag 2023). The DSA aspires to protect users' fundamental rights in the online space and enable a safer digital environment.

Perhaps most significantly under the DSA the very large online platforms (VLOPs) and very large online search engines (VLOSes)—platforms and engines that have more than 45 million users per month, which equals 10 percent of the EU population—are liable for the published content and its moderation, and if they do not comply with the rules defined in the DSA, they can be sanctioned (Frosio and Geiger 2023; Quintais, Appelman, and Ó Fathaigh 2023; Turillazzi et al. 2023). The DSA also attempts to account for the current rapid AI development and warns against the automatic procedures, which can lead to systemic risks and unwilling discrimination (Helberger and Diakopoulos 2023). The legitimization narratives of the DSA included the reconciliation of rights applicable offline and online, the necessity of control from the side of the EU, the protection of small companies, the empowerment of citizens and consumers against very huge platforms and search engines, and the creation of generally applicable rules for the digital environment (Husovec 2023; Schlag 2023).

However, the DSA has been implemented with a wide range of concerns and so tempered enthusiasm in the member states. Firstly, formal obstacles exist; EU countries have preexisting national or federal laws and directives that partially cover the issues regulated by the DSA and so can even collide with the DSA in some aspects. In addition, the EU legislation does not have competency in criminal law, so the definition of illegal content is in charge of the countries themselves (Heldt 2022). Due to the false information that DSA sets a kind of collective censorship spread by some politicians and predominantly alternative media producers, it is understandable that the measure has not been unconditionally welcomed in countries under study.

Another EU-wide effort to regulate digital media is the AI Act that formally came into force in August 2024, but all rules will be fully applicable within the next two years, which gives the entities time and space to conform to the AI Act's rules (Thelisson and Verma 2024). This norm falling under the EU's digital single market strategy addresses, among others, detailed rules related to automated content moderation or recommendation systems. The AI Act also raises the question of media responsibility and accountability in the use and adoption of AI-based software as well as AI in general (Helberger and Diakopoulos 2023).

The criticism of the AI Act from the side of business organizations in the countries under study targets the vague and broad definitions that could possibly lead to an overregulation of the sector and a decrease in the competitiveness of EU-based companies. Conversely, civil society and civil rights organizations point out that the Act should take fundamental human rights into consideration, not only prioritize innovations and business growth (Kusche 2024; Wörsdörfer 2024).

The legal norm aiming to support free democratic media, entitled the European Media Freedom Act (EMPFA), was proposed in 2022 and is fully operational from August 2025 (European Commission 2024b; Seipp et al. 2023). This law covers the areas of freedom of speech and decision (e.g., editorial independence, protection of journalistic sources, and independence of PSM) and transparency in media management (e.g., customization, audience measurement).

The main point of judgment of this norm lies in its definition of media, where "the narrow service-based approach to defining 'media' under Article 2 EMFA appears to be in conflict with the functional approach to defining media under European and international human rights law" (Seipp, Fathaigh, and van Drunen 2023, 39). Due to that, it is questionable who the EMFA gives protection to, and whether potentially vulnerable subjects, such as journalistic startups or individual journalists, will receive the same level of safeguarding as LOPs and VLOSes or large media houses (Seipp et al. 2023). The nonnegotiable differences in media spheres of EU countries are also highlighted by the critics of EMFA while emphasizing that the standardized approach cannot work effectively (Cantero Gamito 2023).

Despite the aforementioned challenges and never-ending debates, the EU legislation governing digital media and freedom of speech is being implemented in the EU member states. The countries under study that do not form a part of the EU, namely the UK and Norway, have the freedom to consider the ideas and rules in this legislation and their possible implementation. The UK has the intention to lead in the digital/media age, while the Online Safety Act (OSA) related to children's safety in the use of social media is a point of long-term discussion (Neudert 2023). Norway is actively involved in the realm of media legislation in Europe; hence their representatives comment on the proposals of EU-wide laws and norms, including the DMA and DSA (Maher 2024). The digitalization of the public sector progresses through the Norwegian digitalization agency Digdir falling under the Ministry of Digitalization and Public Governance (Eriksson et al. 2023).

National Regulations for Digital Media Platforms in the Countries under Study

As described above, the EU sets general regulatory frameworks for digital media, although national regulations of member states are still important. National laws and regulations must adapt these general principles to an individual member state's needs and conditions. This ensures that the regulation of digital media is effective in the countries concerned. Governments are still pushing for regulation to protect users and ensure transparency. The process is complex because different actors with different interests are involved, and poorly designed laws could negatively affect certain groups of people (Kokshagina et al. 2023).

Germany has one of the strictest and most complex legislations in the EU, related to its historical experience with totalitarian regimes. That is why it has several laws regulating content in traditional media and digital media platforms. These regulations mainly supervise the regulation of hate speech and extremist content. Among the main forms of national regulation of social media platforms is the so-called Network Enforcement Act (*Gesetz zur Verbesserung der Rechtsdurchsetzung in sozialen Netzwerken Netzwerkdurchsetzungsgesetz*—NetzDG), which contains specific requirements for social media platform providers. This law was the first such regulation in the world to prohibit major platforms from moderating harmful content at their discretion. Thus, it has set standards for handling complaints and mandated transparent reporting on content moderation (Gorwa 2021). The Act was drafted by former federal minister of justice Heiko Maas (SPD) and was approved in 2017. The Act does not introduce new regulations for online content management but focuses on better enforcement of existing laws on social networks. Its provisions apply to all platforms with over 2 million users (Shavit et al. 2024).

NetzDG obliges social networks and online platforms to respond quickly to complaints about illegal content (Wagner et al. 2020). Owners and operators of digital platforms must identify and remove illegal content quickly. A post must be removed within twenty-four hours of its reporting, and all other unlawful content within seven days. In addition, these platforms must fulfil certain documentation and reporting obligations to the relevant authorities (Gollatz, Riedl, and Pohlmann 2018). For example, they must clearly describe the number of complaints they received, their reasons, and how long they took to respond. Penalties for noncompliance with these regulations can reach up to 50 million euros. The law faced criticism. Opponents believed platforms may tend to overcensor content to avoid fines and potentially overlook satire or other forms of commentary, posing a threat to free speech. Some even claim that NetzDG violates constitutional and European laws and possibly international law (Claussen 2018). Critics are urging cooperation to make this law effective. According to Claussen (2018), legislators should work with social media users, media law experts, and nonprofit organizations.

In Germany, media policy is also changing due to federal states that have interstate agreements. One was the Treaty on Broadcasting (*Rundfunkstaatsvertrag*), one of the central legal bases for public media, replaced by the Interstate Treaty on Media (*Medienstaatsvertrag*—MStV) in 2020. This pact aimed to update the regulatory framework according to the possibilities of the digital media environment. While public broadcasting continues to be subject to regulation, it also focuses on social media. Media intermediaries include platforms that distribute media content in bulk and may not even create it themselves (such as Facebook, X, TikTok, or Google). The Interstate Media Treaty emphasizes transparency and nondiscrimination, expecting these platforms to publish the reasons for displaying certain content and explain how their algorithms work. At the same time, it must not systematically prioritize or limit content from specific sources. Content creators on social media may also violate other laws in Germany (e.g., the Criminal Code, Data Protection Act, Youth Protection Act, Copyright Act). These laws are also relevant to social media users (Shavit et al. 2024).

In Austria, regulating digital media platforms consists of several essential laws designed to regulate their operation, accountability, and transparency. These are the Communication Platforms Act (*Kommunikationsplattformen-Gesetz*—KoPl-G, BGBl. I Nr. 151/2020), Digital Platform Registration Law (*Digitale Plattformen-Meldeplichtgesetz*—DPMG, BGBl. I Nr. 108/2022), and Hate on the Web Combat Act (*Hass-im-Netz Bekämpfungs-Gesetz*—HiNBG, BGBl. I Nr. 148/2020) (Shavit et al. 2024).

The Communication Platforms Act (KoPl-G) is a part of the strategy of Austrian legislation aimed at detecting and punishing hate speech and increasing the accountability of digital platforms. Similar to Germany's NetzDG, this regulation in Austria is supposed to focus on fighting hate, false information, and other illegal content. Digital platform providers should delete an offending post as soon as possible. Under this law, platforms are responsible for the content posted by their users and must take measures to minimize the risk of spreading illegal content. KoPl-Gl and NetzDG are pioneers in platform regulation and are considered sources of inspiration for the DSA. Therefore, the fundamental legislation of the EU focused on regulating digital services (Gruber 2023). In 2023, Google Ireland, Meta Platforms Ireland, and TikTok took Austria's communication platform law to court due to its alleged conflict with EU law. The Austrian court appealed to the Court of Justice of the European Union, which subsequently ruled in favor of these companies (Society for Computers & Law).

Ireland is also aware of the need to regulate digital media and wants to strengthen its position. The primary tool for regulating social media platforms is the Online Safety and Media Regulation Act (OSMR), which came into force in December 2022. The Coimisiún na Meán (Media Commission) was established by the OSMR in 2023. This Act abolished the Broadcasting Authority of Ireland (BAI) and replaced it with a new commission, which took over its functions in broadcast regulation. In addition, Coimisiún na Meán is in charge of, among other things, the regulation of online security. It is part of Ireland's efforts to ensure the media environment remains safe, fair, and trustworthy. One of the Commission's biggest challenges is regulating global digital platforms under Irish law (Coimisiún na Meán n.d.).

Germany, Austria, and Ireland are very active in their national regulation of digital media. Outside of EU regulations, new laws or amendments to older laws or new commissions regulating the behavior on social media are being created in these countries, which reflect their unique legal and cultural contexts. On the contrary, Spain, Belgium, and the Czech Republic use existing legal regulations or are oriented toward European regulations. Some of their national laws focus on different aspects, such as content on social media, protection of minors, or advertising.

The main legislation in Spain in the field of digital media includes the Audiovisual Law No. 13/2022 (*Ley General de Comunicación Audiovisual*) and the Data Protection and Digital Rights Law No. 3/2018 (*Ley de Protección de Datos y Garantía de los Derechos Digitales*) (Shavit et al. 2024). The Audiovisual Law also focuses on new digital platforms. Streaming platforms, VOD services, influencers, and YouTubers in Spain also have obligations (Red Bee Media 2023).

In Belgium, regional media regulators are responsible for enforcing media legislation. The Federal Public Service Economy oversees consumer protection issues in the online environment. Much disinformation and fake news have spread on social media in recent years. Under Belgian law, disinformation is not explicitly regulated, but there are laws and initiatives aimed at controlling illegal content (EDMO BELUX 2.0 2023).

In the fight against disinformation, measures are taken to monitor and flag false or manipulative information in the Czech Republic. Although the Czech Republic does not have specific regulations aimed directly at social media, in March 2023 the National Office for Cyber and Information Security (NÚKIB) warned about the security risks associated with using the TikTok application. This warning reflects concerns about potential security threats arising from the amount of data collected about users, the methods of data collection, and the application's connection to the political environment of the People's Republic of China. In the Czech Republic, social media regulation is governed by several key areas. These include, for example, the protection of personal data, which is ensured through the European General Data Protection Regulation (GDPR) that sets out the rules for collecting and processing personal data, including those obtained through social networks. In addition, some laws govern online content, such as defamation, hate speech, and copyright protection (Shavit et al. 2024).

Norway and Great Britain are outside the EU. Both countries are trying to balance freedom of expression and protection of users in digital media.

However, they are also affected by the European legislation. Although Norway is not a member of the EU, it is a member of the European Economic Area (EEA), so Norway also has to adopt many European laws, including the Digital Media Regulation.

According to the Norwegian government, the internet should be an open and accessible space for sharing and receiving information. At the same time, it should be a space where human rights are protected. The Norwegian Constitution guarantees freedom of expression and guarantees the right to express anything that is not prohibited by other laws. For example, the Norwegian Penal Code (specifically section 185) protects against expressions of hatred against minorities and prevents the spread of hatred that could disrupt social order. This law requires high standards for what can be considered criminal speech. Norway has tried to curb behavioral advertising on platforms like Meta following a ruling by the Court of Justice of the European Union. The Norwegian Data Protection Authority has banned the tracking and profiling of users in the country, but this does not mean a complete ban on personalized advertising on Facebook or Instagram (Shavit et al. 2024).

The regulation of digital media platforms in the UK has undergone significant changes in recent years, particularly in connection with Brexit. The Online Safety Act is one of the most debated rules in recent years. At the time of this law's draft, there was much debate about obligations and penalties for violations. The Online Safety Act focuses on children and young people to keep them safe in the internet environment and away from harmful content. The Act also introduced new criminal acts connected with violations of regulations on digital media platforms (Government of the United Kingdom n.d.). The Age-Appropriate Design Code, known as the Children's Code, also focuses on children and young people. The regulatory framework sets privacy standards for online services for children and young users. The UK Data Protection Authority created this code. The UK also has other laws that regulate social media. These include, for example, the Defamation Act of 2013, the Counter-Terrorism and Border Security Act of 2019, and the Terrorism Act of 2000 (Shavit et al. 2024).

The national regulation of digital media platforms represents an area of law and politics that is constantly changing, and it is precisely to new technological trends that individual regulations must respond. Laws and other rules often differ from country to country, especially with the political system or freedom of speech.

Media Content Regulation and Measures Targeted against Disinformation

The concept or idea of freedom of speech is universally understood and applied across EU member states or generally in Europe. What might be different is the understanding of the general concept and attempts to find a right balance between free speech and other values in the EU countries. Alongside the freedom of expression comes the attempts to protect public order, prevent hate speech or defamation, protect minorities, and so on. From a practical point of view, it makes sense to look into the national states and the role of the EU itself, especially the various institutions involved in the process, such as the European Court of Human Rights (Woods 2006).

Article 11 corresponds to Article 10 of the European Convention on Human Rights, which reads as follows:

> 1 Everyone has the right to freedom of expression. This right shall include freedom to hold opinions and to receive and impart information and ideas without interference by public authority and regardless of frontiers. This article shall not prevent States from requiring the licensing of broadcasting, television, or cinema enterprises.
>
> 2 The exercise of these freedoms, since it carries with it duties and responsibilities, may be subject to such formalities, conditions, restrictions or penalties as are prescribed by law and are necessary in a democratic society, in the interests of national security, territorial integrity or public safety, for the prevention of disorder or crime, for the protection of health or morals, for the protection of the reputation or rights of others, for preventing the disclosure of information received in confidence, or for maintaining the authority and impartiality of the judiciary. (Council of Europe 1950, art. 10.1)

As we can see in other parts of Article 10.1 the understanding of the concept might differ from country to country. One example is a former EU member, the UK, where the concept of freedom of speech has evolved over centuries and is influenced by the Magna Charta. The logic is to enable the greatest possible freedom of speech and simultaneously follow strict libel laws such as the Defamation Act 2013, which made it significantly easier for individuals to sue for defamation. The UK also has a very comprehensive set of rules against hate speech. Another example could be France, which had the roots of freedom of expression during the Great French Revolution and the fact that it is part of the constitution. The historical experience is also reflected in the German Constitution, where freedom of speech has a prominent position. However, even more attention is paid to prohibiting attempts to promote or spread extremist ideologies (Grimm 2005).

However, this brings a new situation. Previously, national principles and legislation norms had the fundamental role. With many new challenges (such as social media regulations and AI), EU legislation has been more weighted, and the member states have gradually adopted it. As von Ungern-Sternberg (2023) states, due to online communication, it can be observed that democratic opinion-forming, the domain of national law, is more and more becoming a question of EU law, and it brings many challenges to communication in the digital space, primarily because of how fast hate speech or disinformation can be dismissed and because of the attempts to protect the European citizens against surveillance, deception, and even manipulation (von Ungern-Sternberg 2023).

If we look at the balance between freedom and regulation, the analyzed countries have very different approaches, from overall legal frameworks to more detailed or specific case-focused approaches. What they share in common is the fact that all laws, regulations, and norms are often reactions or responses to specific affairs, or they are focusing on concrete topics. The goal is often to prevent the problems (or generally protect); however, in reality, they do not prevent problems. Rather, they try to fix it afterward. This section basically looks into the fundamental questions of whether freedom and equality can be achieved or protected through regulations. Regarding democracy and freedom protection, many countries focus on specific and concrete issues that could be considered harmful (Shavit et al. 2024, 7–8). This is not only interesting but rather a logical consequence of the fact that democracy and values are often part of the countries' constitutions. However, new phenomena bring new challenges and threats. To name a few—the COVID-19 pandemic, Russian aggression in Ukraine, the protections of LGBTQIA+, rising antisemitism, and the massive spread of disinformation of various kinds from various actors.

Disinformation and its impact on society are other pressing issues in democratic societies. It brings a paradox. There is always a possibility that by fighting for human rights and trying to prevent disinformation from harming human rights and democracy, we might introduce many measures that can hurt human rights and democracy. There are many elements of good-quality democracy, but counter-disinformation measures can also have a prejudicial impact on human rights and democracy. A study by the European Parliament brings various examples from the member countries (Colomina et al. 2021, 2–7). Ireland is working toward forming a national counter-disinformation strategy focused on countermeasures to support independent journalism and the establishment of regulatory and research mechanisms. Defending Democracy Taskforce is an effort to prevent foreign interference with its democratic institutions and practices, such as using disinformation on social media in the UK (Shavit et al. 2024, 7–8).

The COVID-19 pandemic can be used as an example of the massive spread of disinformation with the motivation to harm and disintegrate the global community and, specifically, the EU (Bechmann 2020). Many criticized the response of the EU to the "infodemic," and the pandemic showed many challenges to European integration (Vériter et al. 2020). Many countries, such as Ireland, Belgium, and Austria, did not regulate content. Germany, too, did not have any media regulations for COVID-19. However, Spain launched a campaign against disinformation. A former EU member—the UK—established the Counter-Disinformation Unit, and similar tendencies were seen in the Czech Republic, where various NGOs engaged in fact-checking (Shavit et al. 2024, 8). On the contrary, the response to Russian war in Ukraine is an example of a united stand of the EU. The EU took the initiative to block the pro-Russian media RTL. National approaches differ from no regulation to strict limits. In February 2022, the Czech government implemented a three-month ban on disinformation media. Consequently, the internet providers blocked various pro-Russian disinformation servers and raised a public debate about freedom of speech (Lazarova 2022).

Many EU member countries have different approaches on how to protect minorities, specifically sexual minorities, in the media. Evidently, the protection of minorities has historically been part of value attitudes, but the method and degree are different. In general, the rights of LGBTQIA+ minorities are secured and anti-hate speech legislation applied in the Czech Republic, Belgium, Ireland, Spain, and many other countries within the EU. In the case of Austria, the court can order the suspension of websites that violate privacy rights (the Austrian Hate on the Web Act). In Germany, representations of different minorities are obligatory for the public service media (Shavit et al. 2024, 9).

Fact-Checking as a Frontline Response

Fact-checking has emerged as a principal strategy for addressing disinformation in the digital age. When the Duke Reporters' Lab began tracking fact-checking initiatives in 2014, it identified forty-four organizations globally (Stencel 2018). By 2019, this number had quadrupled to 188 across more than sixty countries (Stencel 2019), and in 2024—dubbed the "year of elections"—at least 457 programmes were active in 111 countries (Stencel et al. 2024). Although the rate of new initiatives has decelerated, this expansion highlights an increased recognition of, and urgency around, the issue of combating false information on social media platforms. It is also a recognition of the limits of online content moderation that, despite advances with AI, continues to have significant constraints in terms of both their ability to identify disinformation in a wide range of languages and gaps in their effectiveness of picking up more nuanced statements of disinformation (such as parables) or other multimedia content (including video) (De Gregorio and Stremlau 2023).

The rise of fact-checking initiatives parallels growing concerns over disinformation, concerns that have been intensified by recent high-stakes events as described earlier (cases such as the Brexit referendum and the 2016 US election; the COVID-19 pandemic as termed by the World Health Organization an "infodemic"; and the ongoing Ukraine conflict). At least on paper, and as a signal that organizations, governments, and civil society are attempting to respond, fact-checking initiatives have become flagship projects to promote anti-disinformation efforts. The High-Level Expert Group on Fake News and Online Disinformation recognized fact-checking as central to its recommended strategies, which in turn influenced the EU's 2018 Code of Practice on Disinformation (European Union 2018). Nonetheless, fact-checking has not been universally accepted or easily applied; while many consider it essential, others criticize or even restrict it, sometimes enacting laws that criminalize what they deem to be "false news" from fact-checking groups themselves.

While fact-checking provides a resource for mitigating disinformation, it has notable limitations. Primarily reactive fact-checking generally addresses disinformation only after its circulation. The diversity of fact-checking methodologies—such as ante hoc (prepublication verification) versus post hoc (postpublication review)—further raises questions about effectiveness. While initially fact-checking in newsrooms that gained popularity in the 1920s aimed at preventing errors prepublication, it has since shifted largely to external, post hoc verification in response to the overwhelming volume of digital information (Graves 2016). Although consensus on the value of fact-checking persists, empirical studies present mixed evidence regarding its impact on misinformation beliefs or dissemination (Fridkin et al. 2015; Garrett and Weeks 2013; Walter et al. 2020). Some studies argue that fact-checking might inadvertently reinforce misperceptions due to cognitive biases like the backfire effect (Nyhan and Reifler 2010), while others highlight concerns around ideological biases within fact-checking (Park et al. 2021). Particularly in 2024, with elections taking place in more than sixty-four countries, the ability of fact-checking to actually reach social media users with relevant and trusted information remains unclear. Further empirical research is essential to assess their impact, including differentiating between the wide range of fact-checking organizations (and how they are affected by those that fund them).

This also raises the important question of how fact-checking organizations are "governed" or whose standards they are to abide by as they are forced to navigate a complex web of influences, shaped by state regulations, journalistic norms, transparency commitments, and platform policies governing online content (Cavaliere 2020). Social media companies wield significant influence, implementing rules that directly affect fact-checking efforts (Gillespie 2017), including introducing notable constraints on the mission and scope of fact-checking organizations. For instance, Facebook exempts specific political speech from fact-checking, positing that political statements are essential to democratic dialogue. Content created or shared by politicians is thus excluded from misinformation flags, though third-party content shared by politicians remains eligible for review (Facebook 2021). This exemption allows an area of unverified information to circulate widely.

This convergence of regulatory frameworks (as discussed in previous sections) along with the initiatives of civil society and corporations creates a fact-checking environment characterized by both public and private governance. The International Fact-Checking Network (IFCN) has played a central role in establishing standards for fact-checking, promoting transparency, nonpartisanship, and methodological rigor as criteria for IFCN-certified membership. Responding to public and regulatory pressure, platforms like Facebook and Google have provided grants and funding to fact-checkers. Initiatives such as Facebook's Journalism Project and Third-Party Fact-Checking Program have fostered collaborations with IFCN-certified organizations, effectively positioning fact-checkers as de facto content moderators on these platforms. However, these partnerships also reflect social media companies' broader goal of moderating content without fully encroaching upon freedom of expression—a significant tension in regulating digital information.

Furthermore, fact-checking on social media is subject to platform-specific rating systems, where content labeled as "false," "altered," or "partly false" faces visibility reductions rather than outright removal. Severe or repeated infractions can lead to further sanctions, such as monetization restrictions. Yet these measures are inconsistently applied, and platform algorithm transparency remains limited, complicating public oversight of this private regulatory ecosystem. Fact-checkers themselves have minimal insight into or influence over algorithmic decisions that amplify or suppress content, constraining their capacity to counter disinformation effectively.

As fact-checking organizations operate within this complex regulatory landscape, with European disinformation laws and digital regulatory policies aiming to balance combating harmful content with preserving media freedom, a nuanced examination of fact-checking's efficacy is crucial to aligning these objectives within a transparent media governance framework.

Conclusion

This chapter presented various regulatory and nonlegal approaches to the potentially harmful online content in the European media environment. With a particular focus on eight countries under study—Austria, Belgium, Czechia, Germany, Norway, Spain and the UK—it expounded the national responses to current societal and information threats and the concerns about how to treat disinformation without jeopardizing media and speech freedom. The different perspectives of the studied countries reflect historical and cultural realities, while they are also continuously shaped by current local (and global) events.

In the case of the COVID-19 pandemic, the governments mainly relied on fact-checking organized by Very Large Online Platforms (VLOPs) for their content, specifically (dis)information about the COVID-19 vaccine. However, in the UK, the government's Counter Disinformation Unit intensely focused on health and COVID-19 disinformation, followed it, and referred it to social media companies. It continues to do so with the war in Ukraine, supported by the Defending Democracy Taskforce. In 2022 Czechia, which Russia has traditionally considered as a part of its influence area, intensified its efforts to fight Russian disinformation media and switched them off for three months. However, a new governmental envoy for media and disinformation, who was supposed to deliver a law against disinformation, had not survived more than a year in his function and was never replaced due to the public opposition against any limitations on press freedom.

Freedom of speech has been the core argument for other countries, especially Norway, Ireland, and Spain, to avoid developing any specific legislation regarding disinformation. Germany banned *Russia Today* on its territory before it was officially banned on the EU level, but in line with very regionally divided Belgium, there were not any specific measures applied against (Russian) disinformation. In Austria, the Communication Platforms Act, according to which unlawful content when reported must be taken down by the provider immediately, cannot be used against platforms based in foreign countries (that is the case of most VLOPs).

Regardless of the differences, the primary democratic societies' and international institutions' interest should be to protect democracy and human rights and not to permit their violation by disinformation producers and foreign influence actors in a hybrid war. Nevertheless, the battle against harmful content cannot lead to media or speech freedom limitations. The measures taken need to be nuanced enough so they cannot be possibly misused as censorship tools against the progressive societal movements, as were, for example, feminism or environmentalism in the past, or currently LGBTQIA+ rights that have often developed as alternative ideologies on alternative media platforms. Therefore, they should not serve as a means to silence critical voices (Nieminen 2024), especially in countries experiencing democratic backsliding, such as Hungary or Slovakia.

Acknowledgment

The research was supported by Resilient Media for Democracy in the Digital Age (ReMeD), an international multidisciplinary project supported by the European Union's Horizon Europe Research and Innovation Programme, HORIZON-CL2-2022-DEMOCRACY-01-06: "Media for Democracy—Democratic Media," under grant agreement no. 101094742.

Conflict of Interest Statement

No potential conflict of interest was reported by the authors.

Note

1 In this chapter we primarily focus on disinformation although we note that it is often discussed in parallel or together with misinformation. Many of the current legal instruments in Europe, such as the DSA, primarily focus on minimizing harmful content online and protecting users from intentional deception. In practice, however, these new laws oblige platforms to take steps that could impact both misinformation and disinformation.

References

Bayer, Judit. 2024. "The EU policy on disinformation: Aims and legal basis." *Journal of Media Law* 16 (1): 18–27. https://doi.org/10.1080/17577632.2024.2362478.
Bechmann, Anja. 2020. "Tackling disinformation and infodemics demands media policy changes." *Digital Journalism* 8 (6): 855–63. https://doi.org/10.1080/21670811.2020.1773887.
Bennett, W. Lance, and Steven Livingston. 2018. "The disinformation order: Disruptive communication and the decline of democratic institutions." *European Journal of Communication* 33 (2): 122–39. https://doi.org/10.1177/0267323118760317.
Brogi, Elda, and Giovanni De Gregorio. 2024. "From the code of practice to the code of conduct? Navigating the future challenges of disinformation regulation." *Journal of Media Law* 16 (1): 38–46. https://doi.org/10.1080/17577632.2024.2362480.
Cantero Gamito, Marta. 2023. "The European Media Freedom Act (EMFA) as meta-regulation." *Computer Law & Security Review* 48 (2023): 1–15. https://doi.org/10.1016/j.clsr.2023.105799.
Cavaliere, Paolo. 2020. "From journalistic ethics to fact-checking practices: Defining the standards of content governance in the fight against disinformation." *Journal of Media Law* 12 (2): 133–65. https://doi.org/10.1080/17577632.2020.1869486.
Claussen, Victor. 2018. "Fighting hate speech and fake news: The Network Enforcement Act (NetzDG) in Germany in the context of European legislation." *Media Laws* 3 (3): 110–36. www.medialaws.eu/wp-content/uploads/2019/05/6.-Claussen.pdf.
Coimisiún na Meán. n.d. "About us." www.cnam.ie/about-us.
Colomina, Carme, Hector Sánchez Margalef, Richard Youngs, and Kate Jones. 2021. "The impact of disinformation on democratic processes and human rights in the world." *European Parliament: Directorate-General for External Policies of the Union.* https://data.europa.eu/doi/10.2861/59161.
Council of Europe. 1950. "Convention for the Protection of Human Rights and Fundamental Freedoms." *Council of Europe Treaty Series 005.* https://rm.coe.int/1680a2353d.

De Gregorio, Giovanni, and Nicole Stremlau. 2023. "Inequalities and content moderation." *Global Policy* 14 (5): 870–9. https://doi.org/10.1111/1758-5899.13243.

EDMO BELUX 2.0. 2023. "Regulating disinformation: A look up on the legal framework in Belgium." https://belux.edmo.eu/regulating-disinformation-look-up-on-the-legal-framework-in-belgium/?utm_source=rss&utm_medium=rss&utm_campaign=regulating-disinformation-look-up-on-the-legal-framework-in-belgium.

Eriksson, Rikard, Elin Tangnæs, and Pål Ellingsen. 2023. "Innovating the public sector with hybrid interactions." *Nordic Journal of Innovation in the Public Sector* 2 (1): 59–70. https://doi.org/10.18261/njips.2.1.5.

European Commission. 2024a. "Commission services and ERGA partner in support of Digital Services Act enforcement." https://digital-strategy.ec.europa.eu/en/news/commission-services-and-erga-partner-support-digital-services-act-enforcement.

European Commission. 2024b. "European Media Freedom Act." https://commission.europa.eu/strategy-and-policy/priorities-2019-2024/new-push-european-democracy/protecting-democracy/european-media-freedom-act_en.

European Union. 2018. "A multi-dimensional approach to disinformation: Report of the independent high level group on fake news and online disinformation." https://op.europa.eu/en/publication-detail/-/publication/6ef4df8b-4cea-11e8-be1d-01aa75ed71a1/language-en.

Facebook. 2021. "Facebook's approach to political speech." https://about.fb.com. Accessed October 25, 2024.

Fridkin, Kim L., Patrick J. Kenney, Sarah S. Gershon, and Gina Serignese Woodall. 2015. "Spinning debates: The impact of the news media's coverage of the final 2004 presidential debate." *International Journal of Press/Politics* 20 (2): 211–29. https://doi.org/10.1177/1940161214567052.

Frosio, Giancarlo, and Christophe Geiger. 2023. "Taking fundamental rights seriously in the Digital Services Act's platform liability regime." *European Law Journal* 29 (1–2): 31–77. https://doi.org/10.1111/eulj.12475.

Garrett, R. Kelly, and Brian E. Weeks. 2013. "The promise and peril of real-time corrections to political misperceptions." *Digital Journalism* 1 (3): 356–72. https://doi.org/10.1080/21670811.2013.801690.

Gillespie, Tarleton. 2017. "Regulation of and by platforms." In *The SAGE handbook of social media*, edited by Jean Burgess, Poel Thomas Jean, and Alice E. Marwick. Sage Publications. https://doi.org/10.4135/9781473984066.n15.

Gollatz, Kirsten, Martin J. Riedl, and Jens Pohlmann. 2018. "Germany: Removal of online speech in numbers." https://inforrm.org/2018/08/24/germany-removal-of-online-hate-speech-in-numbers-kirsten-gollatz-martin-j-riedl-and-jens-pohlmann/

Gorwa, Robert. 2021. "Elections, institutions, and the regulatory politics of platform governance: The case of the German NetzDG." *Telecommunications Policy* 45 (6): 1–12. https://doi.org/10.1016/j.telpol.2021.102145.

Government of the United Kingdom. n.d. “Online Safety Act: Explainer.” www.gov.uk/government/publications/online-safety-act-explainer/online-safety-act-explainer.

Graves, Lucas. 2016. *Deciding what’s true: The rise of political fact-checking in American journalism*. Columbia University Press.

Grimm, Dieter. 2005. “Integration by constitution.” *International Journal of Constitutional Law* 3 (2–3): 193–208. https://doi.org/10.1093/icon/moi014.

Gruber, Marlene Maria. 2023. “Anpassungsbedarf im österreichischen Kommunikations-Plattformen-Gesetz angesichts des EU Digital Services Acts 2022.” Master’s thesis, Karl Franzens University of Graz. https://unipub.uni-graz.at/obvugrhs/content/titleinfo/8586268/full.pdf.

Helberger, Natali, and Nicholas Diakopoulos. 2023. “The European AI Act and how it matters for research into AI in media and journalism.” *Digital Journalism* 11 (9): 1751–60. https://doi.org/10.1080/21670811.2022.2082505.

Heldt, Amélie P. 2022. “EU Digital Services Act: The white hope of intermediary regulation.” In *Digital platform regulation*, edited by Terry Flew and Fiona R. Martin. Palgrave Macmillan. https://doi.org/10.1007/978-3-030-95220-4_4.

Humprecht, Edda. 2018. “Where ‘fake news’ flourishes: A comparison across four Western democracies.” *Information, Communication & Society* 22 (13): 1973–88. https://doi.org/10.1080/1369118X.2018.1474241.

Husovec, Martin. 2023. “The DSA as a creator’s charter?” *Journal of Intellectual Property Law & Practice* 18 (2): 71–3. https://doi.org/10.1093/jiplp/jpac116.

Juhász, Krisztina. 2024. “European Union defensive democracy’s responses to disinformation.” *Journal of Contemporary European Studies*, February, 1–20. https://doi.org/10.1080/14782804.2024.2317275.

Kokshagina, Olga, Pauline C. Reinecke, and Stan Karanasios. 2023. “To regulate or not to regulate: Unraveling institutional tussles around the regulation of algorithmic control of digital platforms.” *Journal of Information Technology* 38 (2): 160–79. https://doi.org/10.1177/02683962221114408.

Kosters, Lisa, and Oskar J. Gstrein. 2024. “TikTok and transparency obligations in the EU Digital Services Act (DSA): A scoping review.” *Zeitschrift für europarechtliche Studien* 27 (1): 110–45. https://doi.org/10.5771/1435-439X-2024-1-110.

Kusche, Isabel. 2024. “Possible harms of artificial intelligence and the EU AI Act: Fundamental rights and risk.” *Journal of Risk Research*, May, 1–14. https://doi.org/10.1080/13669877.2024.2350720.

Lazarova, Daniela. 2022. “Czech domain operator blocks eight websites spreading disinformation and Kremlin propaganda.” *Radio Prague International*. https://english.radio.cz/czech-domain-operator-blocks-eight-websites-spreading-disinformation-and-kremlin-8743164.

Maher, Imelda. 2024. “Regulatory design in the EU Digital Markets Act: No solo run for the European Commission.” *Journal of Antitrust Enforcement* 12 (2): 273–9. https://doi.org/10.1093/jaenfo/jnae029.

Neudert, Lisa-Maria. 2023. "Regulatory capacity capture: The United Kingdom's online safety regime." *Internet Policy Review* 12 (4): 1–34. https://doi.org/10.14763/2023.4.1730.

Nieminen, Hannu. 2024. "Why does disinformation spread in liberal democracies? The relationship between disinformation, inequality, and the media." *Javnost: The Public* 31 (1): 123–40. https://doi.org/10.1080/14782804.2024.2317275.

Nyhan, Brendan, and Jason Reifler. 2010. "When corrections fail: The persistence of political misperceptions." *Political Behavior* 32 (2): 303–30. https://doi.org/10.1007/s11109-010-9112-2.

Park, Soo Young, H. Chad Lane, and Jesse Fox. 2021. "The role of prior attitudes and feelings in the influence of fact-checking on belief in misinformation." *Digital Journalism* 9 (6): 723–41. https://doi.org/10.1080/21670811.2021.1874887.

Quintais, João Pedro, Naomi Appelman, and Ronan Ó Fathaigh. 2023. "Using terms and conditions to apply fundamental rights to content moderation." *German Law Journal* 24 (5): 881–911. https://doi.org/10.1017/glj.2023.53.

Red Bee Media. 2023. "Red Bee access report." www.redbeemedia.com/app/uploads/2023/04/Red-Bee-Access-Report-English.pdf.

Rowbottom, Jacob. 2024. *Media law*, 2nd ed. Bloomsbury.

Schlag, Gabi. 2023. "European Union's regulating of social media: A discourse analysis of the Digital Services Act." *Politics and Governance* 11 (3): 168–77. https://doi.org/10.17645/pag.v11i3.6735.

Seipp, Theresa, Ronan Ó Fathaigh, and Max van Drunen. 2023. "Defining the 'media' in Europe: Pitfalls of the proposed European Media Freedom Act." *Journal of Media Law* 15 (1): 39–51. https://doi.org/10.1080/17577632.2023.2240998.

Shavit, Anna, Kateřina Turková, Alice Němcová Tejkalová, and Veronika Macková. 2024. "Report on national and EU-wide regulatory frameworks for social media platforms in relation to their role as media distributors." *ReMeD*. https://resilientmedia.eu/?p=1084.

Stencel, Mark. 2018. "Fact-checking: How fact-checking has grown in journalism." https://reporterslab.org/fact-checking-growing-in-journalism.

Stencel, Mark. 2019. "The growth of fact-checking globally." https://reporterslab.org/growth-of-fact-checking-global.

Stencel, Mark, Erica Ryan, and Joel Luther 2024. "With half the planet going to the polls in 2024, fact-checking sputters." www.poynter.org/fact-checking/2024/duke-reporters-lab-fact-checking-cencus-2024/.

Tenove, Chris. 2020. "Protecting democracy from disinformation: Normative threats and policy responses." *International Journal of Press/Politics* 25 (3): 517–37. https://doi.org/10.1177/1940161220918740.

Thelisson, Eva, and Verma Himanshu. 2024. "Conformity assessment under the EU AI Act general approach." *AI and Ethics* 4 (1): 113–21. https://doi.org/10.1007/s43681-023-00402-5.

Turillazzi, Aina, Mariarosaria Taddeo, Luciano Floridi, and Federico Casolari. 2023. "The Digital Services Act: An analysis of its ethical, legal, and social implications." *Law, Innovation and Technology* 15 (1): 83–106. https://doi.org/10.1080/17579961.2023.2184136.

Vériter, Sophie L., Corneliu Bjola, and Joachim A. Koops. 2020. "Tackling COVID-19 disinformation: Internal and external challenges for the European Union." *Hague Journal of Diplomacy* 15 (4): 569–82. https://doi.org/10.1163/1871191X-BJA10046

von Ungern-Sternberg, Antje. 2023. "Freedom of speech goes EU: EU laws for online communication. In *Europäisierung der Meinungsfreiheit: Europäische Normen für die Meinungsbildung im digitalen Raum*, edited by Rainer Hofmann and Stefan Kadelbach. Nomos. http://dx.doi.org/10.2139/ssrn.4387178.

Wagner, Ben, Krisztina Rozgonyi, Marie-Therese Sekwenz, Jennifer Cobbe, and Jatinder Singh. 2020. "Regulating transparency? Facebook, Twitter and the German Network Enforcement Act." In *FAT* '20: Proceedings of the 2020 conference on fairness, accountability, and transparency*, Barcelona, January 27–30, 2020. https://doi.org/10.1145/3351095.3372856.

Walter, Nathan, Jonathan Cohen, R. Lance Holbert, and Yasmin Morag. 2020. "Fact-checking: A meta-analysis of what works and for whom." *Political Communication* 37 (3): 350–75. https://doi.org/10.1080/10584609.2019.1668894.

Woods, Lorna. 2006. "Freedom of expression in the European Union." *European Public Law* 12 (3): 371–401. https://kluwerlawonline.com/journalarticle/European+Public+Law/12.3/EURO2006026.

Wörsdörfer, Manuel. 2024. "Mitigating the adverse effects of AI with the European Union's artificial intelligence act: Hype or hope?" *Global Business and Organizational Excellence* 43 (3): 106–26. https://doi.org/10.1002/joe.22238.

5

Fighting Disinformation in the European Media Context: The Case of Croatia

Barbara Ravbar

Croatian Media System: Overarching Trends

Croatia, a country with a rich and turbulent history, stands at the crossroads of Central and Southeast Europe. Pro-European-oriented and a member of the EU since 2013, Croatia in the past three decades "experienced independence (from the Socialist Federal Republic of Yugoslavia), war, and transformation of its one-party political system and socialist economy to a market economy and a multiparty political system" (Peruško 2013, 709). During this period of transition, the Croatian media landscape also evolved substantially, characterized by processes such as "nationalization, privatization, and marketization" (Peruško 2013, 714), which have shaped the contemporary media environment. On top of that, since 2020, Croatia has faced multiple crises, including a series of earthquakes that caused severe damage to the capital and surrounding areas, the challenges of COVID-19 lockdowns, inflation, and the transition to the euro currency, which caused significant economic changes.

"Along the process of democratization and accession to the European Union, a free press is one of the prerequisites" (Boshnakova and Dankova 2023, 164). In the 2024 World Press Freedom Index, published by Reporters without Borders, Croatia ranked 48th globally, scoring 68.79 points, a decline from its 42nd position in 2023 (RSF, n.d.). This drop has been attributed to various factors, including Strategic Lawsuits against Public Participation (SLAPP) procedures initiated by politicians and business figures; threats, harassment, and online violence against journalists; and declining salaries for journalists since the onset of the COVID-19 pandemic (RSF, n.d.). A further blow to press freedom was the government's proposition of so-called "Anti-leaks" legislation in 2023, whose primary purpose is, according to the Croatian government, to "criminalize unauthorized disclosure of the content of investigative or evidentiary action" (Prtoric 2023). The law has been criticized for threatening whistleblowers with severe penalties, including up to three years in prison, which the president of the Croatian Journalistic Society (HND) called "dangerous," saying that "its initial intention is to undermine journalistic freedoms in Croatia" (Tesija 2023). Following that, the Media Freedom Rapid Response (MFRR)—a European project cofounded by the European Commission whose purpose is to "track, monitor and react to press and media freedom violations in EU member states and candidate countries" (Media Freedom Rapid Response, n.d.)—announced an international mission to assess media freedom challenges in Croatia in September 2024.

"Media freedom and pluralism, together with freedom of expression, are fundamental prerequisites for democratic societies" (Bleyer-Simon et al. 2024, 12). To assess and evaluate risks to media pluralism in a specific country, the Centre for Media Pluralism and Media Freedom at the European University Institute developed the Media Pluralism Monitor (MPM). According to their study, out of thirty-two analyzed countries in 2023 (twenty-seven EU members plus five candidate countries), only Croatia and Turkey are at high risk regarding standards and protections for the journalistic profession, particularly concerning digital safety (Bleyer-Simon et al. 2024, 22). Additionally, they recognized "a significant risk increase" for the protection of freedom of expression (although Croatia is still at the medium-risk band) mainly due to the "misuse of defamation laws and the lack of transparency on online blocks and removals by online platforms" (Bleyer-Simon et al. 2024, 28). Since insult and defamation are ingrained in Croatia's Criminal Act, there are ways for individuals to sue not only newsrooms but journalists as well, which creates "uncertainty and risk about the outcome, which puts pressure on journalists and their freedom to report on sensitive topics in the first place" (Bleyer-Simon et al. 2024, 30).

Despite these challenges, the "Croatian media market is diverse and competitive" (Grbeša and Volarević 2021, 625). Major media outlets are owned by foreign media corporations, such as the Austrian Styria Media Group, which "owns two out of the three bestselling newspapers" (Grbeša and Volarević 2021, 625); the United Group, which owns NOVA TV and cable news channel N1; and Central European Media Enterprises, which owns RTL TV. Although "TV remains an important source of news, well ahead of social media, print's position today (20%) is less than half of what it was eight years ago (43%)" (Peruško

2024, 73). Since 2017, smartphones have replaced computers and laptops as the primary devices for news consumption. However, interestingly, trust in online news, including social media, is declining. Overall, trust in news in Croatia increased from 39 percent in 2017 to a peak of 45 percent in 2021 during the Covid-19 pandemic, and it has since plummeted to 32 percent in 2024 (Peruško 2024, 73), reflecting lowered trust in the postpandemic period.

Media Trust and Spreading of Disinformation during the Covid-19 Pandemic in Croatia and the Balkans

Trust in news and media of one's own country is a profoundly interconnected phenomenon, and the specificity of the Croatian socio-historical context may impact negative trends in media trust compared to other European countries. Croatia, like other Central and Eastern European countries, has a relatively recent past of being part of a country with a nondemocratic political system (the Socialist Federative Republic of Yugoslavia), so up to this day, it deals with its legacy. As Urbániková (2023) claims, trust in the media as "a key social institution" (5) is closely linked to trust in political institutions, politicians, journalists themselves, and the media market, meaning that countries with almost a "cultural habit of distrusting public institutions" (5) will have lower levels of trust. This legacy, combined with a perception that "journalists and media fulfill their owner's assignments and therefore cannot be trusted" (Urbániková 2023, 10), is partially left in the public sentiment since the previous regime. This skepticism toward journalism is further heightened by political actors who "persistently attack the media and try to delegitimize them" (Urbániková 2023, 6), harming the reputation of journalists and the journalistic profession. In Croatia, for instance, the prime minister and other government officials have a history of purposefully evading uncomfortable journalistic questions and accusing journalists of bias. Media skepticism is also fueled by the "rise of 'alternative' media, which spreads disinformation, hoaxes, conspiracy theories, and propaganda" (Urbániková 2023, 5). The term "alternative" is used here as these media outlets often position themselves outside the mainstream media, accusing them of "being sellouts" and "hiding important information from people" (Urbániková 2023, 10). Furthermore, they emphasize that mainstream media reinforces the power of public institutions that work against the interests of the public and the "little man."

The key determinants of disinformation, which the European Commission defines as "verifiably false or misleading information designed, presented and distributed for economic, political or other benefit and with the intention of misleading the public" (Grbeša Zanzerović and Nenadić 2022, 10), are verification, intent, and damages it causes. A comparison of Reuters's data on trust in the news before and after the Covid-19 pandemic reveals that times of insecurity accelerated and amplified the spread of disinformation, which had already been present in some media spaces. So-called "alternative" media, which had begun building audiences through disinformation before the pandemic, expanded their content mainly through social media accounts and channels (Birchall and Knight 2022). It "enabled spreaders to use social networks and the Internet technologies to spread and reinforce disinformation narratives and discourses" (Brautović 2023a, 19) across the Balkan region. This phenomenon is particularly concerning as younger audiences increasingly turn to "partisan commentators, influencers, and young news creators, especially on YouTube and TikTok" (Peruško 2024, 10). Social media's economy of attention incentivizes divisive content that fulfills "identity-based motivations which may be an effective way for capturing attention and engagement" (Harris et al. 2023, 5323). Moreover, "high-profile policy debates can turn on stories and claims by political elites that stretch the truth or fundamentally distort it" (Coddington et al. 2014, 392).

Following the EU's Action Plan against Disinformation from 2018, Cvjetićanin et al. (2019) researched disinformation online using the case of Croatia's neighbor country, Bosnia and Herzegovina. They found "intentionally fabricated false information" (7) in nearly a third of the disinformation content they analyzed, with more than 60 percent of this content addressing political issues (7). Anonymous websites and online portals were identified as the primary sources of disinformation in Bosnia and Herzegovina's online media. Alarmingly, they concluded that "public media frequently use anonymous websites as both sources and amplifiers of disinformation" (Cvjetićanin et al. 2019, 8). Distorting information processes contributes to the "pollution of the communications environment, the promotion of fear and distrust, and the dissemination of information" (Oliviera et al. 2022, 277), which was a visible trend during the times of insecurity linked to the Covid-19 pandemic. A study by Greene et al. (2021) examined the relationship between disinformation dissemination and the pandemic in the Western Balkans (including Albania, Bosnia and Herzegovina, Kosovo, North Macedonia, and Serbia). Their findings revealed that Covid-related disinformation has been used to "shift general public opinion, to exacerbate internal conflict, and to affect the image—positively or negatively—of political leaders" (40). Some of the COVID-related disinformation has been used by "local politicians' desire to protect their image in light of criticism they faced for their response to the pandemic and to justify restrictions imposed" (40). In several cases they also showed "cases of infection among migrant communities in order to attribute blame for spreading COVID-19 to specific actors or groups" (Greene et al. 2021, 41). The spread of disinformation in the region included Croatia as well. Brautović (2023a) discovered that "disseminators of disinformation about Covid-19 have formed transnational disinformation ecosystems consisting of various pages on social networks, channels, groups, and profiles, including alternative and mainstream media originating outside the Croatian border to the rest of Southeast European region" (30). However, the disinformation could also reach Croatian audiences because of the considerable similarities between languages in the Balkan region (Croatian, Bosnian, and Serbian). In the case of Croatia, the analysis revealed polarized clusters formed around "official sources of information about Covid-19 (government), religions (Catholics) and (dis)information (mainstream media, alternative media, spreaders of misinformation about Covid-19, etc.)" (Brautović 2023a, 30).

Further analysis by Grbeša Zanzerović and Vučković (2023) examined Croatian Facebook groups that spread disinformation. They discovered that most Facebook sites within Croatia's disinformation ecosystem originated in Serbia, supporting Brautović's (2023a) findings on transnational disinformation networks in the Balkans. Likewise, their analysis demonstrates that the analyzed Facebook pages were prone to conspiracy theories and "uncovering the real truth," with the populist discourse being prevalent in almost 60 percent of sites (Grbeša Zanzerović and Vučković 2023, 99). These results correlate with another Croatian study by Tonković et al. (2021), who found that almost a quarter of their respondents believed in conspiracy theories related to the pandemic and that "believing in Covid-19 conspiracies was associated with lower education, lower economic standard, higher importance of religion, and declaring no political self-identification" (7). Blanuša et al. (2023) also examined the relationship between vaccination and belief in Covid-19 conspiracy theories, finding that individuals who believed in such conspiracies will have more negative attitudes "towards the justification of preventive measures, greater difficulties in their acceptance and greater general willingness to oppose the reintroduction of measures" (150).

Furthermore, there was a strong correlation between unvaccinated participants and participants who strongly believed in conspiracy theories about Covid-19. Both groups had higher distrust in institutions that encouraged people to get vaccinated. The authors concluded that efforts to promote vaccination must combat disinformation and build trust in the institutions advocating for these measures (Blanuša et al. 2023, 150).

Current research indicates that facing immense global crises, such as the Covid-19 pandemic, left a substantial and lasting impact on how people consume media, not only in Croatia and the Balkans but also worldwide. A decline in trust toward institutions, journalists, and journalism creates a significant disadvantage in combating the spread of disinformation. As new actors and processes increasingly influence journalistic practices and media content distribution (Grbeša Zanzerović and Nenadić 2022, 14), the position of journalists is more unstable than ever. With the news cycle accelerating, journalists are forced to hyperproduce content without thorough fact-checking. This creates a dilemma: to be first in delivering news (maximizing clickability and attracting readers) or to be 100 percent accurate. "The tension between speed and accuracy in journalism is not new, but it has been intensified by the emergence and relevance of the Internet and social media" (Grbeša Zanzerović and Nenadić 2022, 19). Another common tactic is relying on "churnalism" (Davies 2008), which is "recycling" news from PR companies, news agencies, or social media without conducting additional research outside the newsroom. Since online news users in Croatia still predominantly do not pay for online news or digital subscriptions, newsrooms rely on advertising and sponsorship for revenue. To cut costs, they collaborate with journalists with less experience, offering short-term or unstable contracts. In this environment, the "media is part of the problem, and the victims, at the same time" (Grbeša Zanzerović and Nenadić 2022, 14). Moreover, the rise of online platforms has democratized news reporting, where anyone with a smartphone and an internet connection can report on almost anything with a potentially viral international reach. While increased access to content creation can empower individuals to participate in communication processes, more and more people are turning to social media as their primary source of news, creating a cacophony of sources that are not always credible. While social media can serve as a valuable source of information and a tool for quality reporting, especially in situations when access to the event is difficult or impossible for journalists (e.g., during the early stages of the Russian invasion of Ukraine, platforms like X provided journalists access to real-time information), not all online content has journalistic value. With an "increasing focus on partisan commentators, influencers, and young news creators, especially on YouTube and TikTok" (Peruško 2024, 10), concerns about the truthfulness of information available online, especially in social media, are on the rise. With 2024 being the election super year with 3.7 billion voters in seventy-two countries (UNDP n.d.), the European Digital Media Observatory, whose goal is to "strengthen and enable collaboration among a multidisciplinary community of stakeholders tackling online disinformation" (EDMO n.d.), reports that the spread of disinformation reached its peak just before the elections for the European Parliament in 2024. In April 2024 alone, the thirty-six international organizations in EDMO's fact-checking network published 1,716 fact-checking articles (Canetta and Panizio 2024, 2). Notably, "EU-related disinformation reached its highest level since EDMO's dedicated monitoring began" (2), driven by "the false narrative alleging the participation of the EU or its member countries in ground operations in Ukraine" (3) and EU's policies and laws. In response, fact-checking organizations are increasingly mobilized to confront spreading disinformation, especially in politics.

Disinformation in Croatia: From Digital to Physical Spaces

The dissemination of disinformation has actual consequences that can often spill into the offline world. For instance, the spread of Covid-19-related disinformation fueled public protests against pandemic measures in 2020 and 2021. In September 2020, the "Rights and Freedoms Initiative" orchestrated a major protest opposing Covid-19 regulations. In its press release, the initiative claimed its mission was to "advocate for the preservation of the achievements of a democratic society in which decision-making based on panic and propaganda or rewriting instead of reviewing cannot be tolerated" (Inicijativa Prava i Slobode n.d.). Furthermore, they called for respecting human rights, freedoms, knowledge, solidarity, and mutual understanding while gathering in large crowds without respecting recommended public health measures at the pandemic's peak. Notably, the initiative's website did not disclose any names nor provide an impressum, though a list of coordinators responsible for organizing events in over ten Croatian cities was made available. The event recurred in 2021, featuring a four-hour program with sixteen speakers and attracting several thousand participants in Zagreb alone. Some politicians from prominent right-wing Croatian political parties participated in and endorsed the event. The speakers at this "Festival of Freedom" criticized Covid-19-related "censorship" and "propaganda," accusing mainstream media of being instrumental in disseminating vaccine-related misinformation. Since then, smaller protests have occurred throughout Croatia. In May 2021, Croatia participated in the global "World Rally for Freedom," during which protesters marched against Covid-19 measures. Similarly, in November 2021, protesters marched through Zagreb against mandatory Covid-19 certificates required to access schools, official institutions, and travel. In February 2022, a protest against Covid-19 measures for children targeted the use of facemasks in schools and opposed vaccination for minors.

On a localized scale, disinformation circulating in online spaces has led to physical damage to public property. For example, in April 2020, the municipality of Bibinje in southern Croatia initiated the installation of publicly accessible Wi-Fi infrastructure as part of the EU-funded Wifi4EU project. However, this equipment, valued at approximately €15,000, was vandalized overnight due to the spreading of disinformation, saying that the municipality was driving residents into accepting harmful 5G signals. The disinformation gained such traction that the municipality issued an official statement clarifying that the project was intended to establish Wi-Fi access and posed no health risks.

Fact-Checkers: Roles and Challenges

The primary role of fact-checkers worldwide is to systematically provide "publishing assessments of the validity of claims made by public officials and institutions with an explicit attempt to identify whether a claim is factual" (Walter et al. 2019, 351). First fact-checking organizations, "dedicated to publicly evaluating the truth of political claims," were formed in the United States in the early 2000s (Graves and Cherubini 2016, 6) and, since then, have spread worldwide. These organizations primarily focus on checking political statements from "debates, speeches, interviews, and news releases, limiting the topics to claims that can be definitively proven or disproven" (Amazeen 2016, according to Harris et al. 2023, 351). Despite their nonpartisan nature, high standards of transparency, and reliance on independent research, fact-checkers can face skepticism from the public. "Even simple factual questions can leave surprising room for disagreement, and fact-checkers often come under attack from critics who disagree with their verdicts" (Graves and Cherubini 2016, 6). A number of studies have explored the public's willingness to accept fact-checkers' conclusions and whether exposure to fact-checked information leads to changes in beliefs—with mixed results. While people are generally skeptical when navigating the news content they get on social media (Fletcher and Nielsen 2018), the positive effects of corrective information provided by fact-checkers will not consistently achieve the desired outcome. Brandtzaeg et al. (2017) found that journalists viewed fact-checking services as a "useful starting point and supplement in verification and fact-checking" (1124). However, social media users exhibited more extreme positive and negative reactions. Social media users who were skeptical of fact-checkers "arguably displayed the least nuanced position, sometimes even associated with a position of informational disbelief where any online information is seen as potentially untrustworthy" (Brandtzaeg et al. 2017, 1124). Carson et al. (2022) revealed that "fact-checking had a clear negative influence on readers' trust in the original news story" (816), meaning that fact-checking could backfire because the readers perceived the news media's coverage as less trustworthy in general. Additional elements, such as photographs, can influence how audiences respond to fact-checked statements. Garrett et al. (2013) found that textual and photographic information with no direct connection with the false statement also reduced the corrective effects of the message, concluding that "less relevant information included in the message" (14) can affect evidence presented by the fact-checkers.

Furthermore, Nyhan and Reifler (2010) discovered that responses to corrections vary by ideology; in some cases, corrections not only fail to change beliefs, but they "actually strengthen misperceptions among ideological subgroups in several cases" (323). On a more positive note, research indicates that fact-checking can be effective in specific circumstances. Ecker et al. (2019) found that simple retractions, where fact-checkers repeat a false claim while labeling it false, reduced belief in misinformation (48). On the same trace, refutations "may lead to immediate belief reduction" (49). However, at the same time, the effectiveness of retractions done after a week of delay "was worryingly low" (50). Amazeen et al. (2016) also discovered that corrections were effective in a way that "those who saw a correction were significantly more accurate in their assessment of the controversial statement than those who did not see a correction" (39). Furthermore, they found that including a rating scale in correcting a statement is more effective, mainly when "used to correct non-political misinformation" (42). In their study Robertson et al. (2020) concluded that audience perceptions of fact-checking websites depend on awareness, attitudes, and visiting behavior and that "interest in politics and mainstream/liberal news consumption are large and significant predictors of fact-checking awareness, attitudes, and behavior" (231).

Despite the importance of their work, fact-checkers face complex relationships with their audiences. While certain groups hold negative attitudes toward fact-checkers, other research indicates positive audience responses to corrected media content. A strong relationship with traditional media organizations is another key factor in strengthening fact-checking organizations worldwide. As online platforms increasingly hire fact-checkers "to try and reduce the amount of disinformation and misinformation on their platforms, this sometimes means removing certain content from traditional media sources" (Grbeša Zanzerović and Nenadić 2022, 25). This has created tensions between fact-checkers and journalists in South-East Europe, where UNESCO has documented objections from the media regarding the handling of their content by fact-checking organizations (25). In response, UNESCO emphasized the importance of strengthening the relationships between journalists and fact-checkers in 2021.

Fighting Disinformation in Croatia: The Case Study of Faktograf

As of 2024, two fact-checking organizations and one public platform for fact-checking operate in Croatia. Točno tako (Eng. "Exactly so") is a newly established collaborative platform (October 2024) that verifies information. The EU's Recovery and Resilience Mechanism finances the platform as part of the National Recovery and Resilience Plan, overseen by the Ministry of Culture and Media and the Agency for Electronic Media. The objectives are to "strengthen society's resilience to disinformation by reducing the number of disinformation and misinformation in the public space, media, and on social media, and to strengthen information reliability and security when consuming media content and using social networks, as well as strengthening the quality of journalism and credible reporting" (TOČNO tako n.d.). Within this project, 5 million euros is intended for the establishment of new independent fact-checkers, the strengthening of information-checking systems and procedures, the establishment of special units for fact-checking in existing media editorial offices, and training and development of digital tools to assist in the work of fact-checking.

Faktograf and AFP are two established fact-checking organizations. Both are members of the International Fact-Checking Network (IFCN) and participate in Facebook's Third-Party Fact-Checking Program. AFP Fact Check is one of the departments of Agence France-Presse (AFP), a news agency in France. It has been active since 2017 and has over 100 journalists working in twenty-six languages (AFP Fact Check n.d.). Their main goal is to "investigate dubious claims circulating on the Internet that have been widely shared, and which can affect the public in a harmful way" (AFP Provjera činjenica n.d.). They cover social media, blogs, websites, communication apps, and other public forums. Every European country's headquarters has a journalist who tracks disinformation in their country and their language. One of their fact-checking offices is in Croatia, which joined AFP Fact Check in 2023. While AFP Fact Check is a major player in global fact-checking, this chapter will focus on Faktograf, Croatia's first and only locally established fact-checking organization. Given the focus on disinformation in Croatia and Croatian fact-checking services, it is essential to examine Faktograf's practices and challenges in the Croatian media landscape. Launched in 2015 as a nonprofit, copublishing media project between the Croatian Journalistic Association and GONG, a "civil society organization aimed at improving democratic processes and institutions and democratic political culture" (GONG n.d.), this nonprofit model sets Faktograf apart from AFP Fact Check, which is part of a larger, multilingual, for-profit global news agency. The structure and resources of Faktograf are inherently shaped by its nonprofit status, leading to different operational approaches and financial constraints compared to AFP.

In 2018, GONG became an independent publisher of the fact-checking web portal Faktograf.hr, and since November 2021, Faktograf has become a separate association. The Faktograf Association for Informed Public functions as a "non-profit media organization that advocates for the development of good journalism, critical thinking, and an informed public" (Udruga Faktograf n.d.), and the association publishes the fact-checking web portal Faktograf.hr. The purpose of Faktograf.hr is to use a fact-checking method and reliable sources to "evaluate the accuracy and validity of the statements of politicians, as well as other publicly relevant political actors, to prevent unfounded views from being expressed enough times in public discourse gets the status of a fact" (Faktograf n.d.). In their work, Faktograf.hr focuses on monitoring the statements of Croatian politicians and other prominent political actors. They also monitor the claims published in other digital and social media. Their topics are selected by following media reports and public discussions on social media. Brautović (2023b) conducted interviews through an online focus group with four members of the Faktograf.hr newsroom—Petar Vidov (editor-in-chief), Ana Brakus (executive director), Sanja Despot (deputy editor-in-chief), and Ivana Živković (editor of communications)—about their everyday newsroom practices as fact-checking media organization in Croatia. Every morning the editor-in-chief chooses the main topics that will be covered, analyzed, and checked. The criteria they implement when considering the topic for the day are the spread of disinformation, capacity to expand, severity of disinformation, and potential influence on elections (Brautović 2023b, 13). Faktograf's fact-checkers also use two software tools: Facebook interface, which they have special access to as members of Meta's Fact-Checking Program, and which can detect disinformation spreading in the assigned language; and CrowdTangle, which detects viral disinformation (Brautović 2023b, 14). Since they prioritize topics of public interest (Faktograf n.d.), they also allow their users to suggest topics they would like to see fact-checked and analyzed. Their website has multiple columns, such as "Accuracy Assessment," which focuses on the statements of politicians and political actors whose statements get verified; "Exposed," which focuses on the accuracy of claims made by digital media outlets and users on social media; and "Under the Magnifying Glass," which is focused on in-depth checks and reporting on the social and political topics, without expressing opinions. Faktograf provides information on the categories and sources they use when fact-checking and assessing accuracy on their website. They use official sources such as data and announcements of public institutions and other public authorities, scientific research, data from civil society organizations and international organizations, opinions of relevant experts, and media sources. In its work, Faktograf relies "primarily on primary sources and always tries to refer readers to a large number of different relevant sources of data on the topics covered" (Faktograf n.d.). They also implement the reviews of fact-checked articles so that the article is always edited before publication by at least one person who did not participate in its creation. When the article is created, they publish all the sources used, except if there is an assessment that the publication would put the source at risk. All subjects of the articles, especially if they are victims of violence, are protected in illustrations and photographs on the website.

The Faktograf Association is "politically independent as an organization and media outlet" (Faktograf n.d.). They do not advocate voting for any political party, coalition, or candidate in elections for all levels of government and do not enter into agreements or partnerships with political parties or foundations connected to them, guaranteed by the Editorial Statute. In their work, they ensure impartiality and multiple sources of information. Their website firmly states that they do not unjustifiably focus on individual political parties and candidates on the political spectrum, and their employees are forbidden from holding positions in political parties or at any level of government. Fact-checkers of the Faktograf.hr web portal who are active in civil society organizations and civic initiatives, except professional journalistic organizations, are obliged to inform the executive director and editor-in-chief about it and will be removed from reporting on those topics to prevent conflict of interest.

Throughout the years, they have been financially supported by, but not limited to, the National Endowment for Democracy, Google News Initiative's Innovation Fund, the Balkan Trust for Democracy, the Agency for Electronic Media, the European Commission, the European Fund for Media and Information, the US Embassy in Croatia, and through Facebook's Third-Party Fact-Checking Program (Faktograf n.d.). As part of Facebook's program, their rating of the content (rated as incorrect, partially incorrect, lacking context, or edited/manipulated photos/videos) can reduce the reach of Facebook posts that fact-checkers evaluate. If the publisher corrects the information, their rating will be withdrawn, and their social media reach will be approved. Except for the collaboration with Meta, Faktograf is a member of the IFCN (The Poynter Institute, n.d.), an international network of organizations dedicated to fact-checking that focuses on "statements by public figures, major institutions, internet and social media postings, and other widely circulated claims of interest to society" (The Poynter Institute 2024). They are also a member of the European Fact-Checking Standards Network, which represents "the voice of European fact-checkers who uphold and promote the highest standards of fact-checking and media literacy in their effort to combat misinformation for the public benefit" (EFCSN n.d.).

Threats and Attacks: Faktograf's Work and Public Response

Although they publish only information that has been proven correct and verified multiple times, Faktograf is still a target of criticism. Although no studies have yet tackled the audiences and public perception of Faktograf's work, other news outlets and politicians have targeted their writing multiple times. Since Faktograf is a member of Meta's special program for fact-checking news on Facebook, there are multiple Croatian online news portals whose reach was limited on Facebook because Faktograf evaluated their content as untrue or misleading. This spiked anger and resentment among publishers whose content was flagged and their reach on social media limited. For example, one media outlet claimed that Faktograf does "media mobbing" because it flagged their content as incomplete and inaccurate information on the Covid-19 pandemic, and another one claimed that Faktograf punishes their opponents without reason and makes their jobs purposefully harder. Except for publicly speaking out against Faktograf, media outlets whose content was flagged as misleading or disseminating disinformation started publishing texts online attacking and questioning Faktograf, its fact-checkers, editors, and their potential biases and expertise. For example, an online platform called Hrvatski Fokus (Croatian Focus) published a text calling Faktograf's work unconstitutional and accusing them of censoring all conservative and right-wing news outlets. Another web portal, logično.com, called Faktograf's journalists "unprofessional and uneducated peddlers of globalist propaganda" because of their writing about the Covid-19 pandemic (Logično 2023). Narod.hr, published by the conservative religious association In the Name of the Family, which is most famous for its annual anti-abortion parade titled "The March for Life," also heavily critiqued Faktograf. Faktograf flagged texts from Narod.hr regarding vaccines and the spread of Covid-19, which reduced the reach of their posts on Facebook. Narod.hr heavily critiqued Faktograf and said that they carry out censorship of all those who have different opinions and thereby violate the right to freedom of expression (Narod 2020).

There are multiple examples of marginal online newsletters that attack Faktograf.hr, mainly when it comes to their fact-checking of Covid-19-related articles. Online media whose reach has been limited mostly accuse Faktograf of censorship (although Meta is the one who limits the reach, not Faktograf), destroying freedom of speech, spreading leftist, liberal agenda, and questioning Faktograf's work ethic, accuracy, and motives for exercising "censorship." Attacks on Faktograf's work especially increased during and after the Covid-19 pandemic, which "correspond to the development of social tensions and the greater involvement of publicly influential people in opposing epidemiological measures and the spread of disinformation" (Faktograf 2023, 8). During 2020 and 2021, Faktograf got "almost 40 threats of physical violence and death" (9), which were reported to the police. In December 2021, they suffered an organized DDoS cyber-attack; hackers from Russia and Indonesia attempted to enter their website 27 million times, causing their website to crash. In January 2022, Faktograf's editor-in-chief, Petar Vidov, received a threat via SMS. At the same time, in 2021, Faktograf's fact-checkers reported receiving death threats after a Croatian businessman with a semi-large following on his Facebook profile posted that Faktograf has a private relationship with Facebook, and that in collaboration with them, Faktograf censors Facebook posts that question stuff of public interest openly, cutting their audience reach, and therefore limiting the legally guaranteed freedom of speech in the Croatian public space. He also announced that he would go to court if they did not stop limiting his reach. Faktograf was flagging his content because of his Facebook posts connected to the Covid-19 pandemic, where the businessman posted that "experts" in the Croatian media are actually "proponents of the totalitarian regime." In a public post, Faktograf openly wrote that they have been receiving violent threats, as well as death threats, after the businessman's post and that they cannot censor anyone's content on Facebook. They can only check it and rate its truthfulness. From then on, Meta has been deciding if that content aligns with Facebook's terms of service and community standards. If not, they will reduce the reach of posts flagged as inaccurate, manipulative, or miscontextualized by Faktograf. The businessman afterward raised a lawsuit against Faktograf, which was dismissed in 2022. The main narratives when it comes to the attacks on Faktograf are: (1) Faktograf censors and restricts freedom of speech on social media, (2) global centers of power are financing Faktograf, and they earned much money during the pandemic, (3) they are biased and extremely left-wing-oriented, (4) their fact-checking is targeted toward the media and individuals who speak against the mainstream agenda, (5) they are not experts (Faktograf 2023, 38). In July 2024, online threats became a reality when Croatian journalist Melita Vrsaljko of Faktograf and Faktograf's Climate Portal were physically attacked while working on a documentary coproduced by the Climate Portal. Vrsaljko was working on a story about an illegal garbage dump emerging on a public property in Nadin, near Zadar. While passing with her cameraman, an older man attacked her at the place of filming. Upon coming home, the daughter of the attacker showed up, and when Vrsaljko opened the door, the woman started hitting her and tried to take away her mobile phone (Faktograf n.d.).

Unfortunately, harassment of fact-checkers is a harmful and dangerous trend throughout Europe. In 2023, as part of the Decoding the Disinformation Playbook project, led by the International Press Institute, forty-one fact-checking media outlets from twenty-eight European countries participated in a study to assess the potential harassment of European fact-checking organizations. Preliminary results from the study showed that "9 out of ten fact-checking organizations that participated in the survey experienced smear campaigns and online abuse from politicians, government officials, media pundits, and public figures" (International Press Institute 2023). Furthermore, seven out of ten respondents who were harassed online also experienced stalking, smear campaigns, hate speech, and doxing. As Faktograf wrote in their report, heightened social tensions during the pandemic also frequented the harassment. "Initiatives, petitions, or legislative initiatives which would limit the work of fact-checking organizations were recorded in four countries, including Croatia" (Faktograf 2023, 8), with most harassment happening online.

Conclusion

This chapter focused on the spread of disinformation during the Covid-19 pandemic and the efforts of Faktograf, Croatia's first locally established fact-checking organization. Although fact-checkers' work is mainly based on reviewing political statements and Faktograf's work was especially prominent during the Croatian election in 2024, this chapter highlights the activities and challenges they encountered while combating disinformation connected to the Covid-19 pandemic. The global health crisis, coupled with widespread insecurity, fueled the spread of disinformation. Studies conducted in the Balkan region (Grbeša Zanzerović and Nenadić 2022; Brautović 2023a, 2023b; Greene et al. 2021; Grbeša Zanzerović and Vučković 2023) emphasize how the Covid-19 pandemic amplified disinformation networks, leading to the emergence of transnational disinformation networks across the region. Croatia's historically volatile socioeconomic circumstances, exacerbated by the health and economic uncertainties of the pandemic, a series of earthquakes in 2020 and 2021, and the transition from the national currency to the euro in early 2024, have further deepened public mistrust, and as of 2024 only 32 percent of Croatians trust media (Peruško 2024, 73). This distrust is compounded by what Urbániková (2023, 5) describes as a "cultural habit of distrusting public institutions." Political actors, particularly from the conservative spectrum, have attacked mainstream media, accusing them of bias, and marginal online publications, masquerading as advocates for the "little man," have proliferated, spreading disinformation and accusing mainstream outlets of hiding important information. While this chapter focused on the dynamics in Croatia and the Balkans, these trends reflect broader European tendencies. Across the EU, trust in the media and journalism has deteriorated since the pandemic, compounded by disinformation, skepticism toward fact-checkers, and fast-paced changes in the media market.

In the hyperproduction-driven media environment, journalists—particularly those working on digital platforms—face huge pressure to meet deadlines. Fact-checkers, in contrast, provide slower-paced, in-depth analyses, offering valuable support to journalists pursuing accuracy and truth. Faktograf's fact-checkers, with years of experience in various Croatian media organizations, possess a unique understanding of the domestic media landscape, its challenges, and the daily realities of journalistic work. Despite their contributions, fact-checkers like Faktograf are often viewed with skepticism by some parts of the public and online platforms, who label them as "censors" or "propagandists." Nonetheless, their role in today's media ecosystem is essential. Faktograf examines news content and investigates viral social media narratives, striving for thorough, unbiased verification. While some individuals may remain unconvinced of fact-checkers' rigor, their continued presence is necessary. As pressure on journalists in digital media intensifies, fact-checkers should be viewed not as rivals but as allies. Their collaboration has the potential to address shared challenges, enhance media monitoring, and contribute to the overall integrity of the Croatian media space.

Conflict of Interest Statement

No potential conflict of interest was reported by the author.

References

"AFP Fact Check." n.d. https://factcheck.afp.com/.

"AFP Provjera činjenica." n.d. https://provjeracinjenica.afp.com/

Amazeen, Michelle A., Esther Thorson, Ashley Muddiman, and Lucas Graves. 2016. "Correcting political and consumer misperceptions: The effectiveness and effects of rating scale versus contextual correction formats." *Journalism & Mass Communication Quarterly* 95 (1): 28–48. https://doi.org/10.1177/1077699016678186.

Birchall, Clare, and Peter Knight. 2022. *Conspiracy theories in the time of COVID-19*. Routledge. https://doi.org/10.4324/9781003315438.

Blanuša, Nebojša, Mislav Tonković, and Aida Vranić. 2023. "Bihevioralni Korelati Teorija Zavjere o Covid-u 19." In *Covid-19 Dezinformacije i Teorije Zavjera u Hrvatskoj*, edited by Nebojša Blanuša and Anita Brakus. Gong. https://pro-fact.gong.hr/wp-content/uploads/2023/02/COVID-19-dezinformacije-i-teorije-zavjera-u-Hrvatskoj.pdf.

Bleyer-Simon, Krisztina, Daniela Da Costa Leite Borges, Edoardo Brogi, Roberto Carlini, Julia Kermer, Ivana Nenadic, Mark Palmer, Pier Luigi Parcu, Umberto Reviglio, Michele Trevisan, Stefania Verza, and Monika Žuffová. 2024. *Monitoring media pluralism in the digital era*. European University Institute. https://doi.org/10.2870/193899.

Boshnakova, Daniela, and Denitsa Dankova. 2023. "The media in Eastern Europe." In *The media systems in Europe*, edited by Andrea Miconi and Stylianos Papathanassopoulos. Springer. https://doi.org/10.1007/978-3-031-32216-7.

Brandtzaeg, Petter Bae, Asbjørn Følstad, and María Ángeles Chaparro Domínguez. 2017. "How journalists and social media users perceive online fact-checking and verification services." *Journalism Practice* 12 (9): 1109–29. https://doi.org/10.1080/17512786.2017.1363657.

Brautović, Marin. 2023a. "Provjera Činjenične Točnosti u Hrvatskoj: Izbor Tema i Postupci Razotkrivanja Dezinformacija na Faktograf.hr-u." In *Covid-19 Dezinformacije i Teorije Zavjera u Hrvatskoj*, edited by Nebojša Blanuša and Anita Brakus. Gong. https://pro-fact.gong.hr/wp-content/uploads/2023/02/COVID-19-dezinformacije-i-teorije-zavjera-u-Hrvatskoj.pdf.

Brautović, Marin. 2023b. "Mapiranje Ekosustava Dezinformacija o Covid-u 19 u Hrvatskoj." In *Covid-19 Dezinformacije i Teorije Zavjera u Hrvatskoj*, edited by Nebojša Blanuša and Anita Brakus. Gong. https://pro-fact.gong.hr/wp-content/uploads/2023/02/COVID-19-dezinformacije-i-teorije-zavjera-u-Hrvatskoj.pdf.

Canetta, Tommaso, and Elisa Panizio, eds. 2024. "EU-related disinformation peaks in April." European Digital Media Observatory. https://edmo.eu/wp-content/uploads/2024/05/EDMO-35-Horizontal.pdf.

Carson, Andrea, Andrea Gibbons, Alex Martin, and Jeffrey B. Phillips. 2022. "Does third-party fact-checking increase trust in news stories? An Australian case study using the 'Sports Rorts' affair." *Digital Journalism* 10 (5): 801–22. https://doi.org/10.1080/21670811.2022.2031240.

Coddington, Mark, Logan Molyneux, and Regina G. Lawrence. 2014. "Fact-checking the campaign." *International Journal of Press/Politics* 19 (4): 391–409. https://doi.org/10.1177/1940161214540942.

Cvjetićanin, Tijana, Emir Zulejhić, Darko Brkan, and Biljana Livančić-Milić. 2019. "Disinformation in the online sphere: The case of BiH." Citizens' Association "Why

Not." https://zastone.ba/app/uploads/2019/05/Disinformation_in_the_online_sphere_The_case_of_BiH_ENG.pdf.
Davies, Nick. 2008. *Flat earth news*. Chatto & Windus.
Ecker, Ullrich K. H., Zachary O'Reilly, Jesse S. Reid, and Ee Pin Chang. 2019. "The effectiveness of short-format refutational fact-checks." *British Journal of Psychology* 111 (1): 36–54. https://doi.org/10.1111/bjop.12383.
"EDMO" n.d. https://edmo.eu/about-us/edmoeu/.
European Fact-Checking Standards Network (EFCSN). n.d. "European Fact-Checking Standards Network (EFCSN)." https://efcsn.com/.
Faktograf.hr. n.d. "About the association." https://udruga.faktograf.hr/en/about-the-association/.
Faktograf.hr. 2023. "When disinformation campaigns fuel hate and harassment. Case study: Faktograf.hr." https://faktograf.hr/site/wp-content/uploads/2023/03/preliminary-survey-report-final.pdf.
Fletcher, Richard, and Rasmus Kleis Nielsen. 2018. "Generalized skepticism: How people navigate news on social media." *Information, Communication & Society* 22 (12): 1751–67. https://doi.org/10.1080/1369118x.2018.1450887.
Garrett, R. Kelly, Erik C. Nisbet, and Emily K. Lynch. 2013. "Undermining the corrective effects of media-based political fact-checking? The role of contextual cues and naïve theory." *Journal of Communication* 63 (4): 617–37. https://doi.org/10.1111/jcom.12038.
Gong.hr. n.d. "What is GONG?" https://gong.hr/en/who-are-we/what-is-gong/.
Graves, Lucas, and Federica Cherubini. 2016. *The rise of fact-checking sites in Europe*. Reuters Institute for the Study of Journalism. https://apo.org.au/node/70883.
Grbeša Zenzerović, Marijana, and Ivana Nenadić, eds. 2022. *Jačanje Otpornosti Društva na Dezinformacije: Analiza Stanja i Smjernice za Djelovanje*. Agency for Electronic Media. www.aem.hr/blog/2010/02/18/publikacije/.
Grbeša Zanzerović, Marijana, and Marijana Vučković. 2023. "Analiza Sadržaja Dezinformacija o Covid-19 na Facebooku: Teme, Izvori i Diskursi." In *Covid-19 Dezinformacije i Teorije Zavjera u Hrvatskoj*, edited by Nebojša Blanuša and Anita Brakus. Gong. https://pro-fact.gong.hr/wp-content/uploads/2023/02/COVID-19-dezinformacije-i-teorije-zavjera-u-Hrvatskoj.pdf.
Grbeša Zanzerović, Marijana, and Marina Volarević. 2021. "Media in Croatia: From freedom fighters to tabloid avengers." *Publizistik* 66 (3–4): 621–36. https://doi.org/10.1007/s11616-021-00683-y.
Greene, Samuel, Gregory Asmolov, Adam Fagan, Olga Fridman, and Bogdan Gjuzelov. 2021. *Mapping fake news and disinformation in the Western Balkans and identifying ways to effectively counter them*. European Union, European Parliament's Committee on Foreign Affairs.

Harris, Emily, Sam Rathje, Claudia Robertson, and Jay Van Bavel. 2023. "The role of media in political polarization: The SPIR framework of social media and polarization." *International Journal of Communication* 17: 20. https://ijoc.org/index.php/ijoc/article/view/19014.

Inicijativa. n.d. "Inicijativa – Prava I Slobode – inicijativa.hr." https://inicijativa.hr/.

International Press Institute. 2023. "Harassed, threatened, and sued: The state of fact-checking in Europe." https://ipi.media/harassed-threatened-and-sued

Logično.hr. 2023. "Američki FBI se popišao po Indexu i Faktografu." *Vijesti - Logično*, May 3. www.logicno.com/politika/americki-fbi-se-popisao-po-indexu-i-faktografu.html.

Media Freedom Rapid Response. n.d. "Monitoring media freedom." www.mfrr.eu/monitor/.

Narod.hr. 2020. "Nova Cenzura Od Faktograf.hr I Raskrinkavanje.ba Nakon Što Je FB Uvažio Žalbu Narod.hr-a." December 20. https://narod.hr/hrvatska/nova-cenzura-od-faktograf-hr-i-raskrinkavanje-ba-nakon-sto-je-fb-uvazio-zalbu-narod-hr-a.

Nyhan, Brendan, and Jason Reifler. 2010. "When corrections fail: The persistence of political misperceptions." *Political Behavior* 32: 303–30. https://doi.org/10.1007/s11109-010-9112-2.

Oliveira, Alexandra F., Maria João Brites, and Carolina P. B. Cerqueira. 2022. "Intergenerational perspectives on media and fake news during COVID-19: Results from online intergenerational focus groups." *Media and Communication* 10 (4): 277–88. https://doi.org/10.17645/mac.v10i4.5712.

Peruško, Zrinjka. 2013. "Rediscovering the Mediterranean characteristics of the Croatian media system." *East European Politics and Societies* 27 (4): 709–26.

Peruško, Zrinjka. 2024. "Croatia." In *Reuters Institute Digital News Report 2024*, edited by Nic Newman, Richard Fletcher, Craig T. Robertson, Amy Ross Arguedas, and Rasmus Kleis Nielsen. Reuters Institute for the Study of Journalism. https://doi.org/10.60625/risj-vy6n-4v57.

The Poynter Institute. n.d. "International fact-checking network: Poynter." July 10. www.poynter.org/ifcn/.

Prtoric, Jelena. 2023. "Croatia: 'Anti-leaks' legislation and new media law proposal spell trouble for journalists." *IPI Media*, October 31. https://ipi.media/croatia-anti-leaks-legislation-and-new-media-law-proposal-spell-trouble-for-journalists/.

Reporters Without Borders. 2024 . "Croatia." https://rsf.org/en/country/croatia.

Robertson, Craig T., Rodrigo R. Mourão, and Emily Thorson. 2020. "Who uses fact-checking sites? The impact of demographics, political antecedents, and media use on fact-checking site awareness, attitudes, and behavior." *International Journal of Press/Politics* 25 (2): 217–37. https://doi.org/10.1177/1940161219898055.

Tesija, Vedran. 2023. "Croatia's proposed media law condemned as 'death for journalism.' " *BalkanInsight*, July 20. https://balkaninsight.com/2023/07/20/croatias-proposed-media-law-condemned-as-death-for-journalism/.

"TOČNO Tako." n.d. www.tocnotako.hr/o-nama.

Tonković, Mirko, Filip Dumančić, Maja Jelić, and Damir Č. Biruški. 2021. "Who believes in COVID-19 conspiracy theories in Croatia? Prevalence and predictors of conspiracy beliefs." *Frontiers in Psychology* 12. https://doi.org/10.3389/fpsyg.2021.643568.

Udruga Faktograf. n.d. https://udruga.faktograf.hr/.

UNDP. n.d. "A 'Super Year' for Elections." www.undp.org/super-year-elections.

Urbániková, Marína. 2023. "Journalists as liars, servants, and sellouts? On the declining trust in the media in the Czech Republic and Slovakia." *Global Media Journal: German Edition* 12 (2): 1–14. https://doi.org/10.22032/dbt.55519.

Walter, Nathan, Jonathan Cohen, R. Lance Holbert, and Yael Morag. 2019. "Fact-checking: A meta-analysis of what works and for whom." *Political Communication* 37 (3): 350–75. https://doi.org/10.1080/10584609.2019.1668894.

6

Perceptions Toward Disinformation and Regulation in Romania: A Case Study on Public Policy Support

Flavia Durach, Alina Bârgăoanu, Loredana Vladu, and Iuliana Călin

Introductory Remarks

Across democratic societies around the globe, there is growing consensus among policymakers, experts, and civil society representatives that the risks posed by contemporary disinformation need to be tackled both in general and concerning particular circumstances. Nevertheless, the paths to action in this respect may vary, and implementing policies for countering disinformation is a matter of heated democratic debate (Leiter 2024). Policies for tackling disinformation can be perceived by the public as an intrusion on free speech and a form of censorship, making it less likely to be supported blindly (Freiling et al. 2023). Consequently, gaining public support for regulation and other measures is essential for political leaders and policymakers to ultimately be accountable to their electorate.

In this context, our chapter analyzes public perceptions of disinformation and regulatory responses to it in Romania, aiming to identify predictors of public support for regulation initiatives in this field. The research data are sourced from a more extensive study conducted in the EU-funded project "Strategic Planning to Strengthen the Disinformation Resilience and the Management of Hybrid Threats" (SIPOCA/SMIS 2014+: 865/136668) implemented jointly by the Romanian Ministry of Foreign Affairs and the National University of Political Studies and Public Administration (Bucharest) between 2020 and 2023. The implementation period of the project coincided with three periods of crisis with solid repercussions for international relations and for tackling disinformation: the COVID-19 pandemic, the war in Ukraine (bordering

Romania), and the Israel–Hamas war. Thus, context was appropriate for investigating public perceptions related to the pressing topic of coming up with systemic responses, including new or updated regulatory frameworks, to disinformation.

Romania presents an interesting and relevant case study. The country's geographic position on the eastern border of the EU, its role as a pillar of NATO's security in Southeastern Europe, and the fact that it shares a border with Ukraine make Romania a target for Kremlin-aligned anti-NATO, anti-EU disinformation narratives (Bârgăoanu and Durach 2023, 221–36). For example, in an unprecedented sequence of events, the Constitutional Court in Romania annulled the first round of the presidential elections 2024 based on declassified intelligence alleging that Russia ran a coordinated online campaign to promote the far-right candidate—an outsider who was virtually unknown to the general public prior the elections—who unexpectedly won the first round (Cole 2024). Romania's resilience to disinformation is affected by factors such as a preference to use social media for news (Buturoiu et al. 2023), low trust in the national institutions and in journalists (Pricop 2024), and the vulnerabilities of traditional mass media organizations (Free Press Unlimited 2021).

It is worth mentioning that, as an EU member state, Romania is covered by relevant EU regulations for managing digital risks, including disinformation, such as the General Data Protection Regulation (Regulation (EU) 2016/679) of 2016 and the Digital Services Act Package (Regulation (EU) 2022/2065—Digital Services Act, and Regulation (EU) 2022/1925—Digital Markets Act of 2022).

Literature Review

The Third-Person Effect as a Predictor of Support for Regulation

According to the literature, public support for measures to address online disinformation has been explored mainly through the lens of the third-person effect (TPE) theory, which originated in the work of W. P. Davison (1983). A consistent body of studies on the behavioral component of TPE focuses on people's eagerness to engage in or support censorship of what is perceived as harmful media content for others (Xu and Gonzenbach 2008).

Support for governmental restrictions is one of the most consistently tested behavioral outcomes of TPE concerning internet pornography, election polls, and television violence (Cheng and Luo 2021). As evidence suggests, there is a behavioral component involved in the case of disinformation as well; individuals who presume that others are more susceptible to disinformation than themselves are more prone to support countermeasures, such as regulation and sanctions to media organizations and internet users (Cheng et al. 2021; Tang et al. 2021), media literacy interventions (Jang and Kim 2018), governmental restrictions and corrective action during the COVID-19 pandemic (Cheng and Luo 2021), and content moderation (Riedl et al. 2022). Additionally, the use and knowledge of nonregulatory solutions, such as fact-checking websites, reduce support for regulation in mature democracies, with a great emphasis on protecting freedom of speech (Cheng et al. 2021).

Other Factors that Influence Public Support for Regulation

The present study goes beyond the framework of TPE by exploring other factors that might influence support for regulatory responses to disinformation, such as people's fact-checking behavior, perceived exposure to disinformation, knowledge of disinformation effects, habits for checking information, and trust. These factors can contribute to individual resilience to disinformation, which in turn could influence, one way or another, support for regulation.

Fact-checking is one of the main pillars for addressing disinformation, although the results do not always align with expectations (Batista Pereira et al. 2022). A meta-analytic review on the effectiveness of fact-checking in correcting political disinformation (Walter et al. 2020) indicated that fact-checking has a significantly positive overall influence on political beliefs. Educating the public on source credibility can help individuals and institutions reflect on the authenticity of online information (Rodrigo et al. 2024). In conclusion, individuals who engage in fact-checking practices could grow more aware of the severity of the phenomenon and, potentially, become more supportive of regulation.

Perceived exposure to disinformation, especially in the case of heavy social media users, can in turn influence perceptions of the severity and amplitude of the disinformation phenomenon and support for countermeasures. Social media is one of the superspreaders of disinformation and, simultaneously, one of the primary sources of news, especially for younger audiences (Aïmeur et al. 2023; Muhammed and Mathew 2022). Individuals who spend more time on social media may perceive that they are exposed to more disinformation and are more concerned about the effects on other users who have interacted with it (Jones-Jang et al. 2021). In a study in five Arab countries, people who reported high perceived exposure to disinformation were also inclined to think that measures to stop the spread of fake news online were necessary either by governments, tech companies, or laypersons (Martin and Hassan 2020). Thus, we explore the possibility that people who report more significant exposure to disinformation would be more open to supporting regulation in this regard.

Knowledge about the effects of disinformation can also play a role in policy support. Perceptions of disinformation effects on oneself and others were associated in a recent study with several behaviors, including support for regulation (Lee 2021). Consistent with these findings, evidence from a representative survey in Taiwan shows that individuals who perceive more risks stemming from disinformation and a more significant influence also prefer more complex measures against it (Zheng and Lu 2021). Potentially, better knowledge and awareness of the documented effects of disinformation can influence support for regulation, similar to perceptions. We explored this possibility in our study.

The ability to engage in correct information behavior (i.e., assessing information carefully before dissemination) could indicate a heightened awareness of the necessity to enforce regulations against disinformation. We investigated the possibility that, given their enhanced civic online reasoning abilities, individuals who engage in corrective information behavior are more supportive of regulation for tackling disinformation. To the best of our knowledge, no studies have explored this relationship.

Disinformation can account for a decrease in *trust in political institutions* (Bârgăoanu et al. 2021; Invernizzi and Mohamed 2019) and *trust in the media* (Vaccari and Chadwick 2020). Political distrust can reduce support for different types of governmental policies (Achimescu et al. 2021; Hammar and Jagers 2006; Macdonald 2021). To date, there is minimal literature on the predictors of policy attitudes in the context of disinformation. However, evidence suggests that trust in media and democracy is positively related to policy support (Freiling et al. 2023). Starting from these insights, we investigate trust's role in news, media, and media regulatory authorities in public support for regulatory responses to disinformation.

Responsibility for Tackling Disinformation

There is growing emphasis at the level of policymakers, supranational institutions, and organizations (EEAS n.d.; NATO Parliamentary Assembly

2021), fact-checkers, and the research community (Gill and Goolsby 2022; Gori 2024) that a whole-of-society approach is desirable for tackling disinformation comprehensively. The role of national governments and supranational institutions remains central in coordinating policy responses and in pressing for more regulation in the field (Cipers et al. 2023; Tenove 2020). Against this background, we investigate public perceptions of the preferred stakeholders to regulate the information environment (i.e., no actor/the public should protect itself, state institutions, media/journalists).

Methodology

This study aims to assess people's perceptions of possible new or updated media regulatory policy in Romania and their resilience to disinformation through a quantitative approach.

Based on the theoretical underpinnings discussed in the first sections of the chapter, we aim to answer the following research questions:

- RQ1: What are the predictors of public policy support to address disinformation in Romania?
- RQ2: According to the Romanian public, who should regulate the information environment?
- RQ3: What is the profile of Romanians who are resilient to disinformation?

In answering these questions, we used a national survey with an online panel (N = 1070) using soft quotas for age, gender, occupation, and geographical region in Romania. Data were collected by Cult Market Research, a Romanian-recognized market research company, in June 2022. The survey explored people's news consumption, trust in the information received through different media channels, trust in media, fact-checking, and correct informing behavior, and perceived exposure to disinformation and knowledge of disinformation effects. The sample had a mean age of forty-five years with a standard deviation of 15.80 years and was gender-balanced, with 51 percent women and 49 percent men. The sample comprised 41 percent of employees in the private sector, 19 percent in the public sector, and 40 percent unemployed. The sample was skewed toward urban residents, who accounted for 62 percent of the participants.

Measurements

Dependent Variables in the Model

Support for regulation was assessed with two statements measuring people's opinions on freedom of expression and on the uncensored use of the internet on a four-point Likert scale (1 "very important" to 4 "not important at all"). Low scores indicate low support for regulation. For items grouped in one factor, α equaled .605, an acceptable value for scale reliability in exploratory studies. See the appendix for the full wording of statements. The final variable was computed as the mean of the two items in the factor (M = 1.49; SD = .64), suggesting that the respondents are generally against a possible regulation of the internet or the content they provide publicly. This variable is not normally distributed in the population (according to the Shapiro-Wilk test, Sig. <.05), and approximately 2 percent of cases are outliers.

Antecedents in the Model

News consumption was measured with a four-point Likert scale (1 "daily" to 4 "never"), asking people how often they receive news on topics of interest. The variable was recoded into a new variable on a scale from 1 "never" to 4 "daily" so that low scores represented low levels of news consumption (M = 3.45; SD = .88).

Social media consumption for people with access to social media was measured with a four-point Likert scale (1 "daily" to 4 "never") on the frequency of receiving, sharing, and commenting on the news. The variables were recoded into new variables on a scale from 1 "never" to 4 "daily" so that low scores represented low levels of social media consumption. The number of items grouped into one factor, α = .750, was computed as the mean of three items in the factor (M = 2.61; SD = .96).

Trust in news was measured for both mainstream media and social media through a battery of five questions on a nominal scale (1 "rather trust", 2 "rather distrust") asking people if they are inclined to trust or not trust information from TV, radio, and websites (for mainstream media) or social media and influencers (for social media). Variables were recoded into new variables, also on a nominal scale (1 "rather distrust" and 2 "rather trust"), so that low scores represented low levels of trust in the news. For the items of mainstream media grouped into one factor, α equaled .695 (an acceptable value for scale reliability in exploratory studies), which was computed as the mean of three items in the factor (M = 1.59;

SD = .39). The items for social media were also computed in one factor, with a grouping factor of an acceptable value, $\alpha = .625$ (M = 1.37; SD = .43).

Trust in media was measured for both mainstream media and social media using a four-point Likert scale (1 "very much" to 4 "very little") asking people how much they trust the sources of news and information—TV channels, radio stations, newspapers, online or print publications (for mainstream media), social media (Facebook, Instagram, TikTok) and instant messaging platforms (for social media). All variables were recoded into new ones on a scale from 1 "very little" to 4 "very much" so that low scores represented low levels of trust in media. The items for mainstream media were grouped into one factor ($\alpha = .781$; M = 2.45; SD = .75). The items for social media and instant messaging platforms were also computed as one factor ($\alpha = .774$; M = 2.09; SD = .83).

Trust in media regulatory authorities was assessed through three questions about people's trust in the National Audiovisual Council, the National Council for Combating Discrimination, and the National Authority for Management and Regulation in Communications using a four-point Likert scale (from 1 "very much" to 4 "very little"). The variables were recoded into new ones on a scale from 1 "very little" to 4 "very much" so that low scores represented low levels of trust in media regulatory authorities. The items were grouped into one factor (loadings from .761 to .823; $\alpha = .852$), which was computed as the mean of three items in the factor (M = 2.28; SD = .85).

Fact-checking behavior was measured with a battery of six questions on the frequency of reading the same piece of news from more sources (one item) and fact-checking information on different news channels (five items) on a four-point Likert scale (1 "always" to 4 "never"). For the wording of the items, see the appendix. All variables were recoded into new variables on a scale from 1 "never" to 4 "always" so that low scores represented low levels of fact-checking behavior. The items were grouped into one factor (loadings from .779 to .836; $\alpha = .835$; M = 2.79; SD = .72).

Perceived exposure to disinformation was assessed with a battery of three questions measuring people's perceptions of encountering news or information distorting reality on a four-point Likert scale (1 "to a very large extent" to 4 "to a very small extent/not at all"). Variables were recoded into new ones on a scale from 1 "to a very small extent/not at all" to 4 "to a very large extent" so that low scores represent low levels of perception toward exposure to disinformation. The items were grouped into one factor, $\alpha = .802$. The final variable was computed as the mean of three items in the factor (M = 2.86; SD = .81).

Perceived exposure to disinformation from mainstream media was measured with one question on a four-point Likert scale (1 "to a very large extent" to 4 "to a very small extent/not at all"). This variable was recoded into a scale from 1 "to a very small extent/not at all" to 4 "to a very large extent" so that low scores represented low levels of perception toward exposure to disinformation from mainstream media (M = 2.62; SD = .96).

Perceived exposure to disinformation from social media and instant messaging platforms was assessed through two questions based on people's perceptions of their exposure to disinformation from social media and instant messaging platforms on a four-point Likert scale (1 "to a very large extent" to 4 "to a very small extent/not at all"). The variables were also recoded, mirroring the previous variables, on a scale from 1 "to a very small extent/not at all" to 4 "to a very large extent" so that low scores represent low levels of perception toward exposure to disinformation from social media and instant messaging platforms, respectively. The new items were grouped into one factor, $\alpha = .763$. The final variable was computed as the mean of two items in the factor (M = 2.52; SD = .91).

Knowledge of disinformation effects was measured with a battery of eight questions about people's knowledge of the possible effects of disinformation through a four-point Likert scale (1 "to a very large extent" to 4 "to a very small extent or not at all"). See the appendix for the full wording of the statements. All items, except item 4, were recoded into new variables on a scale from 1 "to a very small extent or not at all" to 4 "to a very large extent" so that low scores represent low levels of knowledge of disinformation effects. All items were grouped into one factor, $\alpha = .739$. To increase the reliability of the scale ($\alpha = .877$), item 4 was excluded. The final variable was computed as the mean of seven remaining items in one factor (M = 3.36; SD = .62).

Correct information behavior was assessed with a scale on people's informing habits (1 "just title," 2 "title and content," 3 "title, content, and comments," and 4 "title and comments"). The answers were recoded from 1 "just title," 2 "title and comments," 3 "title, content, and comments," and 4 "title and content" so that low scores indicate a low level of correct information. The mean score was 3.16, with a standard deviation of .79.

Resilience to disinformation was constructed as a mean of six variables mentioned above (fact-checking behavior, perceived exposure to disinformation, including from mainstream media and social media and instant messaging, knowledge of disinformation effects, and correct information). As the newly formed scale was not completely reliable ($\alpha = .660$), one item (correct information) was deleted, and the others were grouped into one factor ($\alpha = .732$). The final variable was computed as the mean of five remaining items in one factor (M = 2.83; SD = .55), with high scores indicating high levels of resilience to disinformation. According to the Shapiro-Wilk test, this variable is not normally distributed in the population (Sig. < .05), but it has no outliers, with one exception (statistically insignificant).

Control Variables

We used *age*, *education*, and *income* as controls. The respondents were asked to provide their age, including the age category to which they belonged. Education was measured with a three-point ordinal scale (1 "primary or secondary school," 2 "high school or vocational school/postsecondary school," 3 "university"); the sample was divided into 64 percent with medium education and 18 percent with low and high education. Income was gauged on a 1-to-5 scale (from 1 "We do not have enough even for basic needs" to 5 "We can afford everything we need without making sacrifices"). One-third of respondents (37 percent) perceived themselves as having enough for a decent life but could not afford more expensive goods. The mean income perception level was 2.85, with a standard deviation of 1.05, showing moderate variation in income perceptions across the sample.

Findings

Predictors of Public Policy Support

We conducted bivariate correlations between the dependent variable and the antecedents. Support for regulation exhibited moderate negative correlations with fact-checking behavior ($r = -.403$, $p < .01$, N = 1068) and resilience to disinformation ($r = -.333$, $p < .01$, N = 1068). Support for regulation is also negatively weakly correlated with news consumption ($r = -.183$, $p < .01$, N = 1066), social media consumption ($r = -.288$, $p < .01$, N = 934), trust in mainstream news ($r = -.142$, $p < .01$, N = 1054), trust in social media news ($r = -.090$, $p < .01$, N = 1019), trust in mainstream media ($r = -.157$, $p < .01$, N = 1053), trust in social media and instant messaging platforms ($r = -.124$, $p < .01$, N = 1032), trust in media regulatory authorities ($r = -.112$, $p < .01$, N = 1027), perceived exposure to disinformation ($r = -.253$, $p < .01$, N = 1055), perceived exposure to disinformation from mainstream media ($r = -.194$, $p < .01$, N = 1048), perceived exposure to disinformation from social media and instant messaging platforms ($r = -.171$, $p < .01$, $N = 894$), knowledge of disinformation effects ($r = -.161$, $p < .01$, $N = 1054$), and correct information behavior ($r = -.104$, $p < .01$, $N = 1054$).

Gender, age, education, income, and residence were also considered. Women in the survey sample ($M = 1.52$; $SD = .64$) were slightly more predisposed to support regulation than men ($M = 1.46$; $SD = .64$; $t(1066) = 1.51$; $p > .01$), but with no significant difference in population. Support for regulation has weak positive correlations with age ($r = .110$, $p < .01$, $N = 1{,}068$) and weak negative correlations with education ($r = -.145$, $p < .01$, $N = 1068$) and income ($r = -.110$, $p < .01$, $N = 1068$), meaning that people becoming more supportive of regulation with age and low levels of education and income are predictors of high support for regulatory media measures. There are significant differences between people according to their occupation toward support for regulation ($F\ (7{,}1060) = 4.97$; $p < .01$). The analysis with the Games–Howell test revealed that pensioners/people who retired from activity ($M = 1.66$; $SD = .74$) are more supportive of media regulation, followed by students ($M = 1.53$; $SD = .50$) and housewives ($M = 1.52$; $SD = .64$), while unemployed people ($M = 1.28$; $SD = .56$) have the least support for regulation. There are also significant differences between people according to their sector of activity toward support for regulation ($F\ (2{,}1065) = 11.89$; $p < .01$). People not working ($M = 1.60$; $SD = .70$) are more predisposed to support regulation than people working in the public sector ($M = 1.46$; $SD = .60$), the least supportive being people from the private sector ($M = 1.40$; $SD = .58$). Significant differences were also observed among people residing in different areas of the country ($F\ (3{,}1064) = 3.39$; $p < .05$). Thus, rural residents are more supportive of regulatory measures ($M = 1.57$; $SD = .65$) than urban residents, among which Bucharest residents ($M = 1.47$; $SD = .68$) are the most predisposed to support regulation.

Consequently, we ran OLS regressions to test all variables correlated with support for regulation, controlling for age, education, and income (see Table 6.1).

The chosen model was good, with an adjusted R^2 of 0.23, indicating that the variables included in the model accounted for approximately 23 percent of the predictors of public policy support. According to this model, news consumption (in general and from social media), trust in news from mainstream media, fact-checking behavior, knowledge of disinformation effects, and education are negatively associated with support for regulation. *Variables related to resilience to disinformation* were excluded from the model when the tolerance indicator was below .05.

Table 6.1 OLS Regression Model Predicting Support for Regulation.

	B(SE)	BETA
(Constant)	3.705 (0.191)	
News consumption	−0.051 (0.023)	−0.077*
Social media news consumption	−0.053 (0.026)	−0.085*
Trust in news from mainstream media	−0.128 (0.061)	−0.086*
Trust in news from social media	−0.041 (0.058)	−0.028
Trust in mainstream media	0.013 (0.033)	0.016
Trust in social media	−0.018 (0.029)	−0.025
Fact-checking behavior	−0.236 (0.031)	−0.282**
Perceived exposure to disinformation	−0.064 (0.033)	−0.087
Perceived exposure to disinformation from mainstream media	−0.025 (.027)	−0.041
Perceived exposure to disinformation from social media	0.032 (.028)	0.049
Knowledge of disinformation effects	−0.141 (0.031)	−0.144*
Correct information behavior	−0.028 (0.024)	−0.037
Age	−0.001 (0.001)	−0.030
Education	−0.099 (0.037)	−.0.087**
Income	−0.013 (0.019)	−0.024
Adj. R^2	.230	

**p < .01, *p < .05.

In summary, predictors of public policy support are a lack of fact-checking behavior, followed by a lack of knowledge of disinformation effects. Support for regulation is also positively influenced by low levels of trust in news from mainstream media and low levels of news consumption (in general and from social media). In terms of sociodemographics, old age, low levels of education and income, lack of occupation, and rural residence predict support for regulatory measures (RQ1).

Perception of Stakeholders Regulating the Information Environment

Regarding the second research question, most respondents believed they should protect themselves from the influence of fake news (39.3 percent favored self-regulatory measures). Similarly, 36.8 percent of respondents thought that state institutions should protect them, and 21.6 percent believed media/journalists should be involved in this endeavor (RQ2).

Profile of Resilient Individuals

Sociodemographic variables were considered when creating the profile of the most resilient people. There was a significant difference in population by gender, with men ($M = 2.87$; $SD = .56$) being more resilient to disinformation than women ($M = 2.79$; $SD = .55$; $t(1068) = -2.33$; $p < .05$). Resilience to disinformation had a weak negative correlation with age ($r = -.148$; $p < .01$; $N = 1070$) and a weak positive correlation with income ($r = .074$; $p < .05$; $N = 1070$) but no correlation with education. This indicates that young age and high income are among the characteristics of resilient people, while education has no impact on the level of resilience to disinformation. There are significant differences between people according to their occupation in terms of resilience to disinformation ($F (7,1062) = 3.10$; $p < .01$). The analysis with the Games–Howell test revealed that independent entrepreneurs ($M = 2.98$; $SD = .55$) are more resilient to disinformation, followed by students ($M = 2.89$; $SD = .51$), while pensioners/people who retired from activity ($M = 2.72$; $SD = .51$) have the least resilience to disinformation. There are also significant differences between people according to their sector of activity toward resilience to disinformation ($F (2,1067) = 5.44$; $p < .01$). People working in the private sector ($M = 2.89$; $SD = .55$) are more resilient to disinformation than people from the public sector ($M = 2.86$; $SD = .57$), with the least resilient category being the inactive category ($M = 2.77$; $SD = .54$). Differences were also observed among people residing in different areas of the country, but the differences were not significant for population ($F (3,1066) = 2.58$; $p > .05$), with urban residents in large cities ($M = 2.90$; $SD = .60$) and Bucharest ($M = 2.89$; $SD = .51$) being most resilient to disinformation. At the same time, rural residents have low resilience to disinformation (RQ3).

Discussion

Higher Perceived Self-Efficacy Decreases Support for Disinformation Regulation

To the best of our knowledge, this is the first study exploring Romanians' appetite for coming up with possible regulatory frameworks concerning disinformation. Our study contradicts some recent scholarly contributions that revealed direct correlations between the perceived influence of fake news on society and support for proactive coping measures, including anti-disinformation legislation (e.g.,

Cheng et al. 2021; Ho et al. 2022). Contrary to other research (e.g., Freiling et al. 2023), our model reveals that factors such as general news consumption, news consumption from social media, trust in mainstream media news, fact-checking behavior, awareness of disinformation effects, and education levels are negatively correlated with support for regulation. In other words, those who consume news (including news from social media) and trust mainstream media news tend to be less in favor of measures to come up with regulatory responses to disinformation. Moreover, users who adopt fact-checking practices while having better knowledge of disinformation effects are not promoters of disinformation regulatory responses. Another counterintuitive finding is that higher education levels decrease citizens' appetite for disinformation regulatory frameworks. At the same time, our findings seem to align with some of the TPE-related research indicating that individuals exhibiting a lower inclination toward TPE in the context of disinformation (and who do not necessarily believe they are less vulnerable to disinformation than others) tend to be less supportive of countermeasures, including regulations and sanctions against media organizations and internet platforms (e.g., Cheng et al. 2021; Tang et al. 2021).

Regarding support for regulation, a quantitative study conducted in a highly politically charged and divided region—Hong Kong—revealed that individuals are more prone to support anti-disinformation legislation if they perceive fake news as a challenge to society at large rather than a challenge to their own lives (Lee 2022). Thus, if people see disinformation as a societal threat rather than an individual menace, they will probably support appropriate policies and regulations (Lee 2022). Our findings partly align with these conclusions by showing that individual traits regarding general news consumption, including from social media, trust in mainstream media, fact-checking practices, awareness of the effects of disinformation, and education levels, are all negatively correlated with support for regulation.

Tackling Disinformation through Regulatory Frameworks: Finding a Good Balance

Our study suggests that the ability to spot and avoid disinformation tends to diminish people's willingness to align with rules imposed by third parties. Higher-income educated individuals who constantly consume and trust news media and apply good communication "hygiene" on their own might think that their good reasoning and information practices make external regulations useless, redundant, or intrusive. While apparently resilient to disinformation, such individuals show little or no support for regulatory initiatives. At the same time, our research paints the profile of a less resilient individual who is older, has a lower income, and resides in rural areas. People who see themselves as less knowledgeable about disinformation tend to agree that regulatory measures could help them discern between facts and less factual content.

Many public and academic discussions about the cultural concept of 'fake news' have arguably promoted an alarmist narrative, viewing such content as a threat to the security of political and electoral processes, business transactions, consumer confidence, and genuine representation. The fake news phenomenon has often been considered a crisis (Allcott and Gentzkow 2017; Tandoc Jr. 2019). Fake news is seen as a crisis not necessarily because it changes how people read and consume media but also because it disrupts daily political and personal decision-making (Tucker et al. 2018).

However, the arguably alarmist approach—while legitimate—can be manipulated and used to hijack essential rights such as privacy or freedom of speech, especially in weak democracies and authoritarian regimes. A regulatory approach to tackling fake news and disinformation may raise ethical concerns, not due to its potential to censor or eliminate defamatory content (as such legislation is standard in many jurisdictions, EU included) but because early evidence suggests that authoritarian regimes may exploit fake news laws to suppress the distribution of information critical of the government (Cover et al. 2023). Various countries have considered implementing anti-disinformation legislation (Moyakine and Tabachnik 2021). However, two problematic aspects involved in regulating disinformation should be noted. First, while democratic politicians might weaponize the terms "disinformation" and "fake news," authoritarian regimes are also likely to misuse these labels to justify anti-disinformation laws and stifle dissent (Neo 2022). Second, a central issue in debates about the desirability of such laws is whether it is possible to clearly define and operationalize disinformation (Ireton and Posetti 2021), or the notion of "harm" and the causality between such harm and certain media outlets, such as internet sites that publish disinformation (Leiter 2024). Critics of anti-disinformation laws in authoritarian contexts often highlight that these laws use overly broad definitions of disinformation (Fernandez 2019). At the same time, labeling anti-disinformation regulations as intrusive or coercive makes a perfect defamatory argument used by politicians interested in opening the door wide for the perpetrators of disinformation campaigns (Mende et al.

2024). Therefore, designing and implementing regulatory frameworks in order to tackle disinformation should be a balancing act driven by the will to protect democracy and fundamental rights with clarity, precision, and solid evidence.

Limitations

Several limitations could be considered for this study. One of the primary limitations is that the sample skewed toward urban residents and medium-educated individuals, which may affect the generalizability of the results. Additionally, there are differences in the sample between active people working in the public and private sectors, which differ from the real balanced distribution in the population. A more diverse sampling strategy in future studies is essential to capture a broader spectrum of public opinion. Additionally, as the data were collected at a single point in time, they may not accurately reflect how attitudes change in other socioeconomic and political contexts. Therefore, longitudinal studies are needed to examine trends and changes in public policy support over time. While our model accounted for a significant proportion of the variance in predicting support for regulation, future research should consider other psychological, social, and economic variables that could further explain this tendency. Additionally, there could be other scales that can help individuals better grasp disinformation and public perceptions of this phenomenon. Further research could explore the effect of specific political events, policies, or public figures on the development of public policy support.

Conclusions

Our study analyzed public perceptions of disinformation and regulatory responses to it in Romania to identify predictors of public support for regulation initiatives. Our findings indicate that the ability to identify and avoid fake news may reduce individuals' support for regulatory measures. Educated individuals with higher incomes who consume and trust news media and practice good information hygiene may view external regulations as unnecessary or intrusive. On the other hand, individuals with lower self-perceived knowledge about disinformation, who are often older and from rural areas, tend to support regulatory measures. Our research highlights that regulating disinformation is a double-edged sword—it risks being perceived as a constraining strategy (i.e., by educated, higher-income, news-savvy urban individuals). At the same time, it can be considered a lifebuoy by individuals vulnerable to disinformation (i.e., less-educated, politically unaware, rural individuals). This dualism reflects to a certain extent the lack of scholarly and political consensus on the topic of anti-disinformation regulation.

Across democratic societies, there is a growing consensus among policymakers, experts, and civil society representatives that the risks posed by contemporary disinformation need to be tackled, particularly in contexts such as elections, health crises, international conflict, and hybrid and information warfare. In spite of this agreement, the methods for addressing these risks vary, leading to ongoing debates about the best approaches for tackling disinformation. Policies meant to tackle disinformation can have risks, especially if they grant excessive power to government bodies or established actors, which could be used, without adequate guardrails, to manipulate the information and communication ecosystem during critical, disruptive times. The challenge lies in balancing the need to protect democracy with the potential risks of overregulation and government overreach. While it is essential to address the harmful systemic effects of disinformation, policymakers must ensure that regulations are precise, practically available, evidence-based, and publicly accepted and do not infringe on values such as an open society, transparency, privacy, and freedom of expression. At the same time, even coming up with regulations that fulfill these criteria (and many others) is not the end of the game since enforcement is key. In regard to tackling disinformation by regulatory means, there is a pressing need for legitimate power and knowledge to design and enforce regulations, given the gap in expertise between those who seek to regulate technology-related phenomena and those who create and use them.

Appendix: Translated Scales Used in the Research Questionnaire

[Support for regulation_1] How important is it to you to be able to express yourself freely, without any kind of limitation? (only one answer)

1. Very important
2. Important

3. Pretty unimportant
4. Not important at all
98. Do not know/No answer

[Support for regulation_2] How important is it to you to use the internet without restrictions? (only one answer)

1. Very important
2. Important
3. Pretty unimportant
4. Not important at all
98. Do not know/No answer

[Fact-checking behavior_1] How often do you read information about the same topic from at least two sources? (only one answer)

1. Always
2. Many times
3. Less often
4. Never
98. Do not know/No answer

[Fact-checking behavior_2] Do you usually check the information you read/hear to analyze its credibility? (only one answer)

1. Always
2. Many times
3. Less often
4. Never
98. Do not know/No answer

[Fact-checking behavior_3] Do you check information/news before sharing them further on social media or instant messaging platforms? (only one answer)

1. Always
2. Many times
3. Less often
4. Never
98. Do not know/No answer

[Fact-checking behavior_4] Have you checked the news you have recently come across from other media sources? (only one answer)

1. Always
2. Many times
3. Less often
4. Never
98. Do not know/No answer

[Fact-checking behavior_5] Have you also checked out what other people are saying about the news you have come across lately? (only one answer)

1. Always
2. Many times
3. Less often
4. Never
98. Do not know/No answer

[Fact-checking behavior_6] Have you relied on your knowledge and intuition to check the news you have come across lately? (only one answer)

1. Always
2. Many times
3. Less often
4. Never
98. Do not know/No answer

[Perceived exposure to disinformation_1] To what extent do you think you personally have been exposed to fake news or disinformation in recent months? (only one answer)

1. To a very large extent
2. To a large extent
3. To a small extent
4. To a very small extent/Not at all
98. Do not know/No answer

[Perceived exposure to disinformation_2] To what extent do you think your loved ones have been exposed to fake news or disinformation in recent months? (only one answer)

1. To a very large extent
2. To a large extent
3. To a small extent

4. To a very small extent/Not at all
98. Do not know/No answer

[Perceived exposure to disinformation_3] To what extent do you think that the population of Romania has been exposed to fake news or disinformation in recent months? (only one answer)

1. To a very large extent
2. To a large extent
3. To a small extent
4. To a very small extent/Not at all
98. Do not know/No answer

[Perceived exposure to disinformation_mainstream media] To what extent do you think that you personally have been exposed to fake news or disinformation in traditional media (TV stations, radio, newspapers, online or printed magazines) in recent months? (only one answer)

1. To a very large extent
2. To a large extent
3. To a small extent
4. To a very small extent/Not at all
98. Do not know/No answer

[Perceived exposure to disinformation_social media] To what extent do you think you personally have been exposed to fake news or disinformation on social media—Facebook, Instagram, TikTok, and YouTube—in recent months? (only one answer)

1. To a very large extent
2. To a large extent
3. To a small extent
4. To a very small extent/Not at all
98. Do not know/No answer

[Perceived exposure to disinformation_instant messaging platforms] To what extent do you think you personally have been exposed to fake news or disinformation on instant messaging platforms—WhatsApp, Facebook Messenger, Signal, Telegram—in recent months? (only one answer)

1. To a very large extent
2. To a large extent

3. To a small extent
4. To a very small extent/Not at all
98. Do not know/No answer

[Knowledge of disinformation effects] On a scale from 1 to 4, where 1 represents "To a very large extent" and 4 represents "To a very small extent/not at all," to what extent do you think that disinformation and fake news can cause (randomize):

1. Incorrect information of citizens
2. Decrease in trust in state institutions
3. Decrease in journalists' ability to obtain correct information
4. An increase in citizens' capacity to solve the problems of the community to which they belong
5. Decrease in trust among people
6. Increase in societal conflicts
7. Worsening of Romania's image in the world
8. Worsening of the perception of Romanians from the diaspora toward Romania
98. Do not know/No answer

[Correct information] When you inform yourself, you usually read (randomize, only one answer):

1. Just the title
2. Title and content
3. Title, content, and comments
4. Title and comments
98. Do not know/No answer.

Acknowledgment

This work was supported by the European Union through the Operational Programme Administrative Capacity (grant number SIPOCA/SMIS 2014+: 865/136668).

Conflict of Interest Statement

No potential conflict of interest was reported by the authors.

References

Achimescu, Vlad, Dan Sultănescu, and Dana C. Sultănescu. 2021. "The path from distrusting Western actors to conspiracy beliefs and noncompliance with public health guidance during the COVID-19 crisis." *Journal of Elections, Public Opinion and Parties* 31 (1): 299–310. https://doi.org/10.1080/17457289.2021.1924746.

Aïmeur, Esma, Sabrine Amri, and Gilles Brassard. 2023. "Fake news, disinformation and misinformation in social media: A review." *Social Network Analysis and Mining* 13 (1): 30. https://doi.org/10.1007/s13278-023-01028-5.

Allcott, Hunt, and Matthew Gentzkow. 2017. "Social media and fake news in the 2016 election." *Journal of Economic Perspectives* 31 (2): 211–36.

Bârgăoanu, Alina, Nicoleta Corbu, Raluca Buturoiu, and Flavia Durach. 2021. "Managing the COVID-19 pandemic: Predictors of trust in institutions in Romania." *Kybernetes* 51 (7): 2398–415. https://doi.org/10.1108/K-12-2020-0913.

Bârgăoanu, Alina, and Flavia Durach. 2023. "Cognitive warfare: Understanding the threat." In *Routledge handbook of disinformation and national security*, edited by Arcos, Rubén, Irena Chiru, and Cristina Ivan. Routledge.

Batista Pereira, Frederico, Natália S. Bueno, Felipe Nunes, and Nara Pavão. 2022. "Fake news, fact checking, and partisanship: The resilience of rumors in the 2018 Brazilian elections." *Journal of Politics* 84 (4): 2188–201.

Buturoiu, Raluca, Nicoleta Corbu, and Mădălina Boțan. 2023. *Patterns of news consumption in a high-choice media environment: A Romanian perspective.* Springer Nature.

Cheng, John W., Hitoshi Mitomo, Artima Kamplean, and Youngkyoung Seo. 2021. "Lesser evil? Public opinion on regulating fake news in Japan, South Korea, and Thailand: A three-country comparison." *Telecommunications Policy* 45 (9): 102185. https://doi.org/10.1016/j.telpol.2021.102185.

Cheng, Yang, and Yunjuan Luo. 2021. "The presumed influence of digital misinformation: Examining US public's support for governmental restrictions versus corrective action in the COVID-19 pandemic." *Online Information Review* 45 (4): 834–52. https://doi.org/10.1108/OIR-08-2020-0386.

Cipers, Samuel, Trisha Meyer, and Jonas Lefevere. 2023. "Government responses to online disinformation unpacked." *Internet Policy Review* 12 (4): 1–19. https://doi.org/10.14763/2023.4.1736.

Cole, Deborah. 2024. "Romanian court annuls first round of presidential election." *The Guardian*, December 6, sec. World news. www.theguardian.com/world/2024/dec/06/romanian-court-annuls-first-round-of-presidential-election.

Cover, Rob, Ashleigh Haw, and Jay Daniel Thompson. 2023. "Remedying disinformation and fake news? The cultural frameworks of fake news crisis responses and solution-seeking." *International Journal of Cultural Studies* 26 (2): 216–33. https://doi.org/10.1177/13678779221136881.

Davison, W. Phillips. 1983. "The third-person effect in communication." *Public Opinion Quarterly* 47 (1): 1–15. https://doi.org/10.1086/268763.

"EEAS." n.d. "Countering disinformation and building societal resilience." www.eeas.europa.eu/eeas/countering-disinformation-and-building-societal-resilience_en.

Fernandez, Joseph. 2019. "Malaysia's Anti-Fake News Act: A cog in an arsenal of anti-free speech laws and a bold promise of reforms." *Pacific Journalism Review: Te Koakoa* 25 (July): 173–92. https://doi.org/10.24135/pjr.v25i1.474.

Free Press Unlimited. 2021. "Romania." April 14. www.freepressunlimited.org/en/countries/romania.

Freiling, Isabelle, Marlis Stubenvoll, and Jörg Matthes. 2023. "Support for misinformation regulation on social media: It is the perceived harm of misinformation that matters, not the perceived amount." *Policy & Internet* 15 (4): 731–49. https://doi.org/10.1002/poi3.360.

Gill, Ritu, and Rebecca Goolsby, eds. 2022. *COVID-19 disinformation: A multi-national, whole of society perspective*. Springer International.

Gori, Paula. 2024. "Countering disinformation: A whole-of-society approach beyond traditional frameworks—EDMO." https://edmo.eu/blog/countering-disinformation-a-whole-of-society-approach-beyond-traditional-frameworks/.

Hammar, Henrik, and Sverker C. Jagers. 2006. "Can trust in politicians explain individuals' support for climate policy? The case of CO2 tax." *Climate Policy* 5 (6): 613–25. https://doi.org/10.1080/14693062.2006.9685582.

Ho, Shirley S, Tong Jee Goh, and Yan Wah Leung. 2022. "Let's nab fake science news: Predicting scientists' support for interventions using the influence of presumed media influence model." *Journalism* 23 (4): 910–28. https://doi.org/10.1177/1464884920937488.

Invernizzi, Giovanna Maria, and Ahmed Ezzeldin Mohamed. 2019. "Trust nobody: How voters react to conspiracy theories." Social Science Research Network. https://doi.org/10.2139/ssrn.3507190.

Ireton, Cherilyn, and Julie Posetti. 2021. *Journalism, fake news & disinformation: Handbook for journalism education and training*. UNESCO. https://unesdoc.unesco.org/ark:/48223/pf0000376919.

Jang, S. Mo, and Joon K. Kim. 2018. "Third person effects of fake news: Fake news regulation and media literacy interventions." *Computers in Human Behavior* 80 (March): 295–302. https://doi.org/10.1016/j.chb.2017.11.034.

Jones-Jang, S. Mo, Dam Hee Kim, and Kate Kenski. 2021. "Perceptions of mis-or disinformation exposure predict political cynicism: Evidence from a two-wave survey during the 2018 US midterm elections." *New Media & Society* 23 (10): 3105–25. https://doi.org/10.1177/1461444820943878.

Lee, Francis L. F. 2022. "What constitutes disinformation? Disinformation judgment, influence of partisanship, and support for anti-disinformation legislation." *Journalism & Mass Communication Quarterly*, May, 10776990221093940. https://doi.org/10.1177/10776990221093940.

Lee, Taeyoung. 2021. "How people perceive influence of fake news and why it matters." *Communication Quarterly* 69 (4): 431–53. https://doi.org/10.1080/01463373.2021.1954677.

Leiter, Brian. 2024. "Free speech on the internet: The crisis of epistemic authority." *Daedalus* 153 (3): 91–104. https://doi.org/10.1162/daed_a_02091.

Macdonald, David. 2021. "Political trust and support for immigration in the American mass public." *British Journal of Political Science* 51 (4): 1402–20. https://doi.org/10.1017/S0007123419000668.

Martin, Justin D., and Fouad Hassan. 2020. "News media credibility ratings and perceptions of online fake news exposure in five countries." *Journalism Studies* 21 (16): 2215–33. https://doi.org/10.1080/1461670X.2020.1827970.

Mende, Martin, Valentina O. Ubal, Marina Cozac, Beth Vallen, and Christopher Berry. 2024. "Fighting infodemics: Labels as antidotes to mis-and disinformation?!." *Journal of Public Policy & Marketing* 43 (1): 31–52. https://doi.org/10.1177/0743915623118481.

Moyakine, Evgeni, and A. Tabachnik. 2021. "Struggling to strike the right balance between interests at stake: The 'Yarovaya', 'fake news' and 'disrespect' laws as examples of ill-conceived legislation in the age of modern technology." *Computer Law & Security Review* 40: 105512. https://doi.org/10.1016/j.clsr.2020.105512.

Muhammed, Sadiq T., and Saji K. Mathew. 2022. "The disaster of misinformation: A review of research in social media." *International Journal of Data Science and Analytics* 13 (4): 271–85. https://doi.org/10.1007/s41060-022-00311-6.

NATO Parliamentary Assembly. 2021. "Resolution 466: Developing a whole-of-society, integrated and coordinated approach to resilience for allied democracies." October 11. www.nato-pa.int/document/resolution-466-developing-whole-society-integrated-and-coordinated-approach-resilience.

Neo, Ric. 2022. "A cudgel of repression: Analysing state instrumentalisation of the 'fake news' label in Southeast Asia." *Journalism* 23 (9): 1919–38. https://doi.org/10.1177/1464884920984060.

Pricop, Sebastian. 2024. "Studiu IRES. 57% dintre români sunt mulțumiți de modul în care trăiesc / Anularea alegerilor, principalul eveniment din 2024 / Câți ar fi votat cu Călin Georgescu." *HotNews*, December. https://hotnews.ro/studiu-ires-57-din

tre-romani-sunt-multumiti-de-modul-in-care-traiesc-anularea-alegerilor-principa lul-eveniment-din-2024-cati-ar-fi-votat-cu-calin-georgescu-1870048.

Regulation (EU) 2016/679 of the European Parliament and of the Council of 27 April 2016 on the Protection of Natural Persons with Regard to the Processing of Personal Data and on the Free Movement of Such Data, and Repealing Directive 95/46/EC (General Data Protection Regulation) (Text with EEA Relevance). 2016. OJ L. Vol. 119. http://data.europa.eu/eli/reg/2016/679/oj/eng.

Regulation (EU) 2022/1925 of the European Parliament and of the Council of 14 September 2022 on Contestable and Fair Markets in the Digital Sector and Amending Directives (EU) 2019/1937 and (EU) 2020/1828 (Digital Markets Act) (Text with EEA Relevance). 2022. OJ L. Vol. 265. http://data.europa.eu/eli/reg/2022/1925/oj/eng.

Regulation (EU) 2022/2065 of the European Parliament and of the Council of 19 October 2022 on a Single Market For Digital Services and Amending Directive 2000/31/EC (Digital Services Act) (Text with EEA Relevance). 2022. OJ L. Vol. 277. http://data.europa.eu/eli/reg/2022/2065/oj/eng.

Riedl, Martin J., Kelsey N. Whipple, and Ryan Wallace. 2022. "Antecedents of support for social media content moderation and platform regulation: The role of presumed effects on self and others." *Information, Communication & Society* 25 (11): 1632–49. https://doi.org/10.1080/1369118X.2021.1874040.

Rodrigo, Padmali, Emmanuel Ogiemwonyi Arakpogun, Mai Chi Vu, Femi Olan, and Elmira Djafarova. 2024. "Can you be mindful? The effectiveness of mindfulness-driven interventions in enhancing the digital resilience to fake news on COVID-19." *Information Systems Frontiers* 26 (2): 501–21. https://doi.org/10.1007/s10 796-022-10258-5.

Tandoc Jr., Edson C. 2019. "The facts of fake news: A research review." *Sociology Compass* 13 (9): e12724. https://doi.org/10.1111/soc4.12724.

Tang, Shuo, Lars Willnat, and Hongzhong Zhang. 2021. "Fake news, information overload, and the third-person effect in China." *Global Media and China* 6 (4): 492–507. https://doi.org/10.1177/20594364211047369.

Tenove, Chris. 2020. "Protecting democracy from disinformation: Normative threats and policy responses." *International Journal of Press/Politics* 25 (3): 517–37. https://doi.org/10.1177/194016122091874.

Tucker, Joshua A., Andrew Guess, Pablo Barbera, Cristian Vaccari, Alexandra Siegel, Sergey Sanovich, Denis Stukal, and Brendan Nyhan. 2018. *Social media, political polarization, and political disinformation: A review of the scientific literature*. Social Science Research Network. https://doi.org/10.2139/ssrn.3144139.

Vaccari, Cristian, and Andrew Chadwick. 2020. "Deepfakes and disinformation: Exploring the impact of synthetic political video on deception, uncertainty, and trust in news." *Social Media+ Society* 6 (1): 2056305120903408. https://doi.org/10.1177/2056305120903408.

Walter, Nathan, Jonathan Cohen, R. Lance Holbert, and Yasmin Morag. 2020. "Fact-checking: A meta-analysis of what works and for whom." *Political Communication* 37 (3): 350–75. https://doi.org/10.1080/10584609.2019.1668894.

Xu, Jie, and William J. Gonzenbach. 2008. "Does a perceptual discrepancy lead to action? A meta-analysis of the behavioral component of the third-person effect." *International Journal of Public Opinion Research* 20 (3): 375–85. https://doi.org/10.1093/ijpor/edn031.

Zheng, Xia, and Yanqin Lu. 2021. "News consumption and affective polarization in Taiwan: The mediating roles of like-minded discussion and relative hostile media perception." *Social Science Journal*: 1–14. https://doi.org/10.1080/03623319.2021.1933877.

Part 3

Regulations in the European Digital Environment in Relation to Disinformation

7

Legal Aspects of Disinformation

Eva Fialová

The regulation of disinformation poses a challenge for European legislators. The biggest challenge is to reconcile the protection of the rule of law and the democratic state with the protection of freedom of expression. Disinformation causes harm to individuals and society but operates within a gray legal space, lacking uniform European regulation.

In some European countries, regulation exists, but it is often criticized for creating the so-called chilling effect (self-censorship) and overblocking. European regulation of online service providers that have the technical capability to block content does exist, but it does not apply directly to disinformation. Some rules can be derived from the case law of the European Court of Human Rights (hereinafter "ECtHR"), namely from decisions dealing with freedom of expression. The rise of generative AI capable of producing sophisticated deepfakes and synthetic content further complicates the regulatory landscape.

In European law, there is no legally binding definition of disinformation. Some soft-law documents try to define this notion. According to the European Commission's Communication on the European Democracy Action Plan, disinformation is false or misleading content that is spread with an intention to deceive or secure economic or political gain and which may cause public harm (European Commission 2020). On the other hand, disinformation does not include misleading advertising, reporting errors, satire and parody, or clearly identified partisan news and commentary and is without prejudice to binding legal obligations, self-regulatory advertising codes, and standards regarding misleading advertising (European Commission 2022).

Even though lawyers find this definition essential since definitions demarcate the regulated subject, sometimes the legally binding definition may be unsuitable, particularly for volatile issues. The term disinformation may cover numerous types of expression of different forms, content, and effect. Some of the expressions may be harmful, which may not be the case for others. Just as the nature of disinformation is not uniform, the response to it may not be either (McGonagle 2018). This chapter gives an overview of the European legal approach to disinformation.

Disinformation and Freedom of Expression in ECtHR Case-Law

In online contexts, the response to disinformation is typically its blocking, deleting, or deindexing from search results. However, this reaction may raise concerns about restrictions on freedom of expression or, in other words, freedom of speech. At the European level, the most important human rights document is the European Convention on Human Rights (hereinafter "ECHR"). The freedom of expression is guaranteed in Article 10 of ECHR, which says: "Everyone has the right to freedom of expression. This right shall include freedom to hold opinions and to receive and impart information and ideas without interference by public authority and regardless of frontiers. This Article shall not prevent States from requiring the licensing of broadcasting, television or cinema enterprises." This means that the ECHR protects not only the dissemination of information and opinions but also the right to receive them.

Freedom of expression is not boundless. The freedom can be limited by rights and freedoms of others or by other legitimate interests. The conditions for limitation of freedom of expression are enumerated in the second paragraph of Article 10. The exercise of freedom of expression may be subject to formalities, conditions, restrictions, or penalties that are prescribed by law and are necessary in a democratic society, in the interests of national security, territorial integrity, or public safety, for the prevention of disorder or crime, for the protection of health or morals, for the protection of reputation or rights of others, for preventing the disclosure of information received in confidence, or for maintaining authority and impartiality of the judiciary. The ECHR determines the conditions under which freedom may be restricted.

Freedom of expression is regulated similarly in Article 11 of the Charter of Fundamental Rights of the European Union. "Everyone has the right to freedom of expression. This right shall include freedom to hold opinions and to receive and impart information and ideas without interference by public authority and regardless of frontiers. The freedom and pluralism of the media shall be respected." As to the scope of the rights, the Charter refers to ECHR (Art. 52, para. 3).

Complaints on violations of ECHR are dealt with by the ECtHR. Someone claiming that a state that is a party to the ECHR had violated their fundamental right guaranteed by the ECHR and had exhausted all domestic remedies may bring the case to the ECtHR.

The ECtHR assesses whether the speech in question qualifies for protection under Article 10 of the ECHR. The ECtHR has repeatedly emphasized that protection under this article is broad. Protection is not limited to certain types of information or ideas, or certain types of expression. Expressions that offend, shock, or disturb the state or any sector of the population are also eligible for protection (*Handyside v. UK*[1] or *Mouvement raëlien Suisse v. Switzerland*[2]). The application of ECHR is not limited to predefined categories of expression(s). ECHR may also cover expressions of commercial nature or advertising (*Markt Intern Verlag GmbH and Klaus Beermann v. Germany*[3]). Freedom of expression protects not only ideas and information. Article 10 applies also to the form in which such ideas and information are being conveyed, such as photographs (*Verlagsgruppe News GmbH v. Austria*[4]) and even photomontage (*Société de conception de presse et d'édition et Ponson v. France*[5]).

Safeguard against Abuse

In article 17, the ECHR contains a safeguard against the abuse of rights and thus the destruction of democratic rule of law. "Nothing in this Convention may be interpreted as implying for any State, group or person any right to engage in any activity or perform any act aimed at the destruction of any of the rights and freedoms set forth herein or at their limitation to a greater extent than is provided for in the Convention."

This article was introduced during the *travaux préparatoires* in awareness of the fragility of democracy in the postwar world (De Morree 2016). Even though, according to a doctrine, not all fundamental rights are apt for the application of this safeguard, freedom of expression belongs to the group of rights to which Article 17 of the ECHR is applicable.[6] In the ECtHR case-law, Article 17 is evoked in the denial of Holocaust (*Garaudy v. France*[7]), Armenian genocide in 1915 (*Perinçek v. Switzerland*[8]), and promotion of totalitarianism (*Kühnen v. Germany*[9]).

According to the ECtHR, Article 17 "is only applicable on an exceptional basis and in extreme cases and should, in cases concerning Article 10 of the Convention, only be resorted to if it is immediately clear that the impugned statements sought to deflect this Article from its real purpose by employing the right to freedom of expression for ends clearly contrary to the values of the Convention."[10] The key consideration in determining whether statements, whether verbal or nonverbal, lose the protection of Article 10 of the ECHR is whether those statements oppose the fundamental values of the ECHR—for instance, by inciting hatred or violence—or whether the author, through making such statements, sought to exploit the ECHR to engage in actions or conduct intended to undermine the rights and freedoms.[11]

The ECtHR would consider whether the disinformation incites hatred, violence, or directly undermines democratic values. If it does, Article 17 of the ECHR applies, removing the protection of Article 10. However, if the disinformation does not intend to harm democratic values of the ECHR, it would likely still fall under the protection of Article 10.

Four-Step Test

The ECtHR uses a structured approach to assess whether a violation of the ECHR has occurred. To determine this, the court asks a series of questions to evaluate whether the state has failed to uphold the rights guaranteed by the ECHR.

1. The court first examines whether there has been an interference with the protected right. The interference may be in the form of formality, condition, restriction, or penalty (*Wille v. Liechtenstein*[12]). The intervention may not only be a conviction, punishment, or criminal proceedings, but also an obligation to pay damages (*Tolstoy Miloslavsky v. UK*[13]). The ECtHR also examines whether the penalty or other form of interference would have a chilling effect on the person against whom the interference was aimed at, such as preventing an individual from publishing on the same topic (*Metis Yayıncılık Limited Şirketi and Sökmen v. Turkey*[14]).
   In light of the above, blocking, deleting, or deindexing of the disinformation may constitute an interference with this right. According to the ECtHR, such actions (e.g., restricting online content) may be seen as a breach of freedom of expression.

2. If the answer to the first question is positive, that is, the intervention occurred, the ECtHR inquires whether the requirements of the second paragraph have been met. The second question examines whether the interference was prescribed by law.
   The law must be of a certain quality. It has to be accessible and foreseeable. In other words, the law has to be formulated so precisely to enable an individual to regulate their behavior accordingly.[15] If the law permits a discretion of public authorities, the discretion may not be limitless[16] or too broad, especially in criminal law (*Savva Terentyev v. Russia*[17]). The ECtHR held that "it is vitally important that criminal law provisions directed against expressions that stir up, promote or justify violence, hatred or intolerance clearly and precisely define the scope of relevant offences, and that those provisions be strictly construed in order to avoid a situation where the State's discretion to prosecute for such offences becomes too broad and potentially subject to abuse through selective enforcement."[18] The requirements posed on law are not met by vague legal provisions whose interpretation is uncertain,[19] or if the legal provisions contradict each other without any solution to this contradiction (*Goussev and Marenk v. Finland*[20]) or the case-law is not consistent (*RTBF v. Belgium*[21]).
   If a government takes action against disinformation under vague or overly broad legal provisions, the ECtHR might find this interference against the prescribed-by-law rule. The ECtHR may require that any restrictions on disinformation be grounded in exact legal provisions that, moreover, do not allow for different interpretations.

3. The third question is whether a legitimate aim is recognized by the second paragraph of Article 10. The state must prove that the interference pursued one or more of the objectives as described in the second paragraph of Article 10. The interpretation of legitimate aims recognized by the ECHR should be narrow (*Perinçek v. Switzerland*).[22]
   The ECtHR might accept that blocking of disinformation could serve legitimate aims, such as protecting national security or preventing public disorder. However, the ECtHR would assess the specific context and impact of the disinformation to determine whether the interference truly aligns with these aims.

4. The last and most essential question assesses whether the interference is necessary in the democratic society. The interference must correspond to a pressing social need and must be proportionate to the legitimate

aim or aims.[23] The ECtHR also considers the manner in which the statements are made and their direct or indirect potential to cause harm (*Perinçek v. Switzerland*[24]). On the other hand, the ECtHR examines the possible impact of statements, that is, whether the person who made the statement is a well-known blogger, a popular social media user, or a public or influential figure. The lack of prominence presumably limits public attention to the statement and, consequently, reduces its potential impact (*Savva Terentyev v. Russia*[25]).

In some cases, the state has a margin of appreciation. This means that the state may assess the necessity of the interference, but only to a certain extent. The margin of appreciation is, however, subject to the supervision of the court.[26] "The breadth of such a margin of appreciation varies depending on a number of factors, among which the type of speech at issue is of particular importance. Whilst there is little scope under Article 10 § 2 of the Convention for restrictions on political speech …, a wider margin of appreciation is generally available to the Contracting States when regulating freedom of expression in relation to matters liable to offend intimate personal convictions within the sphere of morals or, especially, religion … Similarly, States have a broad margin of appreciation in the regulation of speech in commercial matters or advertising."[27] The state authorities have a broader margin of appreciation when assessing the necessity of restricting freedom of expression, if remarks incite violence against an individual, a public official, or a segment of the population (*Sürek v. Turkey*[28]).

In a case involving disinformation, the ECtHR would consider whether the blocking or deleting of content corresponds to the pressing social need and is proportionate to the alleged legitimate aim. If the disinformation pertained to political debate, the ECtHR would accept narrower margin of appreciation of the state in comparison to other types of expression. If the state is able to demonstrate that the disinformation posed a significant and immediate risk to national security and public order, it might successfully justify restrictive measures. However, if the disinformation merely concerns controversial opinions or critiques, it is more probable that the ECtHR would protect the expression under Article 10, emphasizing the importance of free debate in the democratic society.

On the basis of the four-step test, the ECtHR decides whether or not there has been a violation of the ECHR. The violation of a fundamental right does not imply the violation of the ECHR. This is the case when the interference with the fundamental right has passed the test described above, that is, the interference was prescribed by law, pursued a legitimate aim or aims, and was necessary in the democratic society.

Journalists and Their Role in the Democratic Society

Before discussing the role of a journalist, it is necessary to say that the ECtHR differentiates between facts that may be verified and value judgments, which cannot be verified by its nature[29] but still must be based on sufficient factual basis.[30] In order to distinguish between a factual allegation and a value judgment, it is necessary to take account of the circumstances of the case and the general tone of the remarks (*Brasilier v. France*[31]).

The ECtHR reiterates that the press plays an essential role of a public watch in a democratic society. This role consists in imparting information and ideas on all matters of public interest. The public, on the other hand, has to receive the ideas and information (*Sunday Times v. UK*[32]).

Not only journalists enjoy such protection. The same may be applied to nongovernmental organizations (*Animal Defenders International v. UK*[33]) and bloggers and popular users of the social media conveying information of public interest. The state authorities have to assess the public-interest character of information (*Magyar Helsinki Bizottság v. Hungary*[34]). What is the public interest and debate must be considered on a case-by-case basis. Political issues are a matter of public interest, and so is criminal activity, but the private affairs of a person that do not relate to their exercise of a public office are not (*Axel Springer AG v. Germany*,[35] *Standard Verlags GmbH v. Austria*[36]).

The ECtHR considers the journalistic ethics and veracity of information as important criterion for enjoying the protection of Article 10. The way in which the information was obtained and its veracity are also important factors. The ECtHR emphasized that the protection Article 10 provides to journalists when reporting on matters of public interest is conditioned by their good faith, accurate facts, and reliable and precise information conveyed consistently with journalistic ethics.[37]

> Under the terms of paragraph 2 of Article 10 of the Convention, freedom of expression carries with it "duties and responsibilities," which also apply to the media even with respect to matters of serious public concern. Moreover, these "duties and responsibilities" are liable to assume significance when there is a question of attacking the reputation of a named individual and infringing the "rights of others." Thus, special grounds are required before the media can

> be dispensed from their ordinary obligation to verify factual statements that are defamatory of private individuals. Whether such grounds exist depends in particular on the nature and degree of the defamation in question and the extent to which the media can reasonably regard their sources as reliable with respect to the allegations.[38]

Beyond merely informing, the way information is presented often implies how it should be interpreted. In a world overwhelmed by an abundance of information from traditional and digital media, involving an increasing number of stakeholders, the need to uphold and monitor journalistic ethics becomes more and more critical (*Stoll v. Switzerland*[39]).

If the disinformation is disseminated by the press without adherence to journalistic ethics, such as failing to verify sources or acting in bad faith, the ECtHR would likely rule that the expression does not qualify for protection of Article 10 of the ECHR. Conversely, if the press acted in good faith and reported on a matter of public interest, even if inaccuracies are later revealed, the ECtHR might protect the expression, emphasizing the importance of the role of the press in democratic society.

Expression on Internet

The internet offers a huge opportunity for exercising freedom of expression. However, this opportunity comes with certain risks. Harmful content, such as defamatory statements, hate speech, and speech inciting violence, can now be spread globally in seconds and may remain accessible online (*Delfi AS v. Estonia*[40]). When determining whether an internet service provider must remove comments posted by a third party, the ECtHR has outlined four criteria to balance the right to freedom of expression with the right to protect the reputation of the person or entity mentioned in the comments. Those four criteria are: the context and contents of the comments, the liability of the authors of the comments, the measures taken by the applicants, and the conduct of the aggrieved party and the consequences for the aggrieved party and for the applicants.[41]

The internet, with its accessibility and ability to store and share vast amounts of information, plays a crucial role in public access to news and facilitating the dissemination of information. However, it also presents a heightened risk to the exercise and enjoyment of human rights and freedoms—particularly the right to privacy—compared to traditional press (*Arnarson v. Iceland*[42]).

Website blocking is considered an infringement of freedom of expression (*Ahmet Yıldırım v. Turkey*[43]). The ECtHR "considers that such prior restraints are not necessarily incompatible with the Convention as a matter of principle. However, a legal framework is required, ensuring both tight control over the scope of bans and effective judicial review to prevent any abuse of power ... In that regard, the judicial review of such a measure, based on a weighing-up of the competing interests at stake and designed to strike a balance between them, is inconceivable without a framework establishing precise and specific rules regarding the application of preventive restrictions on freedom of expression."[44] The ECtHR has highlighted in this case the importance of balancing the various interests involved, particularly by evaluating the necessity of blocking access to specific sites. It also noted that authorities should have considered, among other things, that website blocking would inevitably make large amounts of information inaccessible and consequently restrict the rights of internet users to receive information. The ECtHR has determined in several cases that imposing a blanket blocking order on a website is an excessive measure that, according to the UN Human Rights Committee and other international bodies, resembles the banning of a newspaper or broadcaster (*OOO Flavus and Others v. Russia, Bulgakov v. Russia*[45]).

In a case where a website owner was required to remove information about filter-bypassing tools to avoid the blocking of the entire website, the ECtHR ruled that the legislative basis for the order failed to meet the foreseeability requirement (*Engels v. Russia*[46]).

The ECtHR emphasizes that the internet provides unparalleled opportunities for freedom of expression and access to information (*Delfi AS v. Estonia*). However, this freedom is not without limits, as harmful content—such as disinformation, hate speech, and defamatory remarks—can spread rapidly with lasting impacts.

Politicians and other public figures often serve as amplifiers of public discourse, whether intentional or unintentional. A politician who opens a Facebook wall to public increases a chance of excessive and immoderate comments. Among those comments, there were offensive comments the politician failed to disavow. Well-known persons on social media may find themselves liable for comments made by third parties that were posted on their social media accounts without any moderation (*Sanchez v. France*[47]).

Holding politicians accountable for third-party comments acknowledges their role in creating an environment of disinformation. However, this also raises additional issues, such as the extent to which public figures can realistically monitor and moderate large volumes of comments and a chilling effect that may cause a politician's discouragement from using social media to engage with citizens, fearing liability for third-party actions.

Blanket blocking of websites, as seen in *Ahmet Yıldırım v. Turkey* and similar cases, is considered disproportionate and harmful to freedom of expression. However, the ECtHR acknowledges that blocking may sometimes be necessary if narrowly tailored and subject to strict judicial oversight. While overly broad blocking undermines access to information, targeted actions (e.g., removal of disinformation or blocking of specific piece of information) may be in line with the proportionality principle.

The ECtHR highlights the need for a clear and predictable legal framework to ensure that restrictions on online content meet the requirements of legality, necessity, and proportionality. Laws targeting disinformation must define prohibited content with precision to avoid arbitrary enforcement or unintended restrictions on legitimate expression.

The ECtHR case-law gives the legislators guidelines on drafting the legislation aiming to combat disinformation, that is, provisions of criteria and examples for identifying disinformation, specification of the extent of blocking, and judicial review.

European Legislation against Disinformation

The EU and some member states have adopted laws that regulate content. In the EU, this regulation is the Digital Services Act and partly the AI Act; however, this regulation does not explicitly apply to disinformation. On the other hand, certain member states have incorporated disinformation into their legal systems. A closer look will be taken at France, Germany, and Austria.

The Digital Services Act

The Regulation (EU) 2022/2065 of the European Parliament and of the Council of October 19, 2022, on a Single Market for Digital Services and amending Directive 2000/31/EC (Digital Services Act) came into force in February 2024. The Digital Services Act (hereinafter "DSA") regulates online platforms and digital services in order to ensure a safer and more transparent digital environment. It sets rules for content moderation, protects user rights, combats illegal content, and promotes accountability and transparency for online platforms, especially large ones like social media and content-sharing platforms. The goal of the DSA is also to set rules for the liability of online intermediaries for online content. The provisions of the DSA replace the E-Commerce Directive.[48]

The DSA makes a distinction between intermediaries, meaning those who deal with information provided by a user of the service. The regulation recognizes providers of mere conduit (the transmission of information in a communication network or the provision of access to a communication network), caching (the transmission of information in a communication network and its automatic and temporary storage in order to make the access more efficient), and hosting (the storage of information). This distinction is important for the determination of liability rules. While mere conduit and catching play a passive role in the transmission of information, the hosting providers provide the infrastructure that enables the storage, dissemination, and accessibility of online content, which can mean also online disinformation. Pursuant to Article 6 of the DSA, the hosting provider is not liable for the information stored at the request of a recipient of the service, on condition that the provider does not have actual knowledge of the illegal activity or illegal content and is not aware of facts or circumstances from which the illegal activity or illegal content is apparent, or, upon obtaining such knowledge or awareness, acts expeditiously to remove or disable access to the illegal content.

The hosting provider may be liable for illegal content if the provider has an actual knowledge of such content or is aware of the circumstances from which the illegal content is apparent. Another condition for liability is the fact that the hosting provider obtained knowledge but failed to remove or disable the content. Pursuant to Recital 22 of the DSA, the removal or disabling of access should be undertaken while observing the fundamental rights of the recipients of the service, including the right to freedom of expression and of information.

The hosting providers have to implement a notice and take-down mechanism to allow users to notify them of the illegal content (Art. 16 of the DSA). The mechanism has to enable the users, among other things, to describe the reason why they deem the content to be illegal and the location of the content. Notices submitted through this mechanism are considered to give rise to actual knowledge or awareness for the purpose of their liability assessment if they allow the provider to identify the illegality of the information without a detailed legal examination. The service providers have to process the notices and take decisions in respect of the information to which the notices relate, in a timely, diligent, nonarbitrary, and objective manner.

For online providers, assessing competing rights is a challenging task, particularly given that even courts evaluate such conflicts on a case-by-case basis, often employing various tests of proportionality. Providers are not adjudicators, yet they are increasingly expected to make decisions that balance complex rights such as freedom of expression, right to privacy, and personality rights or legitimate interests, all in a high-speed digital environment. The difficulty for service providers lies in the performance of judicial-like assessments of competing rights, often in nearly real time without sufficient expertise.

The main difficulty lies in the fact that rights are rarely absolute and often conflict in ways that require nuanced consideration. For example, the right to freedom of expression may clash with the right to privacy or protection from disinformation and hate speech. Courts typically resolve such conflicts through proportionality tests, which involve weighing the importance of the competing rights in the specific context of the case, assessing the necessity of any restrictions, and ensuring that any measures taken are appropriate and minimally intrusive. This judicial process is context-sensitive and depends on legal expertise, case-law, and evidence. On the other hand, the unmanaged spread of harmful content, such as disinformation or hatred, can cause lack of trust in democratic institutions, harm vulnerable groups, and infringe on individual rights.

The DSA does not impose any general obligation on providers to monitor the information, nor actively seek facts or circumstances indicating illegal activity (Art. 8 of the DSA). This rule is in line with case-law of the Court of Justice of the European Union (hereinafter "CJEU") (Senftleben and Angelopoulos 2020). The DSA introduces voluntary content moderation, also called a Good Samaritan Clause (Art. 7 of the DSA) (Berbec 2024). Under this clause, the service providers are not liable if they, in good faith and with diligence, carry out their own voluntary investigations or have taken other measures aimed at detecting, identifying, and removing or disabling access to illegal content. The service providers may deploy automated systems, for example, artificial intelligence. The voluntary monitoring does not influence exemption from liability (Recital 26 of the DSA). Van Hoboken and O. Fathaigh argue that content monitoring and surveillance are detrimental to the right to privacy and to personal date, let alone access to data by public bodies (van Hoboken and Fathaigh 2021). If the ECtHR were to rule on an interference with the right to privacy, it would apply the same four-step test as described above.

The decision of lawmakers to impose responsibility on intermediaries reflects the pivotal role platforms play as gatekeepers of content. The providers shape the digital environment, influencing how information is accessed, shared, and consumed. It is needless to say that the person who uploaded the information on the online platform remains liable, regardless of the liability of the service provider. On the other hand, Senftleben et al. argue that by delegating the regulation of freedom of expression to online platforms and the creative industry, the state actually outsourced a responsibility for protecting human rights to the private sector (Senftleben, Pedro, and Meiring 2023, 105).

The purpose of the regulation of liability is not to prevent disinformation. The DSA does not even know the term disinformation. The provider may be liable for disinformation, if the disinformation may be assessed as illegal content. Pursuant to Article 3(h) of the DSA, illegal content means any information that, in itself or in relation to an activity, including the sale of products or the provision of services, is not in compliance with Union law or the law of any member state that is in compliance with Union law, irrespective of the precise subject matter or nature of that law. Even though illegal content has to be interpreted broadly, Recital 12 of the DSA does not list disinformation as an example of such content. In order for content to be unlawful even in the case of disinformation, it would have to be defamatory, discriminatory, or otherwise infringe the rights of others; or the disinformation, or a particular type of it, would have to be designated as unlawful by member state or Union law. The special legislation should outlaw disinformation, which is not the case in most member states (Strowel and De Meyere 2023). Moreover, it is usually not the provider who decides about the character of information, but this assessment is done by a fact-checking organization (Peukert 2023).

Artificial Intelligence Act

Generative AI can produce convincing fake texts, images, videos, and audio that mimic real events, individuals, or sources. Deep-fake technology, for example, can create realistic but fabricated videos of public figures or other individuals. AI-generated content may appear to come from reputable sources or mimic the style of authoritative figures, misleading audiences about its credibility.

The Regulation (EU) 2024/1689 of the European Parliament and of the Council of June 13, 2024, laying down harmonized rules on artificial intelligence and amending Regulations (EC) 300/2008, (EU) 167/2013, (EU) 168/2013, (EU)

2018/858, (EU) 2018/1139, and (EU) 2019/2144 and Directives 2014/90/EU, (EU) 2016/797 and (EU) 2020/1828 (Artificial Intelligence Act) (hereinafter "AIA"), contains provisions that aim to make manipulation and deep-fake transparent so that the user knows about the AI-generated content and manipulation. Providers and deployers of generative AI systems that are capable of creating and manipulating content have, pursuant to Article 50 of the AIA, a special obligation to disclose information about the use of artificial intelligence. The providers are organizations and companies that develop AI systems. The deployers are professional users (not end users). The deployers may be business corporations, organizations, and public bodies.

An AI system, including a generative AI system, that is capable of manipulating content is called a limited-risk system (Grieman and Early 2023, 66). AI systems—systems with unacceptable risk—that pose a clear threat to the fundamental rights are prohibited. This includes applications like social scoring by governments and manipulative AI technologies. AI systems that may significantly impact health, safety, or fundamental rights are called high-risk systems. Examples include AI used in critical infrastructure, education, employment, law enforcement, and healthcare. AI systems that are not categorized as systems with unacceptable risk, high-risk, or limited risk are systems with minimal risk and as such their providers and deployers are imposed almost no obligation in the AIA.

The providers have to ensure that AI systems that are intended to interact directly with natural persons are designed and developed in such a way that the natural persons concerned are informed that they are interacting with an AI system, unless this is obvious from the point of view of a natural person who is reasonably well-informed, observant, and circumspect.

The providers of AI systems that can generate synthetic audio, image, video, or text content have to ensure that the outputs of the AI system are marked in a machine-readable format and detectable as artificially generated or manipulated. The providers have to ensure their technical solutions are effective, interoperable, robust, and reliable as far as this is technically feasible, taking into account the specificities and limitations of various types of content, the costs of implementation, and the generally acknowledged state of the art, as may be reflected in relevant technical standards. Those technical solutions may have a character of watermarks, metadata identifications, cryptographic methods for proving provenance and authenticity of content, logging methods, fingerprints, or other techniques (Recital 133 of the AIA). These obligations do not apply if the AI system performs an assistive function for standard editing or does not substantially alter the input data or its semantics.

The deployers of an AI system that generates or manipulates image, audio, or video content constituting a deep-fake have to disclose that the content has been artificially generated or manipulated, unless the content forms evidently part of an artistic, creative, satirical, fictional, or analogous work or program. In that case the transparency obligations are limited to disclosure of the existence of such generated or manipulated content in an appropriate manner that does not hamper the display or enjoyment of the work. Łabuz argues that a particularly harmful type of the deep-fake, namely deep-fake porn, should have been classed as prohibited AI system since the harm for persons affected is immense (Łabuz 2024, 14).

The deployers of an AI system that generates or manipulates text that is published with the purpose of informing the public on matters of public interest have to disclose that the text has been artificially generated or manipulated. This obligation does not apply if the AI-generated content undergoes a process of human review or editorial control and a natural or legal person holds editorial responsibility for the publication of the content, which means AI-generated content in public and private media services.

Information about AI-generated or -manipulated content has to be provided to the end user in a clear and distinguishable manner at the time of the first interaction with the system or exposure to the system. The label and watermarks can be however removed by users equipped with special software, and for nondemocratic state actors (Łabuz 2024, 12).

The implementation of legal rules for the detection and labeling of artificially generated or manipulated content may be the subject matter of codes of practice.

Although the AIA does not directly target disinformation, the AIA may be able to help identify AI-created information or AI-manipulated content. Since the disseminators of disinformation conceal the nature of the information, and will certainly try to remove the labels and metadata identifying the manipulation, there is little chance that the AIA will significantly improve the fight against disinformation.

Strengthened Code of Practice on Disinformation

In 2022 thirty-four online platforms, fact-checkers, research and civil society organizations, including Meta, Google, and TikTok, signed the Strengthened Code of Practice on Disinformation (European Commission 2022). The Strengthened Code of Practice on Disinformation establishes commitments and measures to combat disinformation on digital platforms, emphasizing collaboration among stakeholders, transparency, and the protection of fundamental rights. It defines disinformation as false or misleading content spread with an intent to deceive, encompassing activities such as misinformation, disinformation, operations aiming at information influence, and foreign interference. The Code aims to reduce financial incentives for disinformation by scrutinizing advertising practices, ensuring ads are not placed on platforms spreading false information, and promoting transparency. It also mandates clear labeling and identity verification for political and issue ads, alongside maintaining public repositories to ensure fair political processes.

Joint organizations are committed to dealing with manipulative behaviors like fake accounts, bot-driven amplification, and malicious deep-fakes while ensuring transparent and trustworthy AI systems for content moderation. The Code empowers users through media literacy initiatives and provide them with tools to identify disinformation, and control over content.

Legal Regulation in EU Member States

France

In 2018, France implemented specific legal measures to combat the spread of disinformation, particularly during critical periods like elections. The anti-disinformation law (*loi contre la manipulation de l'information*)[49] aims to address the deliberate spread of false information and to protect democratic processes. The infringement is punished by a sentence of imprisonment and a fine up to €75,000.

The law allows courts to intervene during the three months preceding an election to halt the spread of fake news. Affected parties can petition a judge to remove or block content if it is deemed to harm the integrity of voting These decisions are expedited to ensure timely action, with rulings required within forty-eight hours.

Online platforms are also held accountable under the law. Companies like Facebook, Twitter, and Google are required to disclose the funding sources for sponsored content and ensure transparency in how their algorithms promote information. They must provide tools for users to report fake news and are obligated to remove flagged content promptly. Platforms are also expected to keep users informed about their efforts to combat disinformation.

The law enhances the role of the Conseil supérieur de l'audiovisuel, a regulatory authority for audiovisual media, now integrated into ARCOM (Autorité de régulation de la communication audiovisuelle et numérique), in combating disinformation. The authority may suspend the broadcasting of foreign state-controlled media that spread fake news during electoral periods. This provision targets the influence of foreign propaganda campaigns on domestic political discourse.

The law, however, faced criticism. Concerns have been raised about its potential to restrict free speech and the broad or subjective nature of defining fake news. Some critics question its effectiveness in addressing disinformation in real time (Sauvé and Coutant 2023).

Germany

The *Gesetz zur Verbesserung der Rechtsdurchsetzung in sozialen Netzwerken – Netzwerkdurchsetzungsgesetz* (NetzDG), or Network Enforcement Act, was introduced in Germany in 2017 to combat illegal content, including fake news, on social media platforms. The law required these platforms to remove clearly illegal content, including hate speech, defamation, and disinformation, within twenty-four hours from notification. For less clear cases, platforms had up to seven days to review and decide on the content's legality. The law also mandated that platforms establish transparent systems for users to report content and submit annual transparency reports detailing their moderation efforts. Noncompliance can result in fines of up to €50 million. Some parts of this act were derogated by *Digitale-Dienste-Gesetz* (Digital Services Act), enacted in reaction to the DSA.

The NetzDG has sparked significant debate. Supporters argued that it has been effective in holding large platforms accountable for the content shared on their services and in reducing the spread of harmful disinformation and hate speech. However, critics have raised concerns about its implications for free speech. They argue that strict penalties incentivize platforms to over-censor content, potentially removing legitimate posts to avoid fines. Additionally, some have expressed concern about the privatization of content moderation, as platforms—not courts—ultimately decide what content is permissible (Clasen 2022).

Internationally, the NetzDG has been serving as a model for other countries looking to regulate online platforms. It is seen as a pioneering effort in online content regulation, particularly for its attempt to balance the fight against harmful content with the preservation of democratic values (Zurth 2021).

Austria

The *Kommunikationsplattformen-Gesetz* (KoPl-G), or Communications Platforms Act, is an Austrian law introduced in 2021 to regulate large online platforms and combat harmful content, including disinformation, hate speech, and defamation. The law applies to social media platforms and similar services with a significant user base in Austria, such as Facebook, Twitter, and YouTube.

Under KoPl-G, platforms are required to remove illegal content quickly. If the content is clearly illegal, such as hate speech or fake news, it must be removed within twenty-four hours after being flagged. For more complex cases, platforms have up to seven days to decide whether the content violates the law. Platforms must also create user-friendly systems that allow users to report harmful or illegal content.

Additionally, the law requires platforms to publish annual transparency reports, detailing the number of complaints they received, the actions they took, and the steps they are taking to prevent the spread of illegal content. This ensures public accountability and gives insight into how platforms are managing harmful content. To enforce compliance, the law imposes significant fines of up to €10 million for platforms that fail to meet obligations.

KoPl-G aims to protect users from the negative impacts of harmful content while holding platforms accountable for the material shared on their services. However, comparable to other member states' law, it has faced criticism for potentially leading to over-censorship, as platforms may remove legitimate content to avoid penalties (Amnesty International 2020).

Conclusion

Disinformation threatens public trust in democratic processes and institutions. At the European level, there is no legislation aimed at combating disinformation. The lack of a legally binding definition of disinformation in European law means that different interpretations can lead to inconsistencies. The DSA does address illegal content, but disinformation is not explicitly covered. The rise of advanced technologies, such as generative AI and deep-fakes, will accelerate disinformation. Even though the AI Act focuses on identifying content manipulation, disseminators of disinformation will likely try to circumvent the rules.

At the national level, laws like France's anti-disinformation legislation and Germany's NetzDG provide an example of attempts to tackle disinformation in particular by content removal. Attempts to block disinformation raise concerns of the restriction of freedom of expression. The ECHR protects a broad range of expressions, including those that may be offensive or disturbing, stressing the importance of context in determining what constitutes disinformation. The ECHR enables to limit the freedom of expression under conditions set by the second paragraph of Art. 10. The ECtHR case-law stresses the need for exact and unambiguous law on which the limitations of freedom of expression are based and the proportionality principle in combating disinformation.

Conflict of Interest Statement

No potential conflict of interest was reported by the authors.

Notes

1 Decision of the European Court of Human Rights from December 7, 1976, no. 5493/72 (*Handyside v. The United Kingdom*).
2 Decision of the European Court of Human Rights from July 13, 2012, no. 16354/06 (*Mouvement raëlien Suisse v. Switzerland*).
3 Decision of the European Court of Human Rights from December 18, 1987, no. 10572/83 (*Markt Intern Verlag GmbH and Klaus Beermann v. Germany*).
4 Decision of the European Court of Human Rights from March 14, 2007, no. 10520/02 (*Verlagsgruppe News GmbH v. Austria (No. 2)*).
5 Decision of the European Court of Human Rights from March 5, 2009, no. 26935/05 (*Société de conception de presse et d'édition et Ponson v. France*).
6 Decision of the European Court of Human Rights from March 5, 2009, no. 26935/05 (*Société de conception de presse et d'édition et Ponson v. France*), 75.
7 Decision of the European Court of Human Rights from July 7, 2003, no. 65831/01 (*Garaudy v. France*).
8 Decision of the European Court of Human Rights from October 15, 2015, no. 27510/08 (*Perinçek v. Switzerland*).
9 Decision of the European Court of Human Rights from May 12, 1988, no. 12194/86 (*Kühnen v. Germany*).

10 Decision of the European Court of Human Rights from December 3, 2020, no. 55225/14 (*Pastörs v. Germany*).
11 Decision of the European Court of Human Rights from December 3, 2020, no. 55225/14 (*Pastörs v. Germany*).
12 Decision of the European Court of Human Rights from October 28, 1999, no. 28396/95 (*Wille v. Liechtenstein*).
13 Decision of the European Court of Human Rights from July 13, 1995, no. 18139/91 (*Tolstoy Miloslavsky v. The United Kingdom*).
14 Decision of the European Court of Human Rights from June 20, 2017, no. 4751/07 (*Metis Yayincilik Limited Şirketi and Sökmen v. Turkey*).
15 Decision of the European Court of Human Rights from April 26, 1979, no. 6538/74 (*The Sunday Times v. The United Kingdom*).
16 Decision of the European Court of Human Rights from September 23, 1998, no. 27273/95 (*Petra v. Romania*).
17 Decision of the European Court of Human Rights from February 4, 2019, no. 10692/09 (*Savva Terentyev v. Russia*).
18 Decision of the European Court of Human Rights from February 4, 2019, no. 10692/09 (*Savva Terentyev v. Russia*).
19 Decision of the European Court of Human Rights from October 22, 2007, nos. 21279/02 and 36448/02 (*Lindon, Otchakovsky-Laurens and July v. France*).
20 Decision of the European Court of Human Rights from January 17, 2006, no. 35083/97 (*Goussev and Marenk v. Finland*).
21 Decision of the European Court of Human Rights from September 15, 2011, no. 50084/06 (*RTBF v. Belgium*).
22 *Perinçek v. Switzerland*, para. 12.
23 *The Sunday Times v. The United Kingdom*, para. 19.
24 *Perinçek v. Switzerland*, para. 12.
25 *Savva Terentyev v. Russia*, para. 21.
26 *Handyside v. The United Kingdom*, para. 4.
27 *Mouvement raëlien Suisse v. Switzerland*, para. 5.
28 Decision of the European Court of Human Rights from July 8, 1999, no. 24735/94 (*Sürek v. Turkey (No. 3)*).
29 Decision of the European Court of Human Rights from July 8, 1986, no. 9815/82 (*Lingens v. Austria*).
30 Decision of the European Court of Human Rights from July 1, 1997, no. 20834/92 (*Oberschlick v. Austria (No.2)*).
31 Decision of the European Court of Human Rights from July 11, 2006, no. 71343/01 (*Brasilier v. France*).

32 Decision of the European Court of Human Rights from November 26, 1991, no. 13166/87 (*The Sunday Times v. The United Kingdom (No. 2)*).
33 Decision of the European Court of Human Rights from April 22, 2013, no. 48876/08 (*Animal Defenders International v. The United Kingdom*).
34 Decision of the European Court of Human Rights from November 8, 2016, no. 18030/11 (*Magyar Helsinki Bizottság v. Hungary*).
35 Decision of the European Court of Human Rights from July 10, 2014, no. 48311/10 (*Axel Springer AG v. Germany*).
36 Decision of the European Court of Human Rights from September 4, 2009, no. 21277/05 (*Standard Verlags GmbH v. Austria (No. 2)*).
37 *Axel Springer AG v. Germany*, para. 39.
38 Decision of the European Court of Human Rights from June 19, 2003, no. 49017/99 (*Pedersen and Baadsgaard v. Denmark*).
39 Decision of the European Court of Human Rights from December 10, 2007, no. 69698/01 (*Stoll v. Switzerland*).
40 Decision of the European Court of Human Rights from June 16, 2015, no. 64569/09 (*Delfi AS v. Estonia*).
41 Decision of the European Court of Human Rights from June 16, 2015, no. 64569/09 (*Delfi AS v. Estonia*).
42 Decision of the European Court of Human Rights from September 13, 2017, no. 58781/13 (*Arnarson v. Iceland*).
43 Decision of the European Court of Human Rights from March 18, 2013, no. 3111/10 (*Ahmet Yıldırım v. Turkey*).
44 Decision of the European Court of Human Rights from March 18, 2013, no. 3111/10 (*Ahmet Yıldırım v. Turkey*).
45 Decision of the European Court of Human Rights from November 16, 2020, no. 12468/15 (*OOO Flavus and Others v. Russia*), or decision of the European Court of Human Rights from November 16, 2020, no. 20159/15 (*Bulgakov v. Russia*).
46 Decision of the European Court of Human Rights from November 16, 2020, no. 61919/16 (*Engels v. Russia*).
47 Decision of the European Court of Human Rights from May 15, 2023, no. 45581/15 (*Sanchez v. France*).
48 Directive 2000/31/EC of the European Parliament and of the Council of June 8, 2000 on certain legal aspects of information society services, in particular electronic commerce, in the internal market ('Directive on electronic commerce').
49 Loi n° 2018–1202 du 22 décembre 2018 relative à la lutte contre la manipulation de l'information. www.legifrance.gouv.fr/jorf/id/JORFTEXT000037847559/.

References

Amnesty International. 2020. "Amnesty-Stellungnahme zum 'Hass im Netz' Gesetzespaket." October 15. www.amnesty.at/news-events/news/amnesty-stellungnahme-zum-hass-im-netz-gesetzespaket/.

Berbec, Adriana. 2024. "To what extent can online service providers adopt voluntary content moderation measures without losing their immunity shields? A comparative analysis of online service providers' liabilities in the European Union and the United States." *Journal of Intellectual Property, Information Technology and Electronic Commerce Law* 15 (1): 13–37.

Clasen, Moritz. 2022. "Netzwerkdurchsetzungsgesetz -Überblick über zentrale Regelungen und etwaige Verbesserungs-möglichkeiten." *StudZR-WissOn* 2: 302–24.

De Morree, Paulien E. 2016. *Rights and wrongs under the ECHR: The prohibition of abuse of rights in Article 17 of the European Convention on Human Rights.* Intersentia.

European Commission. 2020. *Communication from the Commission to the European Parliament, the Council, the European Economic and Social Committee and the Committee of the Regions on the European Democracy Action Plan.* COM/2020/790 final.

European Commission. 2022. "The strengthened code of practice on disinformation." https://digital-strategy.ec.europa.eu/en/policies/code-practice-disinformation.

Grieman, Keri and Joseph Early. 2023. "A risk-based approach to AI regulation: System categorisation and explainable AI practices." *SCRIPTed: A Journal of Law, Technology and Society* 20 (1): 56–88.

Łabuz, Mateusz. 2024. "Deep fakes and the Artificial Intelligence Act: An important signal or a missed opportunity?" *Policy & Internet*: 1–18. https://doi.org/10.1002/poi3.406.

McGonagle, Tarlach. 2018. "De Raad van Europa en online desinformatie: laveren tussen zorgen en zorgplichten?" (The Council of Europe and online disinformation: Navigating between concerns and duties of care?) *Mediaforum* 30 (6): 180–4. https://hdl.handle.net/11245.1/286d7d2f-f17e-416b-b7b4-5c2864ec6124.

Peukert, Alexander. 2023. "Who decides what counts as disinformation in the EU?" *Verfassungsblog.* https://verfassungsblog.de/who-decides-what-counts-as-disinformation-in-the-eu/.

Sauvé, Mathieu-Robert, and Alexandre Coutant. 2023. "Loi française contre la manipulation de l'information en période électorale et pratiques professionnelles des journalistes face au phénomène des fake news." *Les enjeux de L'information et de La communication* 5 (2A): 103–22.

Senftleben, Martin, and Christina Angelopoulos. 2020. "The odyssey of the prohibition on general monitoring obligations on the way to the Digital Services Act: Between Article 15 of the E-commerce directive and Article 17 of the directive on copyright in the digital single market." https://ssrn.com/abstract=3717022.

Senftleben, Martin, Quintais João Pedro, and Arlette Meiring. 2023. "How the EU outsources the task of human rights protection to platforms and users: The case of UGC monetization." *Berkeley Technology Law Journal* 38 (3): 101–15.

Strowel, Alain, and Jean De Meyere. 2023. "The Digital Services Act: Transparency as an efficient tool to curb the spread of disinformation on online platforms?" *Journal of Intellectual Property, Information Technology and Electronic Commerce Law* 14: 66. https://heinonline.org/HOL/LandingPage?handle=hein.journals/jipitec14&div=9&id=&page=.

van Hoboken, Joris, and Ronan Ó. Fathaigh. 2021. "Regulating disinformation in Europe: Implications for speech and privacy." *UC Irvine Journal of International, Transnational and Comparative Law* 6: 9. https://heinonline.org/HOL/LandingPage?handle=hein.journals/ucivjtoml6&div=5&id=&page=.

Zurth, Patrick. 2021. "The German NetzDG as role model or cautionary tale? Implications for the debate on social media liability." *Fordham Intellectual Property, Media and Entertainment Law Journal* 31 (4): 1089.

8

Mapping the European Union's Evolving Legislative Efforts to Combat Disinformation

Ethan Shattock

This chapter maps the tailored legislative initiatives that EU institutions have developed in response to online disinformation. Commencing with a discussion of the EU's 2018 Code of Practice on Disinformation (hereinafter "the 2018 Code"), this chapter illustrates the European Commission's development of the 2018 Code and focuses on the background that preceded the 2018 Code. Identifying the 2018 Code as a seminal but piecemeal self-regulatory achievement, this chapter distils the key academic criticisms that have been directed at EU institutions in response to the 2018 Code. This discussion lays foundations for a subsequent analysis of how the EU's Digital Services Act (DSA) could be used to limit the spread of online disinformation. Specifically, this chapter assesses DSA provisions that have been designed to curtail the spread of misleading—including potentially lawful—communications that threaten electoral processes. Within this analysis of the DSA, this chapter examines how the 2022 Code acts as a tool of compliance for the effective implementation of the DSA. Mapping these EU legal developments, this chapter illustrates how EU institutions have transitioned from a voluntary and self-regulatory approach to online disinformation toward a more comprehensive coregulatory framework.

Decoding the Code: The 2018 Code

To understand the relevance of the EU's DSA from the disinformation perspective, it is necessary to first understand the context and development of the 2018 Code. Accordingly, this section first illustrates the concerns that motivated the European Commission's development of the 2018 Code. This section then examines the content of the 2018 Code and considers the piecemeal manner in which the Code's signatories implemented its voluntary commitments. Further attention is given to the prevailing academic and legal criticisms of the 2018 Code as an initially promising but ultimately piecemeal initiative.

Background to the 2018 Code

The 2018 Code was spawned by concerns from EU institutions that online disinformation could distort "the integrity of European elections" (De Cock Buning 2018). The European Commission's initiation of the 2018 Code was a product of the creation of the East StratCom Task Force (ESCTF) as part of the European External Action Service (EEAS) as early as 2015. The ESCTF was chiefly developed in response to the European Council's concerns regarding "ongoing" and repeated attempts by Russian state actors to influence European elections and undermine European integration (Pollicino and Somaini 2020). Motivated by these concerns, the European Parliament launched a 2017 resolution wherein the parliament urged the Commission

> to analyze in depth the current situation and legal framework with regard to fake news, and to verify the possibility of legislative intervention to limit the dissemination and spreading of fake content. (European Parliament 2017)

In response, the Commission convened a High-Level Expert Group (HLEG) and instructed this group to explore the development of "a comprehensive EU strategy for tackling disinformation" (De Cock Buning 2018). The HLEG recommended that the Commission "pursue" a "self-regulatory approach based on a clearly defined multi-stakeholder engagement process" as a "first step" for EU efforts to curb disinformation. The HLEG further advised the Commission to "review" and "ensure the continuous effectiveness" of EU self-regulatory approaches to online disinformation. Such language—encouraging the Commission itself to initiate a self-regulatory instrument—epitomizes why some commentators refrain from describing the 2018 Code as a form of self-regulation per se.[1] Industry self-regulation generally involves voluntary decisions undertaken by private actors to control their actions (Gunningham and Rees 1997). The 2018 Code was not purely borne out of autonomous industry collaborations and was instead spearheaded by the Commission itself. Accordingly, the 2018 Code should not be narrowly construed as a somewhat "unique" form of industry-led self-regulation but rather as an institutionally nudged collaborative effort by technological intermediaries to take more proactive steps to limit the spread of online falsehoods through their respective platforms.[2]

A novel feature of the 2018 Code is that it predominately—if not exclusively—targets "false or misleading" communications that threaten elections but are "otherwise lawful" (European Commission 2018, 1). This delineates the 2018 Code from EU initiatives such as the code of conduct for hate speech and the regulation to prevent terrorist content.[3] As Kuczerawy observes, those initiatives exclusively target online communications that are "understood as illegal" (Kuczerawy 2019). Acknowledging this, the European Parliament characterized the 2018 Code as a preferable method of tackling "harmful and manipulative" but lawful communications (European Parliament 2021, 9). Rather than strictly requiring technological intermediaries to *remove* online communications that fall under this category, the 2018 Code sets out five overarching objectives that Vermeulen calls the "thematic pillars" of the Code (2020, 10). Specifically, these five pillars involve voluntary commitments to tackle disinformation by:

- scrutinizing advertising placements to disrupt advertising revenue of accounts and websites that spread disinformation;
- improving the transparency of political advertising and issue-based advertising;
- improving the integrity of services;
- empowering consumers to report disinformation and access diverse and authoritative content;
- empowering the research community to monitor disinformation through access to platform data (European Commission 2018, 5–9).

The Commission acknowledged that these pillars apply to a "heterogeneous range of stakeholders involved" in the 2018 Code (European Commission 2018, 1). For example, initial 2018 Code signatories not only included social media platforms—such as Facebook (now Meta) and Twitter (now X)—but also internet search providers (ISPs) such as Google and web browsers such as Mozilla. The Commission further acknowledged that EU institutions have limited competencies to regulate online communications during national elections.[4] This partially explains why the 2018 Code does not prescribe legally binding obligations for its signatories to limit the spread of disinformation. Instead, it sets out several sub-commitments that signatories voluntarily "commit themselves to adhere to" under the five pillars.

Related to the diverse nature of technological stakeholders involved, the 2018 Code gives discretion for how the Code signatories may interpret its objectives. For example, pillar 1 merely entails a commitment to "improve the scrutiny of advertisement placements" (European Commission 2018, 4). The 2018 Code contemplates that this commitment could involve the promotion of "brand safety and verification tools" or some engagement "with third party verification companies" (European Commission 2018, 7). Pillar 2 sets out a commitment to improve "transparency" for political and "issue-based advertising" (European Commission 2018, 5). To fulfil this commitment, platforms should inform users on why they are targeted by specific advertisements and clearly differentiate advertisements from "editorial content." Pillar 3 commits signatories to protect the "integrity of platform services," whereby signatories are advised to develop "clear policies regarding identity and misuse of automated bots on their services and to enforce these policies within the EU" (European Commission 2018, 7). The Code anticipates that platforms may pursue "efforts to close fake accounts" but does not specifically advise account closures (European Commission 2018, 3). To empower consumers under pillar 4, signatories commit to invest in tools for users to access "diverse news sources" and "make informed decisions when they encounter online news" (European Commission 2018, 9). To empower researchers and fact-checkers under the fifth pillar, signatories should not dissuade "good faith independent efforts to track disinformation and understand its impact" (European Commission 2018, 8). Signatories further commit to supplying the Commission and independent fact-checkers with relevant data to assist this. Measures here may "include sharing privacy protected datasets, undertaking joint research, or otherwise partnering with academics and civil society organizations if relevant and possible." As Colliver highlights, these commitments reflect voluntary "requests" under the 2018 Code that are dependent "entirely on the will of" signatories to "institute changes" (Colliver 2020).

The Inconsistent Implementation of the 2018 Code

Upon observing how the 2018 Code was implemented by its technological signatories, the Commission described this self-regulatory instrument as an "important and necessary first step" in EU anti-disinformation efforts (European Commission 2020). Carrying out several periodic assessments of the 2018 Code, along with third-party assessors, the Commission issued specific praise regarding how all signatories adopted measures to label political advertisements in the run up to the 2019 European parliamentary elections (ERGA 2019). Moreover, the Commission positively acknowledged how many signatories generated accessible ad libraries through public Application Programming Interfaces (APIs).[5] The Commission further noted how several platforms expanded their "ad transparency tools" from being used in the US context to being used in the 2019 European parliamentary elections. Despite its commendation of these successful aspects of the Code's first pillar, the Commission simultaneously identified the varied approaches regarding how signatories implemented the 2018 Code. The Commission expressly linked these divergences to the lack of uniform interpretations of the terminology under the 2018 Code's pillars. For example, the Commission observed that "political advertising" was interpreted "in varying ways by the platforms and is defined differently at Member State level" (European Commission 2020, 11). Only Facebook (now Meta) provided a definition for "issue-based" advertising when self-reporting its commitment to the Code's first pillar (ERGA 2020, 52).

Alongside these definitional inconsistencies, the 2018 Code signatories also reported a diverse range of measures designed to limit the spread of misleading information. For example, Facebook and Google reported launching measures to label political advertisements with "paid for" disclosures, while Microsoft and Twitter (now X) reported that they had prohibited all forms of political advertising outright (European Commission 2020, 5). All signatories reported removals of accounts on the grounds of preventing "inauthentic behavior" under the Code's third pillar. However, signatories pursued this through various and often unconnected policies. For example, Facebook reported disabling accounts that engage in "coordinated inauthentic behavior," while Google reported closure of accounts that violate its spam policy.[6] Other signatories reported that they had sought to combat inauthentic behavior through the application of commercial policies that pre-dated the 2018 Code's development. This includes Google's existing "misrepresentation policy" and Microsoft's "various ads policies" that were "already in place before the Code's initiation" (European Commission 2020, 36).

Fostering further uncertainty was the opaque manner in how signatories reported their measures to meet the 2018 Code's voluntary commitments. For example, while the Commission praised signatories for expanding ad libraries through public APIs, it identified inconsistencies surrounding "the limited functionalities of APIs, completeness of repositories, and quality of searchable information" regarding "sponsors' identity" and targeting criteria (European Commission 2020, 9). The European Regulators Group for Audiovisual Media Services (ERGA), in assisting the Commission's auditing of the 2018 Code, also observed that signatories often provided no specific information on whether account removals had been directed at accounts that were active or received high engagement at the time of removal (ERGA 2020, 47). Significantly, ERGA further observed that this was compounded by how signatories often reported measures to remove problematic accounts based on policies that were "developed for the USA or published in the USA and have not been adapted or translated yet for the European market" (ERGA 2020, 26). Commenting on the piecemeal nature of data access in this specific area, the Commission questioned:

> While the platforms provide numbers on, for example, how many accounts were closed/removed, taken action against etc., oftentimes, these are provided on a global scale rather than focusing on the EU. (European Commission 2020, 45)

This lack of transparency was a symptom of the larger critique regarding how the 2018 Code allegedly provided no effective framework for researchers and fact-checkers to independently assess signatory measures to combat disinformation. The aforementioned fourth and fifth pillars of the 2018 Code involve signatory commitments to support good-faith research "by providing relevant data on the functioning on their services."[7] This commitment is generally considered to have had yielded very limited success by encouraging signatories to voluntarily collaborate with independent fact-checkers and researchers. For example, Twitter periodically disclosed extensive datasets—on state-sponsored disinformation operations—to independent researchers in alignment with this commitment. Relatedly, Google voluntarily shared a large dataset on visual deep-fakes with research stakeholders to assist with the development of detection methods for synthetic videos (Hao 2019). However, the Commission also noted that signatories largely provided data to independent researchers in an "episodic and arbitrary" manner (European Commission 2020, 11).

An example that epitomizes the Commission's concern is Facebook's collaboration with Social Science One (SS1).[8] This partnership was introduced "to study the impact of social media on democracy and elections" and "generate insights to inform policy at the intersection of media, technology, and democracy" (Social Science One 2018). However, academics have routinely criticized how Facebook "has still not provided academics with anything approaching adequate data access" in these key areas (Social Science One 2019).

The Limitations of the 2018 Code

An inherent limitation of the 2018 Code is its self-regulatory nature. This is epitomized by the abovementioned opacity regarding how the 2018 Code empowered its signatories with discretion to share or withhold data that could be used to comprehensively assess the spread of disinformation and associated responses. As Keller and Leerssen highlight, EU legislative proposals encouraging content moderation "should be informed by empirically grounded assessments of platforms' capacity to comply and the potential unintended consequences of their compliance efforts" (Keller and Leerssen 2020). The abovementioned dearth of "granular" information on how signatories apply commitments contributed to challenges in accurately ascertaining how equipped the 2018 Code signatories have been in responding to falsehoods in a consistent and efficient manner.

A related problem is that the voluntary framework of the 2018 Code enables a lack of scrutiny and due process in the event wherein signatory measures adopted in response to the Code's commitments are unclear and lead to restrictions on lawful content that are potentially unjustified. This is particularly crucial, for example, in cases where platforms may mistakenly identify content containing political satire as content containing harmful disinformation. Due to the aforementioned focus of the 2018 Code on online content that is false but not necessarily illegal, it was designed to encourage signatories to carefully limit misleading but "otherwise lawful" content that undermines democratic elections. Crucially, however, it introduces no procedural framework for ensuring scrutiny and accountability if intermediaries arbitrarily remove such content. This reflects a broader critique of how self-regulation often applies in the context of moderating harmful online content. As McIntyre highlights, self-regulatory instruments often encourage actions to remove harmful online content that "generally escape the publicity which would attach to legislation or judicial decisions" (2012, 277–308). This opacity can make it "difficult for customers to understand what content is being restricted and by whom." Angelopoulos et al., while acknowledging the potential effectiveness of voluntary initiatives in minimizing online "harms," posit that self-regulation encourages content moderation that interferes with the right of internet users to access information "without a clear legal way of redress or appropriate safeguards such as due process" (Angelopoulos et al. 2016). Raising analogous criticisms, Kuczerawy postulates that the 2018 Code induces a "delegated private enforcement" of restrictions on misleading content without viable procedural safeguards to identify unjustified content removals (2019, 10).

There is now well-documented evidence that platforms can engage in "over-removal" of harmful online content if left to self-govern online content. The lack of procedural safeguards in the 2018 Code is significant in this context. While the 2018 Code explicitly cautions its signatories to avoid undermining the right to freedom of expression in their efforts to combat disinformation, it provides virtually no concrete guidance on how to achieve this delicate balance. For example, the 2018 Code urges signatories to be "mindful" of a "delicate balance" between limiting misleading content and preserving access to lawful content (European Commission 2018, 1). Significantly, it deliberately instructs Code signatories that any restrictions on access to false information must be achieved in alignment with the jurisprudence of the European Court of Human Rights (ECtHR) and the Court of Justice of the European Union (CJEU) "on the proportionality of measures designed to limit access to and circulation of harmful content." While helpful in principle, such instructions do not in any way preclude the possibility that private ordering of content removal could lead to unjustified measures that curtail the right to freedom of expression. It is noteworthy and positive that the 2018 Code, where it defines disinformation, seeks to focus on intentional falsehoods while excluding "reporting errors" or "political satire."[9] With the exception of this important caveat, the 2018 Code provides little in the way of qualitative criteria that provides interpretive guidance on the standards of compliance under the European Convention on Human Rights (ECHR) and the Charter of Fundamental Rights of the European Union (CFREU) that the Code expressly alludes to. This feeds into and legitimizes concerns regarding how self-regulation can encourage a "privatization of censorship" by encouraging signatories to moderate misleading content without due process (Monti 2020, 214–25).

A pertinent concern is that, by using broad terminology and outsourcing the task of moderating lawful content to its signatories with minimal scrutiny, the 2018 Code could encourage "over-removal" of legal content. As Keller has uncovered, there is already an array of evidence that intermediaries erroneously remove lawful content when responding to laws to combat harmful online communications (Keller 2015). This concern is heightened in the context of false information, which may often involve lawful content that is spread to promote satirical or humorous messages without any intent to deceive. Further relevant here is the Commission's instruction to signatories that EU institutions will consider further "measures of a regulatory nature" if the 2018 Code is ineffective (European Commission 2018). Arguably, such language encourages signatories to limit the spread of misleading—but not necessarily illegal—communications to evade further regulation in the disinformation field. This reflects McIntyre's observation regarding the attractiveness of self-regulation as a means for industry stakeholders to "ward off more intrusive legislative intervention" in how platforms moderate harmful online content (2013, 277–308). This further reflects Helberger's contention that "commercial interests and corresponding strategic motives" of intermediaries "do not always align well with those of public institutions and democracy" (Helberger, Pierson, and Poell 2018, 1–14). Applying these observations to the 2018 Code, a key uncertainty is that, by floating the prospect of further regulation in the event of ineffective implementation, the 2018 Code provides room for signatories to unintentionally undermine the right to freedom of expression despite expressly cautioning signatories against this.

From Moderation to Mitigation: Disinformation and the DSA

This chapter now identifies the EU's approach to online disinformation through the DSA. The focus here is on the relevant provisions and mechanisms under the EU's "DSA package" that have potential significance from the disinformation perspective. This section first provides a general overview of the DSA before identifying DSA provisions that could be used to control the spread of online disinformation, including potentially lawful forms. Building from earlier analyses of the 2018 Code, and the lack of due process involved in the 2018 Code, this section also assessed how the DSA seeks to protect against excessive removal of online content. This section then maps how the new 2022 Code acts as a tool of compliance for the DSA.

Background to the DSA

The DSA was adopted and published in the official EU journal on October 19, 2022.[10] It updates the "rules for addressing illegal content online" and the "liability exemptions" that have affected intermediaries operating in the EU's internal market since the introduction of the E-Commerce Directive in 2000.[11] Husovec and Laguna observe that the DSA "preserves and upgrades the liability exemptions for online intermediaries that exist in the European framework since 2000" (Husovec and Laguna 2023). Significantly from the disinformation perspective, the DSA also creates and "imposes due diligence obligations concerning the design and operation of" intermediary services in the EU to "ensure a safe, transparent and predictable online ecosystem."[12] This is linked to the explicit acknowledgment in the DSA regarding the "new risks and challenges" spawned by the "digital transformation" and "increased use" of intermediary services.[13] The DSA consists of five chapters:

I. General provisions
II. Liability of providers of intermediary services
III. Due-diligence obligations for a transparent and safe online environment
IV. Implementation, cooperation, sanctions, and enforcement
V. Final provisions.

The DSA introduces layered "asymmetric" obligations in a "tiered" manner and applies its most extensive obligations for Very Large Online Platforms (VLOP/SEs) and Very Large Online Search Engines (VLOSEs).[14] Conversely, it sets out its least extensive obligations for "providers of intermediary services" that sit at the bottom tier of providers under the DSA framework.[15]

Several DSA provisions have a potential relevance in the context of moderating and removing online content containing disinformation. This includes online advertising transparency obligations, content moderation transparency obligations, and due-diligence obligations.[16] Due to the considerable communicative power that VLOP/SEs hold in controlling the free flow of information in political and electoral settings, the analysis below focuses on the due-diligence obligations under the DSA for VLOP/SEs to identify and mitigate risks under Articles 34 and 35 respectively. As these provisions are intimately linked to the European Commission's development of the renewed 2022 Code, focus is also given to how the 2022 Code serves as a tool of compliance for VLOP/SE risk mitigation obligations under Articles 34 and 35 of the DSA.

Risks, Crises, and Disinformation under the DSA

The DSA establishes due-diligence obligations for VLOP/SEs to identify and mitigate "systemic risks."[17] Article 34 requires that VLOP/SEs "shall identify, analyse and assess" the emergence of "any significant systemic risks stemming from the functioning and use made of their services in the Union."[18] Article 34 lists that the assessment of such risks by VLOP/SEs "shall be specific to their services and proportionate to the systemic risks" in light of the "severity and probability" of risks.[19] However, it lists that risks "shall include" the following:

a. the dissemination of illegal content through their services;
b. any actual or foreseeable negative effects for the exercise of fundamental rights, in particular the fundamental rights to human dignity enshrined in Article 1 of the Charter, to respect for private and family life enshrined in Article 7 of the Charter, to the protection of personal data enshrined in Article 8 of the Charter, to the freedom of expression and information, including the freedom and pluralism of the media, enshrined in Article 11 of the Charter, to nondiscrimination enshrined in Article 21 of the Charter, to respect for the rights of the child enshrined in Article 24 of the Charter, and to a high level of consumer protection enshrined in Article 38 of the Charter;
c. any actual or foreseeable negative effects on civic discourse and electoral processes and public security;
d. any actual or foreseeable negative effects in relation to gender-based violence, the protection of public health and minors, and serious negative consequences to the person's physical and mental well-being.

Article 34 does not *explicitly* reference online disinformation as a systemic risk under the DSA. However, it references "any actual or foreseeable negative effect" on "civic discourses, electoral processes and public security."[20] Article 34 also states that when identifying risks, VLOP/SEs must "also analyse whether and how the risks pursuant to paragraph 1 are influenced by intentional manipulation of their service, including by inauthentic use or automated exploitation of the service."[21] Recital 57 DSA further states that "the creation of fake accounts, the use of bots, and other automated or partially automated behaviours" are to be considered risks under Article 34.[22] It is further notable that Article 34 identifies risks that entail "any negative effects" on "the exercise" of fundamental rights.[23] As EU institutions have already identified disinformation as a threat to fundamental rights, dissemination of such content could be considered a risk under this provision's interpretation.[24] Finally, Article 34 addresses "the dissemination of illegal content" as a risk for VLOP/SEs to identify.[25] This is significant because several EU member states now make the dissemination of false information an unlawful offence.[26]

Large platforms must take measures to mitigate the systemic risks that are posed to their services. Article 35 DSA states that VLOP/SEs must adopt "effective mitigation measures" that are "tailored" to risks identified under Article 34.[27] Article 35 does not provide an exhaustive list of "effective mitigation measures."[28] However, Article 35 details that such measures "may include"

a. adapting the design, features, or functioning of their services, including their online interfaces;
b. adapting their terms and conditions and their enforcement;
c. adapting content moderation processes, including the speed and quality of processing notices related to specific types of illegal content and, where appropriate, the expeditious removal of, or the disabling of access to, the content notified, in particular in respect of illegal hate speech or cyber violence, as well as adapting any relevant decision-making processes and dedicated resources for content moderation;
d. testing and adapting their algorithmic systems, including their recommender systems;
e. adapting their advertising systems and adopting targeted measures aimed at limiting or adjusting the presentation of advertisements in association with the service they provide;
f. reinforcing the internal processes, resources, testing, documentation, or supervision of any of their activities as regards detection of systemic risk;
g. initiating or adjusting cooperation with trusted flaggers in accordance with Article 22 and the implementation of the decisions of out-of-court dispute settlement bodies pursuant to Article 21;
h. initiating or adjusting cooperation with other providers of online platforms or of online search engines through the codes of conduct and the crisis protocols referred to in Articles 45 and 48 respectively;
i. taking awareness-raising measures and adapting their online interface in order to give recipients of the service more information;
j. taking targeted measures to protect the rights of the child, including age verification and parental control tools and tools aimed at helping minors signal abuse or obtain support, as appropriate;
k. ensuring that an item of information, whether it constitutes a generated or manipulated image, audio or video that appreciably resembles existing persons, objects, places or other entities or events and falsely appears to a person to be authentic or truthful is distinguishable through prominent markings when presented on their online interfaces, and, in addition,

providing an easy to use functionality which enables recipients of the service to indicate such information.

Article 35 explicitly references that VLOP/SEs may "adapt content moderation practices" as a means of mitigating risks.[29] This suggests that Article 35 could lead large platforms and search engines to engage in more moderation of content containing misleading information during elections. As noted above, however, the list of contemplated measures is broad. This broadness leads Fahey et al. to observe that Articles 34 and 35 of the DSA provide VLOP/SEs with "considerable leeway" to identify and mitigate risks (Fahey et al. 2021). This discretionary nature of the DSA is evident where Article 34 states that VLOP/SEs must identify risks that are "specific to their services."[30] Article 35 also instructs that VLOP/SE "mitigation measures" shall be "tailored to the specific systemic risks identified pursuant to Article 34."[31]

Notwithstanding this discretion for VLOP/SEs to identify and mitigate risks, Article 35(2) provides scope for the Commission to annually "publish comprehensive reports" that highlight "the most prominent and recurrent systemic risks" reported by VLOP/SEs.[32] Article 35(3) further empowers the Commission to publish a set of "best practices" for VLOP/SEs to "mitigate" these recurrent risks.[33] Importantly, however, VLOP/SEs are not required to follow these best practices. The key mechanism for assessing how VLOP/SEs comply with DSA obligations to identify and manage risks is the "independent audit" mechanism under Article 37.[34] This provision requires VLOP/SEs to subject themselves to yearly independent audits to assess their compliance with Articles 34 and 35.[35] Independent auditors—if identifying "negative" elements of VLOP/SE compliance—can issue "operational recommendations on specific measures" to achieve compliance with the DSA's "systemic risk" provisions.[36] Importantly, however, this does not set out an explicit requirement for VLOP/SEs to adhere to such recommendations. This reflects Leerssen's observation that independent auditing under Article 37 generally "revolves around self-assessment" (Leerssen 2023).

While VLOP/SEs appear to have discretion to identify and mitigate online disinformation as a risk under the DSA, the true extent of this discretion is currently uncertain. For example, Article 35 states that the measures taken by VLOP/SEs to address risks may include measures aimed at "initiating or adjusting cooperation with" the DSA's "Codes of Conduct and the crisis protocols referred to in Articles 45 and 48 respectively."[37] Article 45 DSA empowers the European

Commission to "encourage and facilitate the drawing up of voluntary Codes of Conduct at Union level" that are intended to address "specific challenges of tackling different types of illegal content and systemic risks."[38] Article 45 provides a basic framework for VLOP/SEs to participate in these codes of conduct and to "take specific risk mitigation measures, as well as a regular reporting framework on any measures taken and their outcomes."[39] While these codes of conduct are voluntary, Recital 104 DSA states that the "refusal without proper explanation" of VLOP/SEs to "participate in the application of such a Code of Conduct could be taken into account, where relevant, when determining" compliance of VLOP/SEs to prevent systemic risks under the DSA.[40]

Article 35 DSA also references that VLOP/SEs may address risks to coordinate with the "crisis protocols" under Article 48 DSA.[41] Article 48 empowers the Commission to "initiate the drawing up" of "voluntary crisis protocols for addressing crisis situations."[42] It is currently unclear whether specific crisis protocols will be drawn up regarding how VLOP/SEs should address online disinformation in times of crises. These voluntary protocols are only intended to be developed in "extraordinary circumstances affecting public security or public health."[43] However, Recital 108 clarifies that the Commission "may initiate the drawing up of voluntary crisis protocols to coordinate a rapid, collective and cross-border response" to crises.[44]

Significantly, this also references crisis protocols as potentially being developed by the Commission "in addition to the crisis response mechanism" for VLOP/SEs.[45] Article 36, which separately establishes the "crisis response mechanism," empowers the European Commission to temporarily identify "crisis situations" related to the EU's "public security" or "public health."[46] Article 36 also empowers the Commission to require that VLOP/SEs "identify and apply specific, effective and proportionate measures, such as any of those provided for in Article 35(1)" as a means of responding to temporary crises.[47] Thus, while VLOP/SE compliance with crisis protocols under Article 48 is voluntary, it appears possible for the Commission to require VLOP/SEs to take measures against the spread of online disinformation if the Commission identifies a need for such measures as part of a temporary crisis situation under Article 36. This raises an important question regarding whether the DSA could encourage VLOP/SEs to respond to online disinformation in crises without providing detailed guidance on how such responses could be rights-protective. While Article 36 states that the Commission shall "aim to ensure" that the adoption of such protocols avoids "any negative effects on the exercise of fundamental rights" when identifying crises under Article 36, no further guidance is provided on this.[48]

A New Code: The 2022 Code

While the above-discussed DSA provisions have relevance in the online disinformation context, it is also important to examine how the DSA is complemented by the 2022 Code.[49] Spurred by "significant shortcomings" of the 2018 Code, the European Commission communicated in 2021 that a "strengthening" of this instrument was required (European Commission 2021). The Commission published a revised Code in 2022 and described this as a "co-regulatory backstop" to address shortcomings from the 2018 Code "in view of the adoption of the proposed DSA."[50] The link between the 2022 Code and the DSA has particular significance for VLOP/SEs. The 2022 Code explicitly states that the revised Code "aims to become a Code of Conduct under Article 45 of the DSA."[51] It further states that "signing up to all commitments relevant and pertinent to their services should be considered as a possible risk mitigation measure" for VLOP/SEs in alignment with Article 35 DSA.[52] This reflects the stated desire of the Commission to ensure that the EU's continued encouragement for intermediaries to voluntarily address online disinformation through self-regulation is made "credible" by linking the 2022 Code to the DSA as part of the EU's "toolbox for fighting the spread of disinformation."[53]

The 2022 Code sets out more extensive commitments than the 2018 iteration and applies to a wider range of signatories.[54] For example, signatories of the 2022 Code now include interactive platforms such as TikTok and Twitch.[55] In outlining renewed commitments, the Commission aims not only to promote greater consistency in the Code's application but also to devise "an appropriate monitoring mechanism" to assess this through "key performance indicators (KPIs)."[56] Importantly, several key updates in the 2022 Code are designed to fix shortcomings the European Commission identified in the 2018 Code.

As noted, the Commission and ERGA reported inconsistencies on how signatories implemented 2018 Code commitments to prevent disinformation from being disseminated through political advertising. To promote greater consistency in how signatories achieve this, the 2022 Code sets out a more precise—although still voluntary—framework for signatories to implement Code objectives. For example, the revised Code sets out renewed sub-commitments for signatories to:

- ensure efficient labeling of political or issue ads;
- develop a common understanding of political and issue advertising;
- develop verification commitments for political or issue ads;
- develop political or issue ad repositories and minimum functionalities for APIs to access political data.[57]

Important here is the 2022 Code's introduction of new commitments for signatories to ensure "minimum functionalities" for APIs and political ad repositories.[58] This is a specific area where the Commission highlighted inconsistencies in how signatories of the 2018 Code provided access to "searchable information" and targeting criteria of published political advertisements.[59] Addressing these inconsistencies, the revised Code instructs signatories to include granular data on APIs regarding "the number of impressions delivered, the audience criteria used to determine recipients," and "geographical areas" where political advertisements receive high engagement.[60]

Of further relevance are the 2022 Code's commitments for signatories to protect "integrity" of platform services and combat "manipulative behaviour."[61] The revised Code retains this objective but introduces new sub-commitments to

- develop a common understanding of "impermissible manipulative behaviour";
- introduce transparency obligations for AI systems;
- ensure cooperation and transparency.[62]

Through these renewed sub-commitments, the Commission has envisaged that the 2022 Code will "ensure a consistent approach" in how signatories identify "impermissible manipulative behavior" across their services.[63] Unlike the 2018 Code, the 2022 Code lists a prospective—although nonexhaustive—range of behaviors that can be considered impermissibly manipulative. These include:

- creation and use of fake accounts and bot-driven amplification;
- hack and leak operations;
- impersonation and malicious deep fakes;
- nontransparent paid messages or promotion by influencers;
- purchase of fake engagements;
- use of accounts that participate in coordinated inauthentic behavior.

Arguably informed by the variations in how the 2018 Code signatories previously implemented measures to combat manipulative behavior, the 2022 Code places more explicit emphasis on the need for "cross-platform" cooperation in this field.[64] For example, signatories are encouraged not only to combat manipulative behavior on their platforms but also to "proactively" engage with other platforms when identifying potential "cross-platform influence operations."[65]

The Commission has stated that the 2022 Code aims to provide an "appropriate monitoring mechanism" supported by the introduction of KPIs.[66] This reflects a criticism raised by the Multi-Stakeholder Forum on Disinformation when providing feedback on the initial 2018 Code.[67] Preceding the development of the 2018 Code, this forum expressed concerns that the 2018 Code "lacked quantifiable KPIs" as a "mechanism" to measure compliance.[68] Addressing this gap the 2022 Code introduces Qualitative Reporting Elements (QREs) and Service-Level Indicators (SLIs).[69] This is intended to assist in measuring how signatories implement voluntary measures to combat falsehoods.

For example, signatories will identify specific policies adopted "to implement" commitments to "combat manipulative behavior" and provide "metrics to estimate the penetration and impact that e.g. fake/inauthentic accounts have on genuine users."[70] Moreover, signatories that commit to maintaining minimal functionalities of public APIs and ad repositories are encouraged to "detail the availability and features of APIs or other interfaces" and provide "quantitative information on the usage of the APIs such as monthly usage."[71] Further commitments instruct platforms to quantify the engagement of genuine users with "inauthentic" content during election periods.[72] Crucially, the 2022 Code states that platforms should provide information surrounding various QREs and SLIs in a manner that details measures adopted at the member state level. Signatories themselves have discretion to identify relevant criteria under QREs and SLIs in a manner that is "proportionate and appropriate" to their size and range of services offered.[73]

A key shortcoming of the 2018 Code lay in failures of signatories to consistently provide adequate access to information to third-party researchers under the 2018 Code's fourth and fifth pillars.[74] To address this, the 2022 Code endorses proposals from the European Digital Media Observatory (EDMO) to develop a Code of Conduct on Access to Platform Data.[75] The revised Code details new commitments for signatories to provide access to "non-personal and anonymised data" to researchers for disinformation "research purposes."[76]

Relatedly, signatories commit to provide "vetted researchers with access to data necessary to undertake research on disinformation by developing, funding, and cooperating with an independent, third-party body that can vet researchers and research proposals."[77]

The 2022 Code explicitly states that signatories "will align the procedures to vet researchers" as such procedures "may emerge under the framework" of Article 40 DSA.[78] Signatories further commit to cooperate with "an independent, third-party body" that will assist in developing a "governance structure" for accessing data that requires "additional scrutiny."[79] This attempts to not only ensure that adequate access is given to "vetted researchers" in alignment with the DSA but also that any complementary data-sharing framework is compliant with "applicable" EU law such as the GDPR.[80] This development—widely encouraged by academic commentators—reflects an attempt to rectify failures regarding how platforms enable researchers to access crucial data points that shed light on European disinformation campaigns and associated platform actions (Burns 2019).

The 2022 Code—mirroring its 2018 predecessor—references that signatories should not undermine the right to freedom of expression under the ECHR and CFR when operationalizing Code commitments. For example, the revised Code states that signatories should

> strictly respect freedom of expression and include safeguards that prevent their misuse, for example, the censoring of critical, satirical, dissenting, or shocking speech. They should also strictly respect the European Commission's commitment to an open, safe, and reliable Internet.[81]

Furthermore, the 2022 Code retains language from the 2018 Code stating that signatories should be "mindful" of the "delicate balance that must be struck between" the right to freedom of expression and "effective action to limit the spread and impact of otherwise lawful content."[82] Notably, however, the 2022 Code provides no specific clarification on how signatories must achieve the Code's objectives in a manner that ensures protection of ECHR and CFR rights.[83] Further notable is that the 2022 Code appears to expand the 2018 Code's definition of disinformation by highlighting that the notion of disinformation includes "misinformation."[84] Adopting terminology from the Commission's European Democracy Action Plan (EDAP), the 2022 Code defines that disinformation "is considered to include misinformation, disinformation, information influence operations and foreign interference in the information space."[85] This inclusion of misinformation is significant because, as the 2022 Code highlights, the EDAP defines misinformation as "false or misleading content shared without harmful intent though the effects can be still harmful (e.g. when people share false information with friends and family in good faith)."[86] The 2022 Code also states that "impermissible manipulative behavior" may encompass misinformation as defined in this manner.[87]

Conclusion

This chapter has chartered the EU's rapidly evolving legislative initiatives that Union institutions have designed to combat online disinformation. This chapter commenced by tracing the European Commission's development of the 2018 Code. While the 2018 Code can be interpreted as a valuable first step in the EU's anti-disinformation policy, it must also be acknowledged that this instrument has been met with justifiable criticism from academic and legal commentators. As discussed, this is chiefly attributable to the lack of transparency and absence of due process that has characterized the piecemeal implementation of the 2018 Code.

While this chapter has not provided an in-depth analysis of the various human rights issues that arise in connection with the 2018 Code, it has been identified that significant concerns have arisen in connection with the potential for 2018 Code signatories to privately enforce content moderation decisions pertaining to false—but lawful—online content in a manner that could undermine the right to freedom of expression under the ECHR and the CFREU.

Displaying a cognizance of the 2018 Code's limitations, EU institutions have undeniably scaled up EU anti-disinformation legislative efforts under the DSA package. As examined, this is epitomized by the DSA's due-diligence obligations for VLOP/SEs to mitigate systemic risks. These obligations, which have significance in the online disinformation context, epitomize how the DSA extends the range of EU intermediary responsibilities beyond liability for illegal content and toward more proactive obligations to identify and minimize potentially harmful online content. Alongside these key developments, EU institutions have consistently referenced the importance of the right to freedom of expression when issuing guidance on how intermediaries should adopt measures to limit the spread of misleading—but not necessarily illegal—content. Due to the focus of the DSA on tackling harmful content that may often be lawful, it is thus far unclear whether the DSA in practice will promote compatibility with the ECHR and EU Charter standards the 2018 Code expressly references. As this chapter has further identified, the 2022 Code is designed with the dual purpose of rectifying the issues with the 2018 Code and complementing the DSA's due-diligence obligations under Articles 34 and 35.

While these developments in the EU's disinformation policy demonstrate an increased and now-persistent focus on mitigating risks posed to the EU's democratic values posed by disinformation, it remains arguable that the EU's coregulatory approach to disinformation still provides an extensive leeway for intermediaries to restrict misleading content in a manner that may not necessarily be compatible with the right to freedom of expression. It is highly likely that this will be the subject of continued and intensified academic focus on the implementation of the DSA in the disinformation context.

Conflict of Interest Statement

No potential conflict of interest was reported by the author.

Notes

1 On general concepts of self-regulation see Tony Prosser, "Self-regulation, Co-regulation and the Audio-Visual Media Services Directive" (2008) 31(1) *Journal of Consumer Policy* 101; Darren Sinclair, "Self-regulation versus command and control? Beyond false dichotomies" (1997) 19(4) *Law & Policy* 532.

2 This is reflected in academic descriptions of the 2018 Code. For example, Bayer et al. call the 2018 Code "induced self-regulation" while Marsden et al. call the Code an "EU-orchestrated" method of self-regulation. See Judith Bayer and others, "Disinformation and propaganda: Impact on the functioning of the rule of law in the EU and its member states," European Parliament (2019) 105. Chris Marsden and others, "Platform values and democratic elections: How can the law regulate digital disinformation?" (2020) 36 *Computer Law and Security Review* 3.

3 See "The EU code of conduct on countering illegal hate speech online," June 30, 2016; Parliament and the Council, "Proposal for a regulation of the European Parliament and of the Council on preventing the dissemination of terrorist content online," COM (2018) 640.

4 Commission, "Tackling online disinformation: A European approach" (Communication) COM/2018/236 final 1.
5 An API is code that enables two software programs to communicate. Public APIs enable third parties to bulk access machine-readable datasets to assess a range of topics.
6 See Commission, "First results of the EU code of practice against disinformation," January 29, 2019.
7 2018 Code, p. 8.
8 Composed of eighty-three researchers.
9 See 2018 Code.
10 European Parliament, "Digital services: Landmark rules adopted for a safer, open online environment" (2022), www.europarl.europa.eu/news/en/press-room/20220701IPR34364/digital-services-landmark-rules-adopted-for-a-safer-open-online-environment.
11 See explanatory memorandum, DSA.
12 See DSA.
13 See DSA (1).
14 DSA, Arts. 25–33.
15 DSA, Arts. 10–13; also "hosting providers" (Arts. 15–14) and "online platforms" (Arts. 16–24).
16 Set out under Articles 39, 14, and 34 DSA respectively.
17 See DSA Chapter III Art. 34.
18 DSA Chapter III Art. 34(4).
19 DSA Chapter III Art. 34(1).
20 DSA Chapter III.
21 DSA Chapter III Art. 34(2).
22 DSA recital 57.
23 See section 5.3.3.
24 See section 5.2.1.
25 DSA Art. 34(1).
26 Under Art. 2 DSA. On this broader issue see Ronan Ó Fathaigh and others, "The perils of legally defining disinformation" (2021) 10(4) *Internet Policy Review* 2022.
27 DSA Art. 35(1).
28 DSA Art. 35(1).
29 DSA Art. 35(1)c.
30 DSA Art. 34(1).
31 DSA Art. 35(1).
32 DSA Art. 35(2).
33 DSA Art. 35(2).

34 DSA Art. 37.
35 DSA Art. 37(1).
36 DSA Art. 37(4).
37 DSA Art. 35(1)h.
38 DSA Art. 45(1).
39 DSA Art. 45(2).
40 DSA recital 104.
41 DSA Art. 35(1)h.
42 DSA Art. 48(1).
43 DSA Art. 48(1).
44 DSA recital 108.
45 DSA recital 108.
46 DSA Art. 36(1); for a three-month period.
47 DSA Art. 36(1).
48 DSA Art. 36(3)a.
49 Hereinafter '2022 Code.'
50 Hereinafter "the 2022 Code", https://digital-strategy.ec.europa.eu/en/policies/code-practice-disinformation.
51 2022 Code preamble.
52 2022 Code preamble.
53 See Commission, 'Disinformation: Commission welcomes the new stronger and more comprehensive code of practice on disinformation' (June 16, 2022).
54 The 2018 Code is twelve pages with fifteen commitments; the 2022 Code is forty-eight pages with forty-four commitments.
55 "Signatories of the 2022 strengthened code of practice on disinformation" (June 16, 2022), https://digital-strategy.ec.europa.eu/en/library/signatories-2022-strengthened-code-practice-disinformation.
56 Commission, "Guidance on strengthening the code of practice on disinformation" (Communication) COM (2021) 262 final.
57 2022 Code, p. 10.
58 2022 Code, p. 10.
59 2018 Code, p. 9.
60 2018 Code, p. 13.
61 2018 Code, p. 15.
62 2018 Code, p. 17.
63 2018 Code, p. 17.
64 2018 Code, p. 17.
65 2018 Code, p. 17.
66 2022 Code, p. 1.

67 Commission, 'Meeting of the multi-stakeholder forum on disinformation' (July 11, 2018), https://digital-strategy.ec.europa.eu/en/library/meeting-multistakeholder-forumdisinformation.
68 Commission, 'Minutes, fourth meeting of the multi-stakeholder forum on disinformation' (September 17, 2018).
69 QREs are specific policies that platforms implement. SLIs are quantitative details revealing implementations of policies reported under the QRE. Generally, an SLI is a carefully defined quantitative measure of some aspect of the level of service that is provided (including request latency—how long it takes to return response to requests).
70 2022 Code, p. 16.
71 2022 Code, p. 14.
72 2022 Code, p. 13.
73 2022 Code, p. 22.
74 See section 5.2.3.
75 2022 Code, p. 26.
76 2022 Code, p. 28.
77 2022 Code, p. 28.
78 2022 Code, p. 28.
79 2022 Code, p. 28.
80 2022 Code, p. 29.
81 2022 Code preamble.
82 2022 Code preamble, p. 20.
83 2022 Code preamble, p. 4.
84 2022 Code preamble, p. 15.
85 2022 Code preamble.
86 2022 Code preamble.
87 2022 Code preamble, p.15.

References

Angelopoulos, Christina, Annabel Brody, Wouter Hins, Bernt Hugenholtz, Patrick Leerssen, Thomas Margoni, Tarlach McGonagle, Ot van Daalen, and Joris van Hoboken. 2016. "Study of fundamental rights limitations for online enforcement through self-regulation." *Institute for Information Law*. https://eprints.gla.ac.uk/149704/.

Bruns, Axel. 2019. "After the 'APIcalypse': Social media platforms and their fight against critical scholarly research." *Information, Communication & Society* 22 (11): 1544–66.

Colliver, Chloe. 2020. "Cracking the code: An evaluation of the EU code of practice on disinformation." *Institute for Strategic Dialogue*. www.isdglobal.org/isd-publications/cracking-the-code-an-evaluation-of-the-eu-code-of-practice-on-disinformation/.

De Cock Buning, Madeline. 2018. "A multi-dimensional approach to disinformation: Report of the independent high-level group on fake news and online disinformation." Publications Office of the European Union, March 12.

ERGA. 2019. *Report of the activities carried out to assist the European Commission in the intermediate monitoring of the Code of practice on disinformation*. http://erga-online.eu/wp-content/uploads/2019/06/ERGA-2019-06_Report-intermediate-monitoring-Code-of-Practice-on-disinformation.pdf.

ERGA. 2020. *ERGA report on disinformation: Assessment of the implementation of the code of practice*. https://erga-online.eu/wp-content/uploads/2020/05/ERGA-2019-report-published-2020-LQ.pdf.

European Commission. 2018. *2018 code of practice on disinformation*. Publications Office of the European Union. https://digital-strategy.ec.europa.eu/en/library/2018-code-practice-disinformation.

European Commission. 2020. "Assessment of the code of practice on disinformation: Achievements and areas for further improvement." https://digital-strategy.ec.europa.eu/en/library/assessment-code-practice-disinformation-achievements-and-areas-further-improvement.

European Parliament. 2017. *Resolution on online platforms and the digital single market*. Communication (2016): 2276. https://eur-lex.europa.eu/legal-content/EN/TXT/?uri=oj:JOC_2018_331_R_0020.

European Parliament. 2021. "The fight against disinformation and the right to freedom of expression." July 9. www.europarl.europa.eu/thinktank/en/document/IPOL_STU(2021)695445.

European Union. 2018. *A multi-dimensional approach to disinformation: Report of the independent high-level group on fake news and online disinformation*. Publications Office of the European Union. https://op.europa.eu/en/publication-detail/-/publication/6ef4df8b-4cea-11e8-be1d-01aa75ed71a1/language-en.

Gunningham, Neil, and Joseph Rees. 1997. "Industry self-regulation: An institutional perspective." *Law & Policy* 19 (4): 363–414. https://onlinelibrary.wiley.com/doi/abs/10.1111/1467-9930.t01-1-00033.

Helberger, Natali, Jo Pierson, and Thomas Poell. 2018. "Governing online platforms: From contested to cooperative responsibility." *Information Society* 34 (1) 1–14. https://doi.org/10.1080/01972243.2017.1391913.

Hao, Karen. 2019. "Google has released a giant database of deepfakes to help fight deepfakes." *MIT Technology Review*. www.technologyreview.com/2019/09/25/132884/google-has-released-a-giant-database-of-deepfakes-to-help-fight-deepfakes/.

Husovec, Martin, and Irene Laguna. 2023. "Digital Services Act: A short primer." In *Principles of the Digital Services Act*, edited by Martin Husovec and Irene Laguna. Oxford University Press.

Keller, Daphne. 2015. *Empirical evidence of "over-removal" by internet companies under intermediary liability laws*. Stanford Internet Observatory. https://cyberlaw.stanford.edu/blog/2015/10/empirical-evidence-over-removal-internet-companies-under-intermediary-liability-laws.

Keller, Daphne, and Paddy Leerssen. 2020. "Facts and where to find them: Empirical research on internet platforms and content moderation." In *Social media and democracy: The state of the field and prospects for reform*, edited by Nathaniel Persily and Joshua Tucker. SSRC.

Kuczerawy, Aleksandra. 2019. "Fighting online disinformation: Did the EU code of practice forget about freedom of expression?" *Disinformation and Digital Media as a Challenge for Democracy* 6. https://ssrn.com/abstract=3453732.

Leerssen, Paddy. 2023. "Counting the days: What to expect from risk assessments and audits under the DSA—and when?" *DSA Observatory Blog*. https://dsa-observatory.eu/2023/01/30/counting-the-days-what-to-expect-from-risk-assessments-and-aud its-under-the-dsa-and-when/.

McIntyre, T. J. 2013. "Child abuse images and cleanfeeds: Assessing internet blocking systems." In *Research handbook on governance of the internet*, edited by Ian Brown. Edward Elgar.

Monti, Matteo. 2020. "The EU code of practice on disinformation and the risk of the privatisation of censorship." *Democracy and Fake News*. www.taylorfrancis.com/chapters/oa-edit/10.4324/9781003037385-20/eu-code-practice-disinformation-risk-privatisation-censorship-matteo-monti.

Ó Fathaigh, Ronan, Natali Helberger, and Naomi Appelman. 2021. "The perils of legally defining disinformation." *Internet Policy Review* 10 (4): 2022–40. https://policyrev iew.info/articles/analysis/perils-legally-defining-disinformation.

Pollicino, Oreste, and Laura Somaini. 2020. "Online disinformation and freedom of expression in the electoral context: The European and Italian responses." *Misinformation in Referenda*. https://ssrn.com/abstract=3552680.

Social Science One. 2018. "Our Facebook partnership." https://socialscience.one/our-facebook-partnership.

Social Science One. 2019. "Public statement from European Advisory Committee of SS1." https://socialscience.one/blog/public-statement-european-advisory-commit tee-social-science-one.

Vermeulen, Mathias. 2020. "The keys to the kingdom: Overcoming GDPR-concerns to unlock access to platform data for independent researchers." *OSF Preprints* 10. https://doi.org/10.31219/osf.io/vnswz.

9

Prospects of a New Spanish Regulation: Law on Journalism and Media

Ana Azurmendi

Prospects of a New Spanish Regulation on Journalism and Media

The Spanish media landscape is currently experiencing a climate of uncertainty. On September 17, 2024, President Sánchez (from the Socialist Party, PSOE) announced a "Plan for the Democratic Regeneration" of the country, which includes one line of measures addressing media regulation. However, the presentation of the plan did not include an explanation of the announced measures. As a result, it remains unclear how the government's intentions will be translated into legislation.

Nevertheless, the information provided by the government outlines a plan comprising thirty-one measures addressing three areas related to politics: central and regional governments, political parties, and politicians. New obligations for these agents would include accountability at different levels of government with the publication of biannual reports; the celebration of compulsory electoral debates among candidates; the creation of a new prosecution unit countering political corruption; and the reform of the law on "political parties" (Ley Orgánica 6/2022, de "Partidos Políticos"), which adds the obligation to publish the financial status of every politician (Cué 2024).

In the context of journalism and media, the measures are related to three core areas: transparency, disinformation, and the protection of politicians' reputation. A Register of Media will be established, providing information on media owners and advertisers. This will facilitate greater transparency while limiting the state's advertising. Additionally, a specific parliamentary committee will be created with the aim of combating disinformation. In terms of the amendment of legislation, the first works will focus on Law 19/2013 on "Transparency, Access to Information and Good Governance," together with Law 2/1984 on the "Right to Reply" and Law 3/2018 on "Personal Data Protection and Digital Rights," amendments that will be designed to enhance the accuracy of news reporting.

The announced legislative change would also regulate the confidentiality of sources, which is currently protected by a constitutional reference in Article 20. However, in cases of attempts to damage the reputation of politicians in public opinion, this right would be restricted.

A significant number of newspapers, radio stations, commercial television channels, representatives of the journalistic profession and individual journalists have spoken out against the government's plan, arguing that it is an attempt to stifle criticism. Given the fragility of Sanchez's coalition government, there is a reasonable chance that the plan will not become law.

Mapping the Present Legislative and Social Context Regarding Media

Although the abovementioned government plan represents a transitional period for the Spanish regulation of journalism and the media, this chapter will explain the main aspects of the present regulation.

Indeed, one of the central characteristics of the Spanish media law system is the attention given to journalism as a relevant actor of freedom of expression for public affairs. This explains why specific professional rights like the clause of conscience and the confidentiality of sources are considered essential, not only for journalists but also in terms of the effectiveness of freedom of expression in society. Something that requires journalists and the media to be able to do their jobs properly . The duty of transparency helps bo th journalists and citizens exercise control over institutions.

Meanwhile, for extra limitations on freedom of expression made by journalists, the Spanish regulation contemplates the right to reply along with the protection of reputation and privacy.

Disruptive phenomena such as disinformation and hate speech also receive attention under the current regulatory framework. However, both their impact on the quality of democracy and the relevance of digital platforms for its extension require new measures to be considered.

One of the influential aspects that must be taken into account is the impact of European regulation on the media in the Spanish legal system. Notable examples of this influence include action plans to combat disinformation and hate speech, as well as the regulation of digital platforms.

Apart from these regulatory considerations, Vara and Arrese (2024, 143–4) highlight that "Spain's media landscape faces several critical challenges, including public disinterest, mistrust, polarization, misinformation, fragile revenue models, and politicized public media." The authors identify four current trends related to media and democracy in the country. Firstly, a notable decline in media consumption. Secondly, an increase in mistrust in the news, "influenced by citizens' perception that media coverage is conditioned by its political and economic interests." The third trend, according to Vara and Arrese (2024), is the deep polarization of the media outlets. In the sense that "media outlets tend to mirror societal ideological divides, thus fostering a discourse that escalates division, rather than encouraging understanding or unity" (Vara and Arrese 2024, 144). The fourth trend is the growing popularity of social media. In their analysis, Vara and Arrese (2024) cite the *Digital News Report España 2023* (Vara et al. 2024) to illustrate the changing patterns of news consumption. They observe that while television remains the primary medium for news in Spain (56 percent), the percentage of internet users checking news on social networks is on the rise. The data indicates that 39 percent of the audience interacts with social networks for news, with platforms such as Facebook (30 percent) and WhatsApp (27 percent) being the most utilized, while Instagram (21 percent), YouTube (21 percent), and Twitter (18 percent) are witnessing an expansion of their informational reach (Vara and Arrese 2024, 144).

Regulation is certainly not the only way to guarantee freedom of expression, the independence of journalists, or to combat disinformation and hate speech. Nevertheless, it helps public communication to fulfill its expectations in a democratic society. Since communication builds social life, we are more aware of its functions and also of its effects when there are striking failures from the point of view of media responsibility. In this sense, disinformation, hate speech, and the radicalization of messages are currently some of the most worrying issues because they undermine civic coexistence. It is therefore understandable that public communication requires some minimum legal requirements in order to avoid these serious dangers.

Constitutional Protection of the Press

Special Attention to Journalism

The constitutional tradition on freedom of expression adheres to a liberal narrative, which regards this right as a fundamental freedom that should be protected from governmental interference. Nevertheless, the influence of the doctrine of human rights is of even greater relevance through the UN Universal Declaration of Human Rights (1948) and the European Convention on Human Rights (1950).

In any case, as has been said, journalism receives special attention in the Spanish constitutional text. In fact, it recognizes freedom of expression in Article 20, which includes a reference to the interaction between journalism and citizens when the text mentions the right to receive and to disseminate truthful information:

> Article 20.1 a) and d) (these rights) "are recognized and protected: the right to freely express and spread thoughts, ideas and opinions through words, in writing or by any other means of reproduction (… and) the right to freely communicate or receive truthful information by any means of dissemination whatsoever. The law shall regulate the right to the clause of conscience and professional secrecy in the exercise of these freedoms."

The last words on the rights to the clause of conscience and the confidentiality of sources reinforce the idea that journalism is at the center of the constitutional recognition of freedom of expression.

One aspect that draws attention in this context is the use of the adjective "truthful" (or "accurate," but the Spanish term "veraz" corresponds better to "truthful") added to the term "information." This intent of precision by the constitution has an important consequence to journalists. Thanks to the Spanish Constitutional Court, through years of jurisprudence, there is a distinction between a broad freedom of expression, on the one hand, and a specific form of freedom of expression linked to journalism, on the other.

The rationale expressed in many of its sentences is:

> In the Constitution, freedom of expression has the object of thoughts, ideas and opinions, a wide concept in which must be included beliefs and judgments too. Instead of that, (the right to information is) the right to freely communicate and to receive accurate information of facts, or, maybe more restrictively, about facts

> which can be considered publishable as news. (Legal argument 5, Sentence of the Constitutional Court 6/1988)

This argumentation is not only the result of an effort to differentiate rights in relation to certain communicative actions, but also the setting of a red line that a journalist cannot trespass, which is the line of accuracy/inaccuracy in the telling of a news story. At the same time, this requirement of accuracy, once present in a journalistic piece, becomes the main legal reason for the protection of the journalist in the face of any judicial search.

> The distinction between thoughts, ideas and opinions on the one hand and informative communication of facts on the other ... has a decisive importance at the time of setting the legitimacy in the exercise of these rights, therefore, meanwhile facts are subject of proof, thoughts, ideas, opinions and judgments are not subject to a demonstration of their exactitude, just because of their abstract nature, and that makes that it was not required the prove for truth or for having applied proper diligence in its inquiry ... consequently, freedom of expression is wider than the right of information. (Legal argument 2, Sentence of the Constitutional Court 107/1988)

This interpretation has been reinforced not only by the constitutional court's resolutions up to the present day but also by those of the Supreme Court and regional courts. However, the concepts of freedom of expression and the right to information are not entirely distinct, as they encompass several similar aspects. Nevertheless, a key distinction lies in the variety of forms of expression that fall under the umbrella of freedom of expression, which is not limited to journalism. The broad concept of freedom of expression involves a multitude of forms, including paintings, theatrical arts, films, poetry, and public religious celebrations, such as the Easter week parades. In contrast, the right to information specifically refers to journalistic facts and opinions.

Freedom of Expression and an Implicit Reference to Disinformation

Article 20 of the Spanish Constitution focuses on professional journalists when it deals with freedom of expression; nevertheless, it attributes to them the role of empowering citizens. In the sense that by exercising freedom of expression and the right to information in a responsible and ethical manner, journalists facilitate the exercise of these rights by citizens.

This does not constitute an exact equivalent to the role of a “watchdog of the democratic system,” as previously defined by the European Court of Human Rights (Azurmendi and Llorens 2018, 49). Instead, the Spanish Constitutional Court defends some kind of social aspect of freedom of expression, which is primarily reliant on the actions of journalists.

> The possibility of the free exercise of the fundamental rights of freedom of expression and information guarantees the formation and existence of free public opinion, because, given (that the possibility of the free exercise of rights) is a prior and necessary condition for the exercise of other rights inherent to a dynamic democratic system, it becomes, at the same time, one of the pillars of a free and democratic society. (Supreme Court Decision Sentence of the Constitutional Court 52/2002, Legal Argument 4, Supreme Court Decision Sentence of the Constitutional Court 159/1986, Legal Argument 6; 21/2000, Legal Argument 4)

Conversely, a journalist is primarily defined as an individual who facilitates the exercise of citizens’ rights to information and freedom of expression. Professional dedication to this role places journalism and, consequently, journalists in a more profound relationship with these fundamental rights and with citizens. One of the most significant indicators of the special position of the journalistic profession is the conceptual alignment between the accuracy of the news, as enshrined in Article 20 of the Constitution, and the requirement that news research, its elaboration as a news report, and its dissemination be carried out with “professional diligence,” as frequently referenced in constitutional court jurisprudence. This “professional diligence” is exclusively associated with journalists.

> The requirement of truth must be understood to be fulfilled in these cases, provided that, prior to circulation of the news, the journalist has performed the activity of investigation of the facts of public interest, and the investigation has been performed with the level of diligence required of a journalist. (Legal Argument 3, Supreme Court Decision Sentence of the Constitutional Court 1/2005, Supreme Court Decision Sentence of the Constitutional Court 69/2006, and Supreme Court Decision Sentence of the Constitutional Court 68/2008)

The Spanish Constitution does not refer to social media, nor to the phenomenon of disinformation, due to the period of time of its publication, 1978. However, it offers relevant principles that can serve in both cases, such as the need to respect the rights of others when exercising freedom of expression and information, along with the requirement of diligent work as a journalist to guarantee the accuracy of news. Therefore, even if new sources of news have emerged, as in the case of social media, "traditional journalism with its focus on verification and accuracy, is as important as ever, even if it too sometimes promotes misinformation and disinformation" (Soares and Recuero 2021).

Rights of Journalists, Clause of Conscience, and Confidentiality of Sources

In the same Article 20 of the Constitution—which recognizes freedom of expression—it is the reference to two milestone rights that guarantee the independence of journalists: the clause of conscience, and the confidentiality of sources. Although the mention of these rights consists solely of a mandate to the regulators to publish a law on these rights, the fact that they are included in the constitutional text is important. So far, only Law 2/1997 on "the clause of conscience" has been issued. Meanwhile, the confidentiality of sources is still awaiting its legislative development. In contrast to the Spanish Constitution's emphasis on these journalistic principles, there are not many cases in the courts that refer to these rights in the jurisdictional instances.

In essence, the clause of conscience entails two fundamental conditions: first, the journalist in question is an employee; and second, they resign from their position within the company, given that performing the duties of their role gives rise to a conflict of conscience. However, Law 2/1997 introduced the possibility of acting according to one's conscience without having to resign. This may be a more realistic option, given the difficulties that journalists encounter in relation to their professional rights. The law may offer a solution to the dilemma of resigning over a labor conflict between the company and the journalist. However, the objection of conscience provides a more nuanced approach to navigating daily ethical conflicts.

Based on this right, journalists have the prerogative to resign from their positions in any media outlet when there is a change in its ideology, or in its informative standards, or even when there is a structural transformation in the company that affects the functions of journalists. This resignation has to be accompanied by an economic compensation made by the company, similar to the amount of money offered in case of firing.

The objection of conscience is applicable in many other everyday circumstances that motivate the journalist to decline involvement in the preparation of information when it conflicts with the ethical principles of journalism. There is no compensation but the possibility of being free of intervention in that news.

Regarding the confidentiality of sources, Article 20 of the Spanish Constitution of 1978 states very shortly that in the future there will be a law about it. Nevertheless, the plan of President Sánchez includes the regulation of the limits of journalistic secrecy (or journalist's privilege) in combination with the Law of "Official Secrets" of 1978.

Investigative journalism depends on this right. In many cases, there is no way to obtain essential information of public interest. Sources need anonymity and the guarantee that if a judicial or law enforcement authority asks to identify a news source, the journalist will keep their anonymity, even if there is a reasonable risk that they will be held in contempt of court.

In most countries, the confidentiality of sources is generally recognized. In fact, the European Court of Human Rights interprets this journalistic principle as part of the content of freedom of expression (for instance, *Sanoma Uitgevers BV v. Netherlands* 2000; *Nordisk Film & TVA/S v. Denmark* 2008; *Financial Times, The Guardian, The Times and The Independent v. UK* 2009; *Ressiot and others v. France* 2012; *Big Brother Watch and others v. UK* 2018, among others). Although countries like the United States, France, Mexico, or Belgium have specific laws, usually named "shield laws," these laws are more concrete but also at the same time more rigid, considering the exception of anonymity of sources. For example, these include the limit of the documents that could imply secrecy of the state if that content could contain personal data.

The fact is that if the confidentiality of sources is limited to that extent, neither Wikileaks nor the Snowden revelations, nor the truth about the killing of a Brazilian citizen in the London tube due to confusion of the British police, nor much other relevant information would have been known.

Citizenship Rights: Right to Reply and Access to Public Information

Among the measures included in the "Plan for the Regeneration of Democracy" of President Sánchez, some are directly addressed to citizens as participatory agents of democracy, such as the case of the announced changes to the right to reply, which invites individuals to react in media and digital platforms to defend their rights; and access to public information, which will be the issue of a new law.

New Developments in the Right to Reply: The Duty of the Influencers

The current government is aware that the right to reply needs to be updated due to the changes in the media, society, and communication technologies. Some of the proposed innovations concern the necessary process of replying to a publication. Others consist of the inclusion of new actors who have the duty to publish the reply, such as social media influencers. As proposed by the Ministry of the Presidency in its announcement of December 17, 2024, the new law proposal considers as influencers those digital users with more than 100,000 followers on one platform, or with a total of 200,000 in different social media. In addition, the government is asking platforms to offer an easy way for citizens to reply.

The novelty in this case is the requirement for media and social media to include a notice on the site of inaccurate information, saying that this precise news has been rectified, plus the obligation to link both the original information and the reply. Ultimately, these new dispositions push to move away from the current practice of media and social media of publishing multiple versions of information, which is the result of the existing law of the right to reply, toward the dissemination of a more rigorous and accurate information. From this point of view, changes in the current law could also help in the combat against disinformation.

The Right to Access to Public Information

Increasing transparency is a central aim within the "Plan for the Regeneration of Democracy," which includes three areas of access: government, parliament, and journalism. Despite its relevance within the plan, there is no new measure on it yet.

As mentioned before, according to the governmental announcement, transparency in journalism focuses on the specific activities of media companies, including their shareholders, sources of funding, and other relevant details. The present legislative framework concerning transparency is set forth in Law

19/2013 on "Transparency, Access to Information and Good Governance." This legislation is based on the fundamental principle that

> transparency, access to public information and standards for good governance shall be the cornerstones of any political action. Only when the actions of public decision-makers are scrutinized, when citizens can know how the decisions that affect them are made, how public funds are handled or which criteria underlie the actions undertaken by our public institutions, we will be witnessing the start of a process in which public authorities begin to answer the questions of a critical, demanding society that requires participation in public power. (Preamble to the Law)

On the one hand, this regulation increases the transparency of public activities, as it establishes obligations for all public bodies in this regard. On the other hand, it guarantees the right of access to information in accordance with the Spanish Constitution of 1978, which stipulates this in Article 105b.

In addition, it establishes the legal obligation to provide a "transparency portal" in order to offer citizens the most relevant and up-to-date data on the public administration in office (Article 7). There are some limitations, such as national security, defense, international relations, public security, and criminal prevention and investigation, among others.

Hate Speech

In light of the growing number of hate messages on social media (Lopes Silva et al. 2019, 470–1), a variety of strategies have been employed to address this phenomenon among the general public. One of the most accepted policy measures is the promotion of self-regulation. Indeed, major technology companies, including Google (Google Search and YouTube), Twitter, and Facebook, have responded to this trend by implementing new moderation protocols in 2020.

European institutions have also been active in promoting codes of conduct, such as the 2016 European Union Code of Conduct on "Countering Illegal Hate Speech Online," which was agreed upon by the European Commission and the aforementioned platforms.

The underlying causes and reasons for online hate speech remain unclear. However, there is a consensus on the factors that facilitate it, particularly the false sense of anonymity on the internet, the ability to create fictitious ad hoc identities and use them to insult, harass, and threaten others, and the lack of social contact with the target audience (Tontodimamma et al. 2021, 157–8). From this perspective, legal initiatives are regarded as supplementary measures to the comprehensive strategy against hate speech, which encompasses awareness-raising and prevention activities, as well as support for self-regulation (European Commission against Racism and Intolerance ECRI 2015, 10).

The reform of the Spanish Criminal Code by means of Organic Law 1/2015 transposed the 2008 Council Framework Decision on "Combating certain forms and expressions of racism and xenophobia by means of criminal law" (2008/913/JHA). As it happens in most European countries, it is an implementation of measures protecting some groups of the population against this specific violence (Azurmendi 2023). Principles supporting this regulation have to do with the principles of human dignity (Fiscalía General del Estado 2019) and personal identity attributes such as race, ideology or religion, ethnic origin, sexual orientation, gender identity, disability, and, in general, any distinguishing community attributes of identity. This also includes attributes of social exclusion and poverty when the members of these groups are targeted with aggression for having any of these identity attributes.

Actions that Promote a Climate of Violence, Hostility, and Hatred

The Spanish Criminal Code distinguishes between two forms of behavior. In the first set, the actions described have the potential to create a climate of violence, hostility, and hatred against certain groups or individuals. The second form of behavior is motivated by discrimination. However, this motivation does not imply the existence of specific intent, as stated by the Public Prosecutor's Office (Fiscalía General del Estado 2019).

Actions that promote a climate of violence, hostility, or hatred against certain groups or individuals include, on the one hand, actions that incite hatred or violence against these groups or individuals on racist or anti-Semitic grounds or for reasons related to their ideology, religion, ethnic origin, or membership of other minority groups and, on the other hand, actions that deny or glorify crimes of genocide or crimes against humanity.

Moreover, it is considered to include conducts connected with the "glorification of terrorism" along with the "humiliation of victims" (Labiano et al. 2023). Cases of this kind of hate speech have caused notable controversy in Spanish public opinion, in the media, and especially in social media. In particular, the Valtonyc and Hasel cases are relevant here. Both artists were punished with prison because of their songs in 2018 and 2021, respectively. Supporters argued that their lyrics and tweets were protected by freedom of expression, even though they were offensive and provocative. However, critics and Spanish courts found them guilty of hate speech, glorification of terrorism, and incitement to violence (Labiano et al. 2023).

Actions Motivated by Discriminating against the Members of Certain Groups

The second group of actions, whose common motivation is the discrimination of others for belonging to a minority group, includes acts that humiliate or denigrate those groups or their members and the justification of offenses committed against them. These conducts can incite hatred or hostility and promote a climate of violence, which calls for more severe punishment.

Moreover, the implementation of measures will be more challenging in cases involving criminal organizations, given that the regulation of criminal liability of corporate bodies is also included in the legislation.

The Limits of Freedom of Expression: Reputation and Privacy

Reputation

Spanish law has a long tradition of protection of the right to reputation. Until 1982, the Criminal Code (*Código Penal*) was the only legal provision that addressed defamation. Law 1/1982 on "Civil Protection of the Right to Reputation, Privacy and One's Own Image" (Ley Orgánica 1/1982, de Protección Civil del Derecho al Honor, a la Intimidad personal y familiar y a la propia Imagen) enacted civil protection of this right.

From the criminal law perspective, there are two main acts against the reputation of one individual: to attribute an offense falsely (orally—slander; in writing or in the press, etc.—libel), which constitutes the crime of defamation, "calumnia" in the Spanish Criminal Code; and to insult somebody in an offensive way, which constitutes a differentiate crime, named "injuria" in Spanish—injury or insult. This division may seem somewhat vague, but the second form involves falsely attributing acts that are not crimes but simply bad actions.

The major difference between defamation and injury or insult in the legal process is that in the case of defamation, criminal liability disappears if the accusation proves to be true. Because, for instance, news about political corruption would be very difficult to publish if the politicians involved could sue at any time, asking for damages, or appealing repeatedly, regardless of whether the news was true. This would have a chilling effect on journalists. From a different perspective, the need to prove this kind of information promotes the responsibility of journalists. Because many times they must keep the scope without publishing it until they obtain the evidence to demonstrate its accuracy.

At the same time, the Spanish Criminal Code adds some circumstances that can increase liability in cases of defamation: the involvement of the media and committing defamation for a price, award, or promise.

The penalties corresponding to these conducts are severe: if defamation is committed through the media, two years of imprisonment or fines; if a price, award, or promise is involved, special suspension from working as a journalist for six months to two years.

However, there are some elements that modify the initial punishment related to defamation: if a defendant admits this action before the judge, the possibility of imprisonment or suspension is cancelled; at the same time, the forgiveness of a claimant cancels any criminal liability. This is a direct encouragement of prejudicial agreements in cases of defamation, a usual practice when the media are involved in conflicts of this characteristics.

As mentioned above, Law 1/1982 on "Civil Protection of the Right to Reputation, Privacy and One's Own Image" is the main source for tort actions or civil protection of these human rights. With subtle differences, both criminal and civil regulations consider the same illicit conducts against reputation.

Privacy

The right to privacy is a fundamental human right, rooted in the inherent dignity of the individual. In the sense that each person has the right to choose which parts of their personal life to share with others and which to keep private. It's about having control over one's information and deciding what to share and with whom . . . In any case, consent is the determining factor in establishing the legal status of the acts enumerated by the law as invasions of privacy.

Under Spanish legislation, the value of privacy is receiving heightened protection. The initial regulation to protect privacy was the 1982 Law on "Civil

Protection of the Right to Honor, Privacy, and One's Own Image." The 1995 edition of the Criminal Code subsequently incorporated criminal acts against privacy. Similarly, the Constitution of 1978 addressed privacy concerns by establishing fundamental protections for human rights, which occasionally delineate the boundaries of freedom of expression.

The Criminal Code safeguards privacy in two distinct ways: firstly, in general terms, and secondly, in relation to specified matters arising from the use of digital technology. In general, it provides for punishment for the acts of appropriation of documents, letters, messages, personal documents, and sound and video recordings, as well as the use of technical elements to obtain them when the aim of doing so is to trespass upon another's privacy. In specific matters related to digital technology, the Criminal Code delineates the criminal conduct that may be perpetrated with the use of computers, including but not limited to the following: accessing, appropriating, utilizing, and modifying the personal data stored in databases; transferring, disseminating, and disclosing said data; and any other actions that may result in the alteration, misuse, or dissemination of personal data.

Conversely, privacy, together with reputation and personal image, is protected by the law of damages. Law 1/1982 is focused on the activity of journalism, photojournalism, and paparazzi, which often trespass on the privacy of celebrities. It also lists illicit behaviors similar to those included in the Criminal Code with regard to privacy and reputation. In consequence, the question arises as to the consistency of providing two legal avenues for the protection of these rights—namely, criminal and civil law. It is appropriate to question the rationale behind maintaining two distinct legal frameworks that address similar forms of illicit conduct.

It is accurate to conclude that civil law can also result in the effect of a "gag law" through the application of damage compensation. Nevertheless, the Spanish Law of Civil Procedures offers some degree of protection for journalists in the event that a sentence related to freedom of expression is appealed. In such cases, the execution of the sentence may be delayed.

However, there will always be a possibility of misleading use of law—both criminal and civil—with the aim of silencing particular information and, in some cases, the journalist's self-censorship. Consequently, in addition to the implementation of appropriate legislation, it is essential to foster a context of democratic culture that provides a social and political environment that genuinely supports the exercise of human rights. The establishment of this context is not merely a matter of publishing a list of laws and establishing media control bodies.

Conclusions

In Spain, the recent political initiative for a new regulatory framework for media and digital platforms has created an atmosphere of uncertainty about freedom of expression of journalists and media.

Nevertheless, the current regulation related to freedom of expression (from the right to reply to privacy) in many cases does not include any reference to social media and its challenges concerning individual rights. Therefore, there is a true need to update the regulatory system.

The fact that many journalists and editors of media (traditional and online) are speaking out against the measures proposed by the Spanish government in September 2024 as a "Plan for the Regeneration of Democracy" obliges citizens to be cautious about the government initiative. It is necessary to check for oneself whether this is a plan to improve responsible journalism or, on the contrary, an attempt to silence criticism by journalists.

Reputation and privacy receive double legal protection by the criminal law and the tort—or damages—regulation. It seems paradoxical that the same behaviors could correspond to different results: imprisonment under criminal law and just an indication for damages under civil law. It depends on the procedure chosen by the claimant. On the other hand, the measure of imprisonment for actions against reputation appears disproportionate. Actions like hate speech in social media or the disclosure of personal data for lucrative purposes are difficult to address from this perspective. The cases of the Spanish rappers Valtonyc and Hasél show how controversial imprisonment can be when the illegal actions consist of abuse of freedom of expression.

Acknowledgment

The research was supported by Resilient Media for Democracy in the Digital Age (ReMeD), an international multidisciplinary project supported by the European Union's Horizon Europe Research and Innovation Programme,

HORIZON-CL2-2022-DEMOCRACY-01-06: "Media for Democracy—Democratic Media," under grant agreement no. 101094742.

Conflict of Interest Statement

No potential conflict of interest was reported by the authors.

References

Azurmendi, Ana. 2023. "Freedom of expression in social media and legal efforts against hate speech." In *Comments, hate speech, disinformation, and public communication regulation*, edited by Josip Popovac. Agency for Electronic Media.

Azurmendi, Ana, and Carles Llorens. 2018. *Media law in Spain*. Wolters Kluwer.

Council of Europe. 2015. *European Commission against racism and intolerance (ECRI) general policy recommendation N°15 on combating hate speech*. www.coe.int/en/web/european-commission-against-racism-and- intolerance/ recommendation-no.15.

Cué, Carlos E. 2024. "Así queda el plan de regeneración democrática: más control sobre los cargos públicos y límites a la publicidad institucional en los medios." El País. https://elpais.com/expres/2024-09-18/asi-queda-el-plan-de-regeneracion-democratica-mas-control-sobre-los-cargos-publicos-y-limites-a-la-publicidad-institucional-en-los-medios.html.

European Commission. 2016. *The European Union code of conduct on "countering illegal hate speech online."*

European Union. 2008. *Council framework decision 2008/913/JHA, of 28 November 2008, on "combating certain forms and expressions of racism and xenophobia by means of criminal law."* https://eur-lex.europa.eu/legal-content/EN/TXT/HTML/?uri=CELEX:32008F0913&from=ES.

Fiscalía General del Estado. 2019. *Circular 7/2019, de 14 de mayo, de la Fiscalía General del Estado, sobre pautas para interpretar los delitos de odio tipificados en el artículo 510 del Código Penal.*

Labiano, Roncesvalles, Ana Azurmendi, and María-Fernanda Novoa-Jaso. 2023. "The constructive role of the media in hate speech controversies: The Valtònyc and Hasél cases." *Journalism Practice* 18 (2). https://doi.org/10.1080/17512786.2023.2242818.

Lopes Silva, Luis Rogerio, Rodrigo Eduardo Botelho-Francisco, Alison Augusto de Oliveira, and Vinicius Ramos Pontes. 2019. "La gestión del discurso de odio en las plataformas de redes sociales digitales: un comparativo entre Facebook, Youtube y Twitter." *Revista Ibero-Americana de Ciencia d'Informacao* 12 (2): 470492. https://doi.org/10.26512/rici.v12.n2.2019.22025.

Soares, Felipe, and Raquel Recuero. 2021. "How the mainstream media help to spread disinformation about COVID-19." *M/C Journal* 24 (1). https://doi.org/10.5204/mcj.2735.

Tontodimamma, Alice, Eugenia Nissi, Annalina Sarra, and Lara Fontanella. 2021. "Thirty years of research into hate speech: Topics of interest and their evolution." *Scientometrics* 126: 157–79. https://doi.org/10.1007/s11192-020-03737-6.

Vara, Alfonso, and Ángel Arrese. 2024. "Spain. A fast-changing media landscape." In *Media compass. A companion to international media landscapes*, edited by Aljosha Karim Schapals and Christian Pentzold. Wiley-Blackwell.

Vara, Alfonso, María Fernanda Novoa-Jaso, Aurken Sierra, and Roncesvalles Labiano Roncesvalles. 2024. "Digital news report Spain 2023." In *Digital news report*, edited by Reuters Institute for the Study of Journalism. University of Oxford. www.unav.edu/web/digital-news-report.

Part 4

Current Challenges of the European Digital Environment in Relation to Disinformation

10

Hate Speech and Hate Crime in European Digital Environment: Problems, Documented Effects, and Coping Mechanisms

Kateřina Turková

Hate Speech and Hate Crime: Current State

Despite hate having been present all around from the beginning of human history, it has been repetitively awakened or strengthened in situations of danger, or threat, or times, or locations where socioeconomic inequality was elevated (Denti and Faggian 2021; Kaakinen et al. 2018; Sternberg and Sternberg 2008). The topic of online hate speech and hate crime came into the research spotlight at the beginning of the twenty-first century, and after a period of consolidation in the second decade, it has become tempting again in recent years (Schäfer et al. 2024; Tontodimamma et al. 2021; Vandebosch and Rothmund 2024).

Online hate speech and hate crime can be understood from various aspects, while hate crime can contain hate speech. More specifically, online hate speech may be a form of online hate crime (Breazu and Machin 2023; Dreißigacker 2024). Online hate speech is extremely harmful; hence it contains negative stereotypes and direct or indirect expressions of violence (Caiani et al. 2021; Schäfer et al. 2024). This is even more dangerous in times of crisis, such as the COVID-19 pandemic or still-ongoing military conflict in Ukraine (Breazu and Machin 2023; Schulz-Tomančok and Woschnagg 2024). In addition, various social media platforms and channels provide countless options for accommodating and prompt sharing of hateful messages worldwide (Caiani et al. 2021; Matamoros-Fernández and Farkas 2021).

People are involuntarily exposed to hateful content despite they not actively searching for it (Reichelmann et al. 2020). It is then evident that society should counteract, but the question stands as to whether (and which) legal and nonlegal measures should be applied (Gagliardone et al. 2015). This chapter focuses on the two interconnected phenomena that relate to hate—hate speech and hate crime—in the European digital environment. Legislative instruments and legislature dealing with the European digital environment have evolved on national and international levels (Peršak 2022; Windisch et al. 2022). However, the analyses of the current state proved that despite the progress being made, the counteracting schemes against online hate crime and hate speech are not yet fully developed, and in some cases do not correspond with the regulation of those issues offline (Tontodimamma et al. 2021; Vergani et al. 2024).

Contrary to the already mentioned negatives, including not ideal current state and harmful effects, that are further explained in the first part of this chapter, the second part of the text is devoted to the coping mechanisms with hate speech and hate crime that were detected by research conducted in various European countries (e.g., Kuřík et al. 2024; Oehmer-Pedrazzi and Pedrazzi 2024). The author of this chapter argues that further research and expert attention dedicated to the phenomena can help to successfully prevent and counteract hate speech and hate crime in the European digital environment.

The Operationalization Problem

When the topic of hate speech and hate crime comes into the conversation, various ambiguities frequently complicate the dialogue. The first issue connected to online hate speech and hate crime prevention is related to understanding both terms. The operationalization of those concepts in countries around the world differs, while it is affected by both the historical consequences and the cultural and geographical background (Vergani et al 2024; Windisch et al. 2022).

The origin of the definitions varies; hence "hate crime definitions and measurement tools are more likely to originate from Anglophonic countries, especially the USA, but hate speech definitions and measurement tools are more likely to originate from continental Europe" (Vergani et al. 2024, 2). In the United States, the avoidance of governmental censorship of hate speech is crucial, while in the European environment, the concerns primarily touch on the functioning of speech control (Kohl 2022). The overarching core element of hate speech and hate crime reflected in the majority of definitions is the overt or covert intention to harm (Baider 2022; Cedena-de-Lucas 2024).

Despite the European Union's efforts to harmonize legislation in member states, differences still remain (Oehmer-Pedrazzi and Pedrazzi 2024; Peršak 2022; Yar and Steinmentz 2019). For example, German anti-discrimination legislation takes into account gender and sexual orientation, whereas it is not particularly highlighted in the Czech legislature (Gorenc 2022; Kuřík et al. 2024; Kohl 2022). While talking about the approach to sexual orientation, only a minority of EU member states criminalize hate speech targeted to that issue in relation to age (Hietanen and Eddebo 2023). Some countries, such as France and Germany, have already passed laws covering online hate speech (Badouard 2022; De Blasio and Selva 2021), while other states have not acted yet. These discrepancies affect not only the public view but also criminal liability for online hate crime in various European countries, no matter whether they are EU member states or not.

In addition, the distinction of whether the textual and visual content is or is not hateful, degrading, or discriminatory may be disputable and depends on various consequences (Baider 2022; Oehmer-Pedrazzi and Pedrazzi 2024; Yar and Steinmentz 2019). The creation of a "precise, universal, operable definition of online hate speech that is generally accepted by multiple stakeholders—scholars and practitioners, who may come from different, unrelated fields" (Papcunová et al. 2023, 2828) happens to be nearly impossible.

The lack of clarity in definitions of hate speech was also identified by the already published research (Vergani et al. 2024; Yar and Steinmentz 2019), although numerous lists of hate speech indicators and their rationales were compiled. The hate speech indicators usually consist of sexist language, attacking, humiliating minorities and vulnerable individuals, denial of human rights, negative stereotyping, misinterpretation or manipulation of facts, and vulgar or derogatory language (Bayer 2021; Hietanen and Eddebo 2023; Papcunová et al. 2023). The European Union as the key authority in the European digital environment does not define online hate speech specifically, but describes these acts as "hate speech that occurs using information and communication technology" (Hawdon et al. 2024, 817).

Online hate speech is generally discussed from three different perspectives: legal, technological, and social. Whereas the legal definition characterizes online hate speech as "any form of web-based communication that disparages a person or a group on the basis of 'protected' characteristics such as race, ethnicity, gender, sexual orientation or religion" (Vandebosch and Rothmund 2024, 371), the technological approach focuses on the development and implementation of automatic systems detecting online hate, while the strictness of the term itself varies (Tontodimamma et al. 2021; Ullmann and Tomalin 2020). The distinction between purely negative and hateful content, or even prohibited hateful content, causes difficulties (Cinelli et al. 2021; Hietanen and Eddebo 2023).

The social perspective explores the issue by various methods and suggests alternative solutions to the legal norms, such as systemic changes and counter-speech (Vandebosch and Rothmund 2024; Schäfer 2024). These initiatives can be the driving force behind change, as this chapter documents.

The Problem of Localization

For the purpose of this chapter, the author follows the broader approach to conceptualization and understands the terms online hate and online crime universally, as web-based hate (Vandebosch and Rothmund 2024). Nevertheless, it is essential to sum up where the hateful content occurs (Reichelmann et al. 2020). As this substantially differs across the world, this overview is limited solely to the European digital environment, where the percentage of people who witness online hate speech significantly exceeds the ratio in North America (Cedena-de-Lucas 2024; Denti and Faggian 2021; Hawdon et al. 2024). Despite the common belief that online hate and online crime are carried out by organized groups, the current research shows that this is often conducted by individuals as well (Denti and Faggian 2021).

Internet forums happened to be places where people voice their negative stands and disagreements; and logically, hate speech was also located there (Cinelli et al. 2021; Hietanen and Eddebo 2023). The classic internet forums are still sites where the discussants meet; hence emotional and hateful messages occur especially under the news articles covering controversial and polarizing topics, such as climate change (Schulz-Tomančok and Woschnagg 2024).

In the recent era, social media have become the leading platform for public debate and, due to that, also the environment where online hate speech and hate crime cumulate (Badouard 2022; Dubois and Reepschlager 2024; Gorenc 2022). According to a multinational online survey realized in 2018, Facebook apparently hosted the highest percentage of hateful messages; hence around 55 percent of Polish, over 40 percent of Finnish and French, and slightly under 40 percent of Spanish and British respondents claimed that they saw online hate speech there. Interestingly, a similar percentage of Spanish participants (under 40 percent) viewed hateful content on Instagram, which differed from the results in other countries (Reichelmann et al. 2020).

Due to their noncentralistic structure, social media have the power to reshape the way how hate is articulated (Dubois and Reepschlager 2024; Gorenc 2022), while the character of the platform itself plays an essential role. For example, the community character of Reddit enables the rise of toxic subcultures encouraging the expression of hateful opinions (Matamoros-Fernández and Farkas 2021). Alternatively, forms of glorifying violence and political bullying were recorded on X (formerly Twitter) (Baider 2022; Caiani et al. 2021).

Oppositely, it was proven that the overall proportion of hateful messages on social media remains relatively small in relation to all the published content (Kaakinen et al. 2018). The comprehensive analysis of more than 1 million comments under Italian YouTube videos on the topic of COVID-19 did not localize any users who continuously posted hateful content (Cinelli et al. 2021). Also, the amount of hate speech present on TikTok profiles of Spanish and UK populist-right parties was relatively low despite the assumptions (González-Aguilar et al. 2023). Moreover, the attributes of some social media platforms could even limit the effect of hate speech and hate crime (Dubois and Reepschlager 2024). "Longevity of hateful comments online is better regulated in platforms such as Snapchat, where users' comments disappear after a while, thus providing a shorter time exposure and a more limited circle of influence" (Gorenc 2022, 416).

The Counteracting Problem

It was proven that "living hatred" has various negative psychological, physical, and social effects on targeted individuals and groups. We as a society have to take this issue seriously, as hate speech and hate crime happen on a daily basis. Despite the fact that boundaries between the offline and online world have been diminishing, different rules for these harmful acts committed offline and online are still applied (Gorenc 2022; Kuřík et al. 2024).

In the offline world, hate speech and hate crime are being suppressed by law or at least perceived as publicly unacceptable. Thanks to that, it is (hypothetically) possible to identify and punish people who commit them. Even more importantly, this allows protecting the victims of hate speech and hate crimes from additional harm that could be caused, for example, by further dissemination of hateful messages (Dreißigacker 2024; Oehmer-Pedrazzi and Pedrazzi 2024).

Unfortunately, the situation differs in the digital environment. The growth of digital communication has been praised by many because of the opportunity to express opinions openly and freely (Gorenc 2022; Yar and Steinmentz 2019). On the other hand, the anonymity, invisibility, and instantaneousness that characterize the online world (Brown 2018; Chun 2017) can be conducive to the creation of different kinds of hateful content, the rise in the amount of this content and its highly effective, greater and faster spread (Keighley 2021; Üzelgün 2024). It is then problematic for social media to take responsibility for the content published through the platforms, or to implement moderation mechanisms (De Blasio and Selva 2021). The effects of online hate speech and hate crimes on their victims were previously underestimated because the absence of physical interaction reduces the level of harm. However, this hypothesis was rejected in past research (Brown 2018; Kuřík et al. 2024).

The problems connected with tackling and contracting hate crime and hate speech are indisputable. Even if the definition problem mentioned above is somewhat solved, the philosophical dilemma between the protection against harm and censorship of free speech on the internet prevails (Badouard 2022). Beyond that, the connection between online hate and offline violence was evidenced (Reichelmann et al. 2020).

Brown (2018) argues that "all national governments should be working as closely as possible with Internet companies to help find ways of combating online hate speech, with national governments in a sense contracting out the regulation of the Internet to these companies, at least when it comes to day-to-day adjudications on non-illegal hate speech content" (321). Although this idea sounds utopical, it is what the European Union attempts to achieve by its measures (Peršak 2022). Additionally, the collective public counter-speech also improves the online discourse (Buerger 2021), and it works more effectively than strict legal measures in some cases (Bayer 2021).

The Documented Effects and Coping Mechanisms

While talking about the aftermaths of hate speech and hate crimes, it is important to highlight that the disputes about the adequateness, necessity, and best practices in counter-speech are taking place not only in the European area (Schäfer et al.

2024). The reasons for fighting hate crimes and speech are nonnegotiable; hence the previous studies revealed that the harm caused by these behaviors deserves attention (Dreißigacker 2024; Keighley 2021). The documented effects and coping mechanisms applied by victims within the European digital sphere vary, as the literature mentioned below shows.

The research realized in Lower Saxony, Germany, revealed that the victims of online hate crime and speech were negatively influenced by these messages, while their experiences made targeted individuals feel insecure not only online but also outside cyberspace (Dreißigacker 2024). The online experiment aimed at a specific subgroup of German citizens—Muslims—accented the same matter of fact (Obermaier et al. 2023). The results of the survey ascertaining opinions of LGBTQ+ young people predominantly living in the UK were in line with the aforementioned (Keighley 2021), which indicates that this effect of online hate may not be geographically determined.

On the contrary, some other academics do not share this pessimism. Kuřík et al. (2024) conducted semi-structured interviews with Czech, German, Italian, and Portugal citizens who are targeted by hate speech in their daily lives. The results documented the cumulative desensitization against hateful messages. The interviewees claimed that they got used to hate speech and did not take it as seriously as at the beginning of the period when they had to face it. Additionally, the emotional and psychological support provided by family, friends, and even medical professionals helps them to cope with hate speech.

Oehmer-Pedrazzi and Pedrazzi's (2024) representative study that aimed at the perception of the seriousness of online hate against immigrants in Austria also underlined the possibility of overcoming trauma caused by the exposition to online hate speech. The scholars found that "empathic suffering becomes less relevant for egalitarian individuals, which indicates an overwriting process that might be a promising way to counteract socially harmful digital hate perceptions" (Oehmer-Pedrazzi and Pedrazzi 2024, 468).

An article written by Hansen et al. (2024) looked at the phenomena from a slightly different angle, as it focused on the willingness to take part in crowd moderation online. The results of the survey of Danish social media users confirmed that personal motivation is an essential factor influencing the users' reactions and reporting activity, while these actions were rare. The authors stated that the public good analogy can be applied to this issue. However, the results of a German experimental study conducted by Álvarez-Benjumea and Winter (2018) confirmed that content moderation in online discussion can have a normative effect on the authors of hate speech. The fact that hateful messages were deleted lowered the engagement of the participants who had an intention to create or share similar content.

Buerger's (2021) paper described the effect of collective counter-speech realized on social media through groups named "I am here" in local languages. This initiative, originally developed in 2016 in Sweden and called #jagärhär, attempts to react to hate speech under the news articles posted on social media in a vigorous but respectful way. It was proven that polite counteraction can serve more effectively than the prevention of hate speech in certain environments and circumstances. However, the benefits of prevention programs and educational activities with a specific focus were also demonstrated by recent research (Cedena-de-Lucas et al. 2024; Pizzi 2022; Wachs et al. 2023).

Concluding Remarks and Possible Solutions

As this chapter described, the responses to hate speech and hate crime include both legal and nonlegal measures (Gagliardone et al. 2015; Windisch et al. 2022). Gorenc (2022) argued, "Hate speech should be banned because it is inconsistent with the fundamental values of liberal democracy, such as equal respect for all people" (419). However, the ongoing attempts to harmonize the legislative instruments and legislature in the European environment dealing with the cultural and regional specifics, as well as the persuasion of the interventions to the online freedom of speech (Badouard 2022), show that the complete, perfect legal prohibition is nearly impossible. Additionally, imprecise or vague explanations of terms complicate the understanding and usefulness of the existing legal norms (Baider 2022; Peršak 2022).

The detecting and coping mechanisms against hate speech and hate crime vary, as well as their potential value and effectiveness (Buerger 2021; Hansen et al. 2024; Obermaier et al. 2023). In the meanwhile, new forms of hate speech and hate crime occur. For example, it is extremely difficult to reveal and combat visual hate, such as hate images or video content (Oehmer-Pedrazzi and Pedrazzi 2024). However, the benefits of counter-speech in the specific digital environment and country should be tested (Bayer 2021; Denti and Faggian 2021), and they are worth trying.

The aforementioned "I am here" movement preferred further reactions to good counterarguments to hateful messages instead of reacting to the hate speech itself. The harmless and so-called positive content then dominates over harmful one, which will lead to more space for alternative viewpoints and satisfactory communication (Buerger 2021). Together with educational and prevention programs, similar initiatives undisputedly help to cultivate online discussions and spaces (Cedena-de-Lucas et al. 2024; Wachs et al. 2023; Pizzi 2022).

Some academics argue that the European online environment is toxic in its nature (Üzelgün et al. 2024). The author of this chapter disagrees while she sees the online world as the mirror or catalyst of the general problems, and the form of offline and online communication is in our hands. Overall, we as a society should keep in mind Hansen et al.'s (2024) argumentation that low-hate online discussions contribute to public well-being. And this is what we should seek for, at least in the European digital environment.

Acknowledgment

The research was supported by Resilient Media for Democracy in the Digital Age (ReMeD), an international multidisciplinary project supported by the European Union's Horizon Europe Research and Innovation Programme, HORIZON-CL2-2022-DEMOCRACY-01-06: "Media for Democracy—Democratic Media," under grant agreement no. 101094742.

Conflict of Interest Statement

No potential conflict of interest was reported by the author.

References

Álvarez-Benjumea, Amalia, and Fabian Winter. 2018. "Normative change and culture of hate: An experiment in online environments." *European Sociological Review* 34 (3): 223–37. https://doi.org/10.1093/esr/jcy005.

Badouard, Romain. 2022. "Hate speech, fake news and content regulation on social networks in Europe." In *Cyberhate in the context of migrations*, edited by Angeliki Monnier, Axel Boursier, and Annabelle Seoane. Springer.

Baider, Fabienne. 2022. "Covert hate speech, conspiracy theory and anti-semitism: Linguistic analysis versus legal judgement." *International Journal for the Semiotics of Law/Revue internationale de Sémiotique* 35 (6): 2347–71. https://doi.org/10.1007/s11196-022-09882-w.

Bayer, Judit. 2021. "High-impact hate speech by persons of authority: A lower threshold needed?" *Hungarian Journal of Legal Studies* 61 (3): 269–84. https://doi.org/10.1556/2052.2020.00003.

Breazu, Petre, and David Machin. 2023 "Racism is not just hate speech: Ethnonationalist victimhood in YouTube comments about the Roma during COVID-19." *Language in Society* 52 (3): 511–31. https://doi.org/10.1017/S0047404522000070.

Brown, Alexander. 2018. "What is so special about online (as compared to offline) hate speech?" *Ethnicities* 18 (3): 297–326. https://doi.org/10.1177/1468796817709846.

Buerger, Catherine. 2021. "# iamhere: Collective counterspeech and the quest to improve online discourse." *Social Media + Society* 7 (4): 1–17. https://doi.org/10.1177/20563051211063843.

Caiani, Manuela, Benedetta Carlotti, and Enrico Padoan. 2021. "Online hate speech and the radical right in times of pandemic: The Italian and English cases." *Javnost: The Public* 28 (2): 202–18. https://doi.org/10.1080/13183222.2021.1922191.

Cedena-de-Lucas, Beatriz, Mar Amate-García, Francisco D. Fernández-Martín, and José L. Arco-Tirado. 2024. "A service-learning program to prevent online hate speech perpetration among secondary education students: A pilot study." *Journal of Interpersonal Violence*. 08862605241286028. https://doi.org/10.1177/08862605241286028.

Chun, Wendy Hui Kyong. 2017. *Updating to remain the same: Habitual new media.* MIT Press.

Cinelli, Matteo, Andraž Pelicon, Igor Mozetič, Walter Quattrociocchi, Petra Kralj Novak, and Fabiana Zollo. 2021. "Dynamics of online hate and misinformation." *Scientific Reports* 11: 22083. https://doi.org/10.1038/s41598-021-01487-w.

De Blasio, Emiliana, and Donatella Selva. 2021. "Who is responsible for disinformation? European approaches to social platforms' accountability in the post-truth era." *American Behavioral Scientist* 65 (6): 825–46. https://doi.org/10.1177/0002764221989784.

Denti, Daria, and Alessandra Faggian. 2021. "Where do angry birds tweet? Income inequality and online hate in Italy." *Cambridge Journal of Regions, Economy and Society* 14 (3): 483–506. https://doi.org/10.1093/cjres/rsab016

Dreißigacker, Arne, Philipp Müller, Anna Isenhardt, and Jonas Schemmel. 2024. "Online hate speech victimization: Consequences for victims' feelings of insecurity." *Crime Science* 13 (1): 4. https://doi.org/10.1186/s40163-024-00204-y.

Dubois, Elizabeth, and Anna Reepschlager. 2024. "How harassment and hate speech policies have changed over time: Comparing Facebook, Twitter and Reddit (2005–2020)." *Policy & Internet*. https://doi.org/10.1002/poi3.387.

Gagliardone, Iginio, Danit Gal, Thiago Alves, and Gabriela Martinez. 2015. *Countering online hate speech*. UNESCO Publishing.

González-Aguilar, Juan Manuel, Francisco Segado-Boj, and Mykola Makhortykh. 2023. "Populist right parties on TikTok: Spectacularization, personalization, and hate speech." *Media and Communication* 11 (2): 232–40. https://doi.org/10.17645/mac.v11i2.6358.

Gorenc, Nina. 2022. "Hate speech or free speech: An ethical dilemma?" *International Review of Sociology* 32 (3): 413–25. https://doi.org/10.1080/03906701.2022.2133406.

Hansen, Tanja Marie, Lasse Lindekilde, Simon Tobias Karg, Michael Bang Petersen, and Stig Hebbelstrup Rye Rasmussen. 2024. "Combatting online hate: Crowd moderation and the public goods problem." *Communications* 49 (3): 444–67. https://doi.org/10.1515/commun-2023-0109.

Hawdon, James, Ashley Reichelmann, Matthew Costello, Vicente J. Llorent, Pekka Räsänen, Izabela Zych, Atte Oksanen, and Catherine Blaya. 2024. "Measuring hate: Does a definition affect self-reported levels of perpetration and exposure to online hate in surveys?" *Social Science Computer Review* 42 (3): 812–31. https://doi.org/10.1177/08944393231211270.

Hietanen, Mika, and Johan Eddebo. 2023. "Towards a definition of hate speech: With a focus on online contexts." *Journal of Communication Inquiry* 47 (4): 440–58. https://doi.org/10.1177/01968599221124309.

Kaakinen, Markus, Pekka Räsänen, Matti Näsi, Jaana Minkkinen, Teo Keipi, and Atte Oksanen. 2018. "Social capital and online hate production: A four country survey." *Crime, Law and Social Change* 69: 25–39. https://doi.org/10.1007/s10611-017-9764-5.

Keighley, Rachel. 2021. "Hate hurts: Exploring the impact of online hate on LGBTQ+ young people." *Women & Criminal Justice* 32 (1–2): 29–48. https://doi.org/10.1080/08974454.2021.1988034.

Kohl, Uta. 2022. "Platform regulation of hate speech: A Transatlantic speech compromise?" *Journal of Media Law* 14 (1): 25–49. https://doi.org/10.1080/17577632.2022.2082520.

Kuřík, Bob, Marie Heřmanová, and JanCharvát. 2024 "Living hated: Everyday experiences of hate speech across online and offline contexts." *Communications* 49 (3): 378–99. https://doi.org/10.1515/commun-2023-0110.

Matamoros-Fernández, Ariadna, and Johan Farkas. 2021. "Racism, hate speech, and social media: A systematic review and critique." *Television & New Media* 22 (2): 205–24. https://doi.org/10.1177/1527476420982230.

Obermaier, Magdalena, Desirée Schmuck, and Muniba Saleem. 2023. "I'll be there for you? Effects of Islamophobic online hate speech and counter speech on Muslim in-group bystanders' intention to intervene." *New Media & Society* 25 (9): 2339–58. https://doi.org/10.1177/14614448211017527.

Oehmer-Pedrazzi, Franziska, and Stefano Pedrazzi. 2024. "An image hurts more than 1000 words? Sources, channels, and characteristics of digital hate images." *Communications* 49 (3): 421–43. https://doi.org/10.1515/commun-2023-0117.

Papcunová, Jana, Marcel Martončik, Denisa Fedáková, Michal Kentoš, Miroslava Bozogáňová, Ivan Srba, Robert Moro, Matúš Pikuliak, Marián Šimko, and Matúš Adamkovič. 2023. "Hate speech operationalization: A preliminary examination of hate speech indicators and their structure." *Complex & Intelligent Systems* 9 (3): 2827–42. https://doi.org/10.1007/s40747-021-00561-0.

Peršak, Nina. 2022. "Criminalising hate crime and hate speech at EU level: Extending the list of eurocrimes under Article 83 (1) TFEU." *Criminal Law Forum* 33 (2): 85–119. https://doi.org/10.1007/s10609-022-09440-w.

Pizzi, Fabrizio. 2022. "Online hate speech: Education as prevention." *Journal of Inclusive Methodology and Technology in Learning and Teaching* 2 (1). https://doi.org/10.32043/jimtlt.v2i1.26.

Reichelmann, Ashley, James Hawdon, Matt Costello, John Ryan, Catherine Blaya, Vicente Llorent, Atte Oksanen, Pekka Räsänen, and Izabela Zych. 2020. "Hate knows no boundaries: Online hate in six nations." *Deviant Behavior* 42 (9): 1100–111. https://doi.org/10.1080/01639625.2020.1722337.

Schäfer, Svenja, Isabella Rebasso, Ming Manuel Boyer, and Anna Maria Planitzer. 2024. "Can we counteract hate? Effects of online hate speech and counter speech on the perception of social groups." *Communication Research* 51 (5): 553–579. https://doi.org/10.1177/00936502231201091.

Schulz-Tomančok, Andreas, and Florian Woschnagg. 2024. "Credibility at stake. A comparative analysis of different hate speech comments on journalistic credibility and support on climate protection measures." *Cogent Social Sciences* 10 (1): 2367092. https://doi.org/10.1080/23311886.2024.2367092.

Sternberg, Robert J., and Karin Sternberg. 2008. *The nature of hate*. Cambridge University Press.

Tontodimamma, Alice, Eugenia Nissi, Annalina Sarra, and Lara Fontanella. 2021. "Thirty years of research into hate speech: Topics of interest and their evolution." *Scientometrics* 126: 157–79. https://doi.org/10.1007/s11192-020-03737-6.

Ullmann, Stefanie, and Marcus Tomalin. 2020. "Quarantining online hate speech: Technical and ethical perspectives." *Ethics and Information Technology* 22 (1): 69–80. https://doi.org/10.1007/s10676-019-09516-z.

Üzelgün, Mehmet Ali, Iliana Giannouli, Ioanna Archontaki, Klára Odstrčilová, Barbara Thomass, and Cláudia Álvares. 2024. "Transforming toxic debates towards European

futures: Technological disruption, societal fragmentation, and enlightenment 2.0." *Central European Journal of Communication* 35: 82–102.
Vandebosch, Heidi, and TobiasRothmund. 2024. "Online hate: A European communication perspective." *Communications* 49 (3): 371–7. https://doi.org/10.1515/commun-2024-0097.
Vergani, Matteo, Barbara Perry, Joshua Freilich, Steven Chermak, Ryan Scrivens, Rouven Link, Daniel Kleinsman, John Betts, and Muhammad Iqbal. 2024 "Mapping the scientific knowledge and approaches to defining and measuring hate crime, hate speech, and hate incidents: A systematic review." *Campbell Systematic Reviews* 20 (2): 20:e1397. https://doi.org/10.1002/cl2.1397.
Wachs, Sebastian, Norman Krause, Michelle F. Wright, and Manuel Gámez-Guadix. 2023. "Effects of the prevention program "HateLess. Together against Hatred" on adolescents' empathy, self-efficacy, and countering hate speech." *Journal of Youth and Adolescence* 52 (6): 1115–28. https://doi.org/10.1007/s10964-023-01753-2.
Windisch, Steven, Susann Wiedlitzka, Ajima Olaghere, and Elizabeth Jenaway. 2022. "Online interventions for reducing hate speech and cyberhate: A systematic review." *Campbell Systematic Reviews* 18 (2): e1243. https://doi.org/10.1002/cl2.1243.
Yar, Majid, and Kevin F. Steinmentz. 2019. *Cybercrime and society*, 3rd ed. Sage Publications.

11

Visualizing Tortures and Wars: Visual Representation and Photojournalism Ethics of Bucha Massacre in Online Print Media

Barbora Součková and Zuzana Jarolímková

The images of violence have always been there. They are linked to drawing, painting, but also photography. As a medium, photography has been intrinsically related to war, conflict, violence, and death since its invention—it is its constant companion, one of its natures (Sontag 2003).

Recent and ongoing violent conflicts of global significance taking place around the world are no exception. Due to the news media, this image of war is close and familiar to us. It lives with us in our living rooms; we hold it while we watch it on our phones. During wartime, photography usually gets much more space in the news media than in times of peace. Images also tend to reproduce representations from previous conflicts (Allan and Zelizer 2004) that are familiar and recognizable to audiences.

The circulation, omnipresence, and frequency of such images certainly impact how we perceive or understand them. However, the framing of these images, brought to us by the news media, is also crucial, especially in how they deal with these images in terms of the standards, demands, and adherence to them in professional journalistic work. In this chapter, we explore how this works through the example of the war in Ukraine, which was triggered by Russian aggression in February 2022. Since then, its visual representations have flowed to us continuously. Concretely, we focus on the events in the Kyiv suburb of Bucha, which surfaced on April 1 of the same year, as were covered by the online version of the US newspaper *New York Times* and Czech news web *Seznam Zprávy*.

The massacre of civilians occurred in Bucha during the occupation by Russian troops from March 5 to 30, 2022. The occupying forces murdered hundreds of civilians. There was evidence of brutal torture on some of the victims. According to the UN, these acts may fulfill a war crime (UN 2022).

When journalists entered Bucha with soldiers, they saw dead people with their hands tied behind their backs, bodies lying on the streets, dead people were also found in wells or mass graves with signs of torture, and the children's camp became an executing ground (Rainsford 2022). Everything was surrounded by destroyed military techniques. After the liberation, the story of killing and rape was told by survivors (Limaye 2022). Russians denied the crimes as a "provocation" and a "staged performance" by Kyiv (Reuters 2022). The consequences of the Bucha massacre for Russia were beyond international denouncements, isolations, expulsion of diplomats, and more sanctions from the EU (Renic 2024).

Considering these overwhelming events and the fact that the conflict and such events in Ukraine are still ongoing and escalating, the famous publication *Regarding the Pain of Others* (2003) by photography theorist and philosopher Susan Sontag could not be more relevant to us. "The photographs are a means of making 'real' (or 'more real') matters that the privileged and merely safe might prefer to ignore" (Sontag 2003, 7).

We aim to discuss how visual representations of the war in Ukraine are shaped, specifically in the case of the Bucha massacre, and to present how the overall image is constructed. This includes discussing the overall role of images and propaganda in the war and questions about the ethics of journalistic practice itself, which we will then consider through a case study of two media outlets. The focus is not only on the importance of the national context of the Czech Republic (*Seznam Zprávy*) but also on the global significance (the *New York Times*).

Controlling the (Visual) Narrative

The image of war and how we see it (through the news media) evolves. Theorists such as Jean Baudrillard (1995), W. J. T. Mitchell (2011), and Nicholas Mirzoeff (2016) point out that, significantly since the 1990s and the events of September 11, 2001, how war is visually represented has been reduced mainly to the demonstration of technology, militarism, power, conquered targets, and the warfare apparatus. It is essentially as if it were a computer game that lacks any humanitarian impact on the civilian population.

From this period, framed mainly by the so-called war on terror, the image of war has a much more developed function than before. Mitchell (2018) calls this era the "war of images." The redefinition of the role of the image from this time consists mainly in the fact that, beyond documentation and recording, the image, more fundamentally than ever, has its power, which functions as a driving force capable of achieving specific political goals through visuality (Mirzoeff 2016).

> The question for war photography thus concerns not only what it shows, but also how it shows what it shows. The "how" not only organizes the image, but works to organize our perception and thinking as well. If state power attempts to regulate a perspective that reporters and cameramen are there to confirm, then the action of perspective in and as the frame is part of the interpretation of the war compelled by the state. The photograph is not merely a visual image awaiting interpretation; it is itself actively interpreting, sometimes forcibly so. (Butler 2009, 71)

According to Mirzoeff (2016), the Prussian general Carl von Clausewitz would have seen images in this "new war" as a tool to gain political goals. In other words, these can be effective tools, such as state propaganda, with different aims. This is still relevant today because achieving these goals through visual representation has much greater possibilities in terms of platforms or media on which it can operate. This is particularly interesting to consider because although the image can be manipulated easily, it is often perceived as evidence, and its truth is often seen as undeniable (Lábová and Láb 2009).

Focusing directly on war propaganda, it targets actors that are important or needed for the politics of governments involved in war or conflict. Propaganda is an intentional action by an institution or propagandist who tries to gain the support of the public or make them push for the action. This is achieved by various symbols, representations, or messages developed for this purpose (Patrona 2022). Propaganda does not only exist in totalitarian or authoritarian regimes but also democratic governments, as Herman and Chomsky pointed out in 1988. They argue that propaganda and systematic bias exist in the mass media during peace and war. They introduced five filters used in media to decide what to publish, which can even lead to self-censorship: ownership, advertising as the primary income, sources of the news, flak, and anti-ideology (Herman and Chomsky 1988). All these filters influence the final media product (Hanusch 2010).

Propaganda can also be seen as a purveyor of ideology, whose dominant meanings are constructed by the media (Jowett and O'Donnell 2015). The reason why this is so may be based entirely on journalistic practice and media logic. Audiences expect a constant flow of news, especially in conflict situations and times of war. This leads media outlets to find reliable sources, which can be complex and problematic. Governments or major business companies often become the only news sources. Thus, there is no independent perspective and no possibility of critical verification of information because there often is no other in times of war. What may arise from such cooperation is the maintenance of mutual relations. When relations between the government and the media are not good, there is a possibility that there will be no information, no statements, no interviews, and no permission and accreditation for journalists to get into war-affected places (Hanusch 2010; Shoemaker and Reese 2014).

The governments need to have control over the overall representation (including the important visual dimension) of the war to secure the support of the citizens and donors who are financially and materialistically helping them. However, the media outlets sometimes reinforce this (Hanusch 2010).

This is often manifested in the publication of information that may disturb the audience and provoke a specific response that typically stimulates emotions that influence their social attitudes and behavior (Sielska 2023, 138). At the same time, it is often information that reports on the reality of war. This puts the news media into a challenging situation that may sometimes even be an impasse because this forced position can threaten the traditional roles of journalism. However, this is not a new phenomenon; we can observe this since the Falkland War of 1982 when the government tried to control it via the press pool, which strongly influenced the visual representation of war or conflict (Kennedy 2016).

An interesting example of government power over the news media is how the United States used this system during the Gulf War when they appointed photojournalists to the army troops. Behind the control, they hoped that journalists would not go against their "companions" and would not publish any content that would go against US politics. We could see the results—the censorship led to minimal visual explicit coverage, and according to the study of Griffin and Lee (1995), only 27 of 1,104 (2 percent) images published in *Time*, *Newsweek*, *U.S. News*, and *World Report* showed wounded or dead US soldiers. This results in the showcase of military technology and the strength of the American army, and with only slight exceptions, there is no story of human suffering (Kennedy 2016; Stallabrass 2022).

In this example, journalists could have done their role as a check on power, the government, and powerful and influential ones. As Shoemaker and Reese

(2014) point out, there is always the debate about the public right to know and national security during wartime. At the same time, the important roles of journalism are to provide testimony and documentation of events and to make power holders accountable and responsible.

These aforementioned situations, associated with war photojournalism, have been common practice since 1982 when the Falklands War was ongoing (Kennedy 2016). It is known as "embedded journalism." Here, the news reporting only occurs in the company of the army and the military units, which also control the particular narrative that is formed about the war (Sontag 2003). For journalists, this is often the only way they can get to the source of information and the events themselves, and due to this logic, they are, therefore, more likely to agree to report while accompanied by the military (Butler 2009). Even in the context of the war in Ukraine, this needs to be kept very much in mind, as the movement of journalists in the country is not free but only possible with an accreditation permit (Reporting Ukraine Guide 2024).

Thus, the events in Bucha, which were entirely under the control of the Ukrainian Army after the massacre and the liberation of the town from Russian occupation troops, are still only a particular perspective that we are allowed to see through journalistic and photojournalistic production. This brings us back to what Judith Butler (2009) notes. Controlled visual perspectives "actively structured our cognitive apprehension of the war" (Butler 2009, 66). Conversely, regulating a specific visual narrative is not the same as dictating it. Instead, it is how decision-making on what to include in perception, memory, and understanding of war is interpreted in advance by the government and the military. Overall, however, this is consistent with the broad issues of representation and ideology as defined, for example, by Hall (2013).

Shaping the (Visual) Narrative in Ukraine and Bucha

It is crucial to discuss the specific role of image construction and war propaganda, specifically in the case of Ukraine. The main aspect of the Ukrainian propaganda is to gain sympathy and support for their fight. Because of that, they try to arouse sympathy and admiration. The key role is President Volodymyr Zelenskyj (instead of suit, dressed in a military uniform during wartime), who gives speeches and visits hospitals or places of enormous destruction and atrocities, as was Bucha (Sielska 2023; Baysha 2024). He also emphasizes that this is a war for democracy and freedom and calls for the unity of a civilized and democratic world with Ukraine as a getaway to Europe (Baysha 2024, 45).

The representation of Ukrainian soldiers is also important, as it is positive and shows them "in a good light"—how they help people, save animals, or rescue people during shelling. Moreover, they also try to show their strength to Russia (and Russia does the same) to undermine their effort (Baysha 2024).

When media outlets decide that a war is worthy of our emotions, they unrolled the audience to the "dance of militarisation," which mobilizes its sensibilities (Ølgaard 2022, 175). To evoke emotions, make people remember, and spark action, specific language (also visual) must be used to dominate negative emotions prevalent in politics (Sielska 2023). This works in the Czech context, too, resembling the Soviet invasion in 1968 and the Munich Agreement in 1939. With other post-soviet countries such as Poland, Hungary, or Slovakia, there is also the fear that if Ukraine is defeated in the war with Russia, their countries could be the next target of the Russian invasion.

The Bucha massacre itself can be used as an example of war propaganda. Many photojournalists entered the suburb of Kyiv on April 2 after the liberation; however, another "press trip" on April 5 was only accessible with accreditation. Journalists needed to be permitted to enter the scene, and they had pre-selected places for their work. This resulted in the scene with a "crowd" of people around the venues, which were described as vultures (Williams 2022). For those who did take photos there, the experience was intense. Heidi Levine, who published her work from Bucha in the *Washington Post*, said that she was "horrified" by what she had seen in Ukraine and that she "understands that many of my images are challenging to look at, but this is the reality of this war" (Levine 2022).

Photos have always existed in the context, and their meanings are political, especially in wars with sensitive content. States conduct politics internally and externally, and according to Sielska (2023), "in the future, the significant and strongest international actors will not be those with the strongest armies, but those with the most extensive digital networks" (140).

Part of wartime propaganda is also the spreading of disinformation. In the Western country's context, Russia is trying to ground the international support of Ukraine and discredit democratic institutions (Bond 2024). Kremlin's work also shows today's danger of spreading disinformation via social platforms, which resulted in Meta's ban on Russian media outlets that was announced in September 2024 (Isaac and Frenkel 2024).

According to Ahmad and Munk (2025), the information disorder campaign by Russia uses online platforms and algorithms, which often create echo chambers where people see news, leading to information overload and confusion. Moreover, they tailor their propaganda for different audiences and platforms (Bond 2023), which results in a fragmented information ecosystem and responses (Ahmad and Munk 2025).

However, Nathaniel Gleicher, head of security policy at Meta, said they "used a throw-the-spaghetti-at-the-wall-to-see-what-sticks kind of approach" (Bond 2023). This approach aims to saturate the information space with different kinds of false theories and deny what happened—and people are puzzled or disinterested (Bond 2023).

In the case of information about the Bucha massacre, as was mentioned in the introduction, Russians denied the crimes (Reuters 2022) and started an information campaign with the claim that images and videos were false and were staged by actors (Ahmad and Munk 2025).

This is shown, among other things, in the example of our case study. During the period under review, both online media outlets published numerous reports corroborating the events in Bucha and refuting Russian disinformation—the *New York Times* published on April 4 (with updates on April 6) articles with satellite images that showed that the bodies in Bucha lay there for weeks "despite Russian claims" (Browne et al. 2022). In addition, the authors of this article also added maps and videos, which resulted in a complex context for those who did not believe. The role of the image is crucial here because the *New York Times* used photographs, satellite images, or videos as direct evidence that the events actually happened.

The same situation was the case with our second chosen Czech media outlet. *Seznam Zprávy*, on April 7, also used satellite images to prove the event's truth. However, they refer to other analyses from Bellingcat or BBC and the previously mentioned *New York Times*. The images, in that case, support photos of the atrocities. An interesting project of *Seznam Zprávy* was a series of articles called "What They Say in Russia,"[1] where they informed about the opposite narrative about Bucha in Russian media.

Many more projects rebut Russian claims about Bucha and are still ongoing. This shows the urgency of the crises we face in the Ukraine War. However, as a study by Ahmad and Munk (2025) of disinformation about Bucha shows, despite this evidence, those who believe Russian claims do not seek fact-checking articles out and believe what they see or hear. The reason behind this is the war on images and the lack of media and visual education.

Navigating the (Visual) Narrative through Journalistic Ethics

The apparency and increased presence of media coverage of war or conflict are primarily driven by the fact that crises significantly fulfill the criteria of news values. In the case of the war in Ukraine and the Bucha massacre, we can refer to principles such as unexpectedness, unambiguity, relevance, unpredictability, and continuity. In some European media regions (including the Czech Republic), there is also geographical and cultural proximity or reference to elite people (Galtung and Ruge 1965; Brighton and Foy 2007). This fundamentally contributes to the generally amplified media representation of the topic.

Especially in the case of reporting on such events, in which an extraordinary number of situations involving human suffering, death, violence, or fear can be anticipated, there is a need for heightened sensitivity to the ethical standards that photojournalism, like all journalistic practice, must unconditionally adhere to (Silva and Eldridge 2020). Láb et al. (2019) categorize the issues involving the ethics of photojournalism into three levels. It is (1) *the level of production of photographs and the circumstances of their making*, (2) *the content of the image*, and (3) *postproduction and manipulation*. Within these, the three most common ethical issues are discussed: the rights of victims of violence, privacy and its invasion, and falsification of the content of images (Lester 1991).

Basic frameworks that address the ethics of photojournalism include, for example, the Code of Ethics of the National Press Photographers Association (NPPA 2024), which is an international professional organization with a long tradition of being the leader in the field of photojournalism advocating high ethical standards for the work and for the medium of photography itself. Although it does not explicitly name situations related to reporting and photography in war or conflict, the following passages may help define guidelines for how photographers and photojournalists in the field (but also in the newsroom) should be working:

- when photographing or recording subjects, provide full context, avoid stereotypes, and be mindful of minimizing personal biases in your work;

- treat all depicted subjects with respect and dignity, especially vulnerable individuals who were victims of crime or tragedy, and only intrude on private moments of grief when there is a clear and justifiable public need;
- try to be discreet and humble when working with the subject (NPPA 2024).

Moravcc (2020) identifies war and conflict as "anthropogenic emergencies" that, by their nature and increased media coverage, imply a higher number of ethically questionable or problematic situations, during which there may be a higher incidence of ethically objectionable moments that may occur during the journalistic practice. Whether it is field experience while covering events "on the spot" or "from the desk" in newsrooms, at any stage of the editorial process, a moment may arise that contradicts ethical standards or even codes of ethics. Particularly in the context of reporting on sensitive or traumatic events, it appears that "what to show and how" is not always clear. Codes of ethics usually do not provide an answer to all possible situations, so it is a matter of practice as to how such visual materials are handled. A fundamental contradiction is often discussed in newsrooms (sometimes more, sometimes less). It is a question of the role of the news media to report what happened, but it is also a question of respect for the victims of these tragic events, their victimization, or retraumatization. As it turns out, in newsrooms this debate is urgent and still unclear (Mäenpää 2022).

Particularly sensitive are images that directly portray death or the immediate mourning of the bereaved. According to Hanusch (2010, 2013), several factors influence their publication, such as the type of media system, the type of media (such as tabloid, serious, or broadsheets), and the geographical distance in which the death occurs. It is typical, he argues, that Western or Global North media are more likely to take a more restrained approach when it comes to the visualization of death by not depicting dead bodies or explicit actions on dead bodies (with signs of torture, blood, etc.). This also suggests that the implementation of ethical standards has its dimensions, and often, geographical distance rather than morality-based ethical principles determine the practice (Silva and Eldridge 2020). This is also what Sontag notes: "With our dead, there has always been a powerful interdiction against showing the naked face … The more remote or exotic the place, the more likely we are to have full frontal views of the dead and dying" (Sontag 2003, 55–6).

According to other factors influencing the overall photojournalism ethics, Mäenpää (2022) summarizes that these conventions are also often incorporated into the perception of such situations by photojournalists, who often take a self-censoring approach to these types of events (either by not photographing the situation or by using particular visual practices, such as using long shots instead of close-ups), which are less explicit and overall more sensitive.

Case Study: Bucha, in the First Week

As we outlined, we followed the *New York Times* and *Seznam Zprávy* during the first week of liberation of Bucha, from March 31 to April 8, 2022. In total, we included eighty-four photographs published on the topic of the events (*New York Times* n = 41; *Seznam Zprávy* n = 43). First, we conducted a thematic analysis (Braun and Clarke 2022) on these photographs to identify the main themes that emerged in the photographs concerning the ethics of visual representation. In total, we identified five main themes: (1) *Visualizing torture, dead bodies and bereaved*, (2) *Satellite view*, (3) *Military aid*, (4) *Civilian life in the streets*, and (5) *Devastated town.*

At the same time, we conducted a social semiotic analysis (Caple 2013) on twenty photographs, which provided a more detailed description of the ethically problematic moments that can occur during war photojournalism. This also helped us focus on the text that complemented the photographs in captions. We focused on whether the text provided sufficient context and if it was relevant. While we want to highlight some bad practices, it is also important to point out examples of good practices that the news media have done well in reporting and representing this case.

After collecting photographs for the final sample, each of the authors first analyzed the photographs themselves. A discussion between both authors followed, and any disagreements were debated and resolved. This resulted in a presented categorization. The authors then followed the same procedure for applying social semiotic analysis. Findings represent the final work after joint discussions. It is also crucial to mention the positionality of both authors. One of us is still a practicing photojournalist, which provided an additional point of view of critical discussion on ethical visual representation in news media. Moreover, all these skills were used during the analysis itself.

Visualizing Torture, Dead Bodies, and Bereaved

In the case of the Bucha massacre, there was an unprecedented amount of images in the news media that explicitly visualized violence, torture, death, and impact on civilians. This is also included in our first category, which is the most comprehensive and potentially includes the most significant number of problematic situations regarding image construction. For both media outlets that we observed, some photographs depicted the dead in the streets of Bucha (either the victims as the only object of a photograph or in larger scenes with mourners or residents) or in cemeteries. However, the specific photographic approaches used in both media varied, especially in the usage of explicit images on news media websites and the specific editorial process practices.

Seznam Zprávy published a considerable number of pictures showing the dead bodies of victims. The visualization of these scenes can be assessed as sensitive, as the victims were photographed either from a distance or out of focus of the camera. Photographs in which the face of a dead person could be identified were edited in postproduction by blurring. Based on the total number of published images, dead bodies appeared in more than half of the forty-three photographs published by *Seznam Zprávy*, specifically in twenty-four of the forty-three photographs. Some scenes were even repetitive (it was obviously the same scene, just from a different angle). One specifically problematic case in *Seznam Zprávy* is a photograph of a dead person in an open body bag with no visible face. The central motive of this image is the person's open wallet (it is an extreme close-up), where a photograph, presumably of a bereaved child, is visible. We consider the publication of such photograph as inappropriate, as it may victimize the depicted child and the whole situation as insensitive.

The *New York Times* also presented images of the victims of the massacre, that is, explicit photographs of dead bodies, most often taken from behind or from the side, but in such a way that their faces could not be visible. This approach works sensitively not only with the victims themselves and their remembrance but also with respecting relatives or survivors who might identify them. At the same time, they have published such photographs to a much lesser extent than *Seznam Zprávy*; out of the forty-one photographs, thirteen captured dead bodies. This suggests a different approach in editorial processes and gatekeeping and the general sensitivity with which the *New York Times* approached the representation. The publishing practice of such images was more restrained.

The dead bodies of people with their faces slightly visible appeared in the photographs published by both media outlets in two cases. While these were long-shot images, their publication should still be considered.

However, it is necessary to consider the different nature of both media outlets. The *New York Times* is a newspaper with worldwide reach, global influence, and selling. Thus, their economic possibilities are entirely different, and they could have afforded to pay for more than one photojournalist who could get to Bucha. This led to the creation of unique visual content that is tailored to articles. On the contrary, *Seznam Zprávy* has a local domestic reach, and its economic situation is different even though it is one of the most prominent news media outlets in the Czech Republic. Still, they offered their audience original content from Bucha, but most published images were from the wire services.

Additionally, the first category also includes photographs of the bereaved and mourners of dead people. Overall, in the case of both media, we can summarize that they did not explicitly record the grieving and bereaved in the vulnerable moments of personal experience of the immediate tragedy. Instead, photographs of the impact of the Russian occupation on the residents and the city were most common. Thus, there were depicted situations of recovering from the occupation (for example, burying the corpses or removing them from the streets). These were less emotionally intense situations and did not record an exclusively private situation. Directly depicted mourning appeared in units of the photographs; only women were depicted in this role.

For those representations, the geographical and historical closeness plays a significant role. According to the textual representation of these images, *Seznam Zprávy* chose more emotional headlines, which even compared the event in Bucha to the Srebrenica massacre during the war in Bosnia and Herzegovina in 1995. The more urging tone of articles and selection of explicit photos may be connected to the closeness of Russia, the similarities with Czech history, and the fear of Ukrainian defeat, as we already mentioned.

Satellite View

The second category included technical images that captured bird's-eye satellite images of Bucha. These images functioned here as maps, accompanied by captions inside the images that described individual objects on satellite photographs. A poorer visual quality complemented this description, as the photographs were generally of lower resolution. The use of such images appeared in the case of both observed media (the prevalence in units appeared in *Seznam Zprávy*). These images appeared in the coverage of both media mainly as "evidence" (as evidence of the truth of the events in Bucha), showing the deployment of Russian troops around the town or the location of dead bodies in the streets.

Although publishing these photographs intends to provide visual evidence of the event, their overuse could be problematic overall. This is because these types of images reduce the reality of war to a technical view from above, which by its very nature does not draw on the human and civilian perspective of war but rather on the technical-military one. This may distort the overall image of the war by excluding perspectives that cover the civilians and their suffering.

In our analysis, these images were used moderately and well-considerably. They were published only in units of cases (although the number of pictures published was higher for *Seznam Zprávy*). At the same time, it is also essential to include the aforementioned context of their publication, demonstrating that such images can be used appropriately in some instances.

Military Aid

The third category includes images of soldiers and Ukrainian military units in the town that they helped liberate. More often, they were portrayed with only military equipment or with the wreckage of burnt-out remains of Russian tanks. In our sample, there were basically no photographs where military aid was depicted in the context of the civilian population (only one photograph published in *Seznam Zprávy* showed a direct interaction between members of a military troop and one female Ukrainian civilian).

The focus of these images on military equipment and weapons weakens the role of the civilian population in representing the event and reinforces the role of military power. Through these images, a narrative of the liberation of the city as a purely technical military operation can be developed, which may neglect and omit the humanitarian impact on the population and the whole subset of the massacre, which was exclusively civilian. This can be ethically problematic and disrespectful. In this manner, the *New York Times* published eleven images, and *Seznam Zprávy* six images.

Civilian Life in the Streets, and Devastated Town

The last two categories—civilian life in the streets, and devastated towns—involve the smallest number of ethically problematic or questionable situations. The category capturing civilian life on the streets represents the residents dealing with the situation in the town. These are scenes of people returning to their homes, living in improvised conditions. Another prominent characteristic is their bicycle movement around the town, which appears in several images. They often ride on roads where dead bodies are still present. As absurd as these scenes are, we do not consider them ethically problematic because the dead bodies are depicted sensitively, and these photographs instead reflect life in the city after the massacre, which is tragic but existing.

The photographs of the category depicting the devastated town were images without human actors; they showed the remains of the presence of the Russian army, which left behind burnt buildings and cars, with traces of gunfire or munitions. At the same time, the presence of Russian tanks is also a major feature. We do not find problematic representations in these photographs; their use was also reasonable.

The Usage of Photo Captions

We also focus on photos and captions necessary to publish any visual context in media. They should name an author or source and offer a description to the readers so they know what they are looking at. Even though news images should speak for themselves without captions and be easily read, the captions are the specifications that assure readers of the content and add broader context (e.g., that the photo is really from that place and time, not just an illustration for the article).

Twenty photos and captions were equally selected from both websites for analysis. Both media accompanied images with the description of the depicted scene and the day of its creation. However, the *New York Times* was more accurate and detailed in their work, and captions created small stories under photos. Especially with the famous Reuters photo of the hand with red nails from Zohra Bensemra,[2] there was a whole story behind the photo and how the depicted victim was recognized.

Seznam Zprávy, on the other hand, was more concise with captions—shorter and more emotional—and even used quotations from survival victims. Also, the comparisons with Srebrenica occur in the captions. In the article, the photo gallery used the same caption, which describes the place and the context with a date when the photos were taken. The reason for this could be the source of photos, as all analyzed images from Bucha in *Seznam Zprávy* were acquired from news wire services such as Profimedia or Getty Images. In that case, it is difficult for the article's author, who selected and uploaded photos to the webpage, to create proper captions. In such cases, it is particularly challenging for journalists responsible for selecting and uploading photographs in the newsroom to craft accurate and appropriate captions. This difficulty is further heightened in sensitive and emotionally charged contexts, such as Bucha, where careful consideration of publication was required due to the graphic nature of the content.

The cooperation of photos and captions is essential as it speaks about the work's quality and the care given to the final published news content. For accuracy, we can see the good practice of defining the days. Hence, the reader knows precisely when the photographers are in that place, evidenced by the photos and the story itself.

Discussion and Conclusion

Our analysis has shown that dealing with images of tragic or sensitive war events is a specific case that needs special consideration. The biggest problem may arise with photographs showing dead bodies directly. Both studied media followed the practice of covering or anonymizing the faces of dead people—in the case of *Seznam Zprávy*, even in postproduction. However, this may raise further ethical questions about image manipulation, even if the aim is positive. Simultaneously, some photographs did not properly cover the face in a few cases. The specific usage of individual photographs and the intensity of their use, which was notably higher in the case of *Seznam Zprávy*, also turned out to be problematic. While this overuse of images of death and suffering may suggest sensationalism, it may also undermine their relevance. Also, it has been shown that incorporating satellite imagery can be done right, but problems can arise when the imagery overly depicts and demonstrates military units and equipment.

The example of Bucha shows that the government and the army always control the image of war. However, this does not mean that we should reject it. Tragic events must be represented so that they can be critically reflected and evaluated in the broader global discourse because wars have a particular impact on civilians, who suffer and often die during such incidences. At the same time, it is also necessary to perceive the image of death similarly. It must be approached sensitively, carefully, and with respect for the victims and survivors, but this does not mean that the news media should neglect it. This could lead to the sanitization of the war, that is, showing images without any signs of violence, blood, and tragic situations (Robertson 2004). This would contribute to the media's denial of these events.

Sontag insists that we react to the spectacle of war we see with sympathy, indignation, excitement, or sympathy. However, we argue that an additional significant emotional response is apathy. Butler (2009) also points to this, discussing the transitive affectivity of photography, which can also overwhelm and numb in times of war. This was evident, for example, with the images from the Iraq War, which were horrifying, but through their circulation and constant repetition, they eventually became rather banal. So, we ask whether we are not experiencing the same situation with the war in Ukraine. The images from Bucha have shocked the world and contributed to increased political, humanitarian, and civilian support. What about today, almost three years since the conflict began? Could the cruel images of war still shock us?

This question should answer everyone themself. On the other hand, it is necessary to show its reality, even though we, the privileged ones, might not want to see it. To do that, media outlets should always consider the reasoning and care for those they might afflict. Moreover, it does not matter if it is in Ukraine or any other country on the other side of the world.

Conflict of Interest Statement

No potential conflict of interest was reported by the authors.

Notes

1 In original: "Co se píše v Rusku."

2 In the analysis, this photo was the only one of ten not taken by the photographer of The New York Times.

References

Ahmad, Juan, Tine Munk, and Tine Munk. 2025. "Deception as an online weapon: Does the truth matter?" In *Victimisation in the digital age*, edited by Juan Ahmad, and Tine Munk. Routledge.

Allan, Stuart, and Barbie Zelizer, eds. 2004. *Reporting war: Journalism in wartime.* Psychology Press.

Baudrillard, Jean. 1995. *The Gulf War did not take place.* Indiana University Press.

Baysha, Olga. 2024. *War, peace, and populist discourse in Ukraine.* Routledge.

Bond, Shannon. 2023. "How Russia is losing—and winning—the information war in Ukraine." *National Public Radio*, February 28. www.npr.org/2023/02/28/1159712623/how-russia-is-losing-and-winning-the-information-war-in-ukraine.

Bond, Shannon. 2024. "This is what Russian propaganda looks like in 2024." *National Public Radio*, June 6. www.npr.org/2024/06/06/g-s1-2965/russia-propaganda-deepfakes-sham-websites-social-media-ukraine.

Braun, Virginia, and Victoria Clarke. 2022. *Thematic analysis: A practical guide.* Sage Publications.

Brighton, Paul, and Dennis Foy. 2007. *News values.* Sage Publications.

Browne, Malachy, David Botti, and Haley Willis. 2022. "Satellite images show bodies lay in Bucha for weeks, despite Russian claims." *New York Times*, April 4. www.nytimes.com/2022/04/04/world/europe/bucha-ukraine-bodies.html?searchResultPosition=10.

Butler, Judith. 2009. *Frames of war: When is life grievable?* Verso.

Caple, Helen. 2013. *Photojournalism: A social semiotic approach.* Palgrave Macmillan.

Galtung, Johan, and Mari Holmboe Ruge. 1965. "The structure of foreign news." *Journal of Peace Research* 2 (1): 64–91.

Griffin, Michael, and Jongsoo Lee. 1995. "Picturing the Gulf War: Constructing an image of war in *Time*, *Newsweek*, and *US News & World Report*." *Journalism & Mass Communication Quarterly* 72 (4): 813–25.

Hall, Stuart, Jessica Evans, and Sean Nixon, eds. 2013. *Representation: Cultural representations and signifying practices*, 2nd ed. Sage Publications.

Hanusch, Folker. 2010. *Representing death in the news: Journalism, media and mortality.* Springer.

Hanusch, Folker. 2013. "Sensationalizing death? Graphic disaster images in the tabloid and broadsheet press." *European Journal of Communication* 28 (5): 497–513.

Herman, Edward S., and Noam Chomsky. 1988. *Manufacturing consent: The political economy of the mass media.* Pantheon.

Isaac, Mike, and Sheera Frenkel. 2024. "Meta and YouTube crack down on Russian media outlets." *New York Times*, September 17. www.nytimes.com/2024/09/17/technology/meta-rt-russian-tv.html.

Jowett, Garth S., and Victoria O'Donnell. 2015. *Propaganda & persuasion*, 6th ed. Sage Publications.

Kennedy, Liam. 2016. *Afterimages: Photography and U.S. foreign policy.* University of Chicago Press.

Láb, Filip, Sandra Štefaniková, and Martina Topinková. 2019. "Photojournalism in Central Europe: On authenticity and ethics." *Środkowoeuropejskie studia polityczne* 5 (2): 73–89.

Lábová, Alena, and Filip Láb. 2009. Soumrak fotožurnalismu? Karolinum.

Lester, Paul. 1991. *Photojournalism: An ethical approach*. Routledge.

Levine, Heidi. 2022. "What I've seen in Bucha." *Washington Post*, April 8. www.washingtonpost.com/outlook/2022/04/08/bucha-images-photographer/.

Limaye, Yogita. 2022. "Ukraine conflict: 'Russian soldiers raped me and killed my husband.'" *BBC*, April 11. www.bbc.com/news/world-europe-61071243.

Mäenpää, Jenni. 2022. "Distributing ethics: Filtering images of death at three news photo desks." *Journalism* 23 (10): 2230–48.

Mirzoeff, Nicholas. 2016. *How to see the world: An introduction to images, from self-portraits to selfies, maps to movies, and more*. Basic Books.

Mitchell, W. J. T. 2011. *Cloning terror: The war of images, 9/11 to the present*. University of Chicago Press.

Mitchell, W. J. T. 2018. "Spectacle, surveillance, and just war today." In *Visualizing war: Emotions, technologies, communities*, edited by Anders Engberg-Pedersen and Kathrin Maurer. Routledge.

Moravec, Václav. 2020. *Proměny novinářské etiky*. Academia.

NPPA. 2024. "Code of ethics." https://nppa.org/resources/code-ethics.

Ølgaard, Daniel Møller. 2022. "Embodying war, becoming warriors: Media, militarisation and the case of Islamic State's online propaganda." In *Making war on bodies*, edited by Catherine Baker. Edinburgh University Press.

Patrona, Marianna. 2022. "Snapshots from an information war: Propaganda, intertextuality, and audience design in the Russia–Ukraine conflict." *Violence: An International Journal* 3 (2): 253–80. https://doi.org/10.1177/26330024231162636.

Rainsford, Sarah. 2022. "Ukraine: The children's camp that became an execution ground." *BBC*, May 16. www.bbc.com/news/world-europe-61442387.

Renic, Neil. 2024. "The cost of atrocity: Strategic implications of Russian battlefield misconduct in Ukraine." *Ethics & International Affairs* 38 (1): 6–16. https://doi.org/10.1017/S0892679424000054.

Reporting Ukraine Guide. 2024. www.reportingukraine.guide/accreditation.

Reuters. 2022. "Russia denies killing civilians in Ukraine's Bucha." April 3. www.reuters.com/world/europe/russia-denies-killing-civilians-ukraines-bucha-2022-04-03/.

Robertson, Lori. 2004. "Images of war." *American Journalism Review* 26 (5): 44. https://link.gale.com/apps/doc/A124000698/AONE?u=anon~e16ed19d&sid=googleScholar&xid=34c8c81c.

Shoemaker, Pamela J., and Stephen D. Reese. 2014. *Mediating the message in the 21st century: A media sociology perspective*, 3rd ed. Routledge.

Sielska, Zuzanna. 2023. "Emotions during the war: Interplay between emotions and information." In *War in Ukraine. Media and emotions*, edited by Agnieszka

Turska-Kawa, Agnieszka Kasińska-Metryka, and Karolina Pałka-Suchojad. Palgrave Macmillan.

Silva, Miguel Franquet Santos, and Scott Eldridge II. 2020. *The ethics of photojournalism in the digital age*. Routledge.

Sontag, Susan. 2003. *Regarding the pain of others*. Picador.

Stallabrass, Julian. 2022. *The Look of War*. Art Monthly.

United Nations. 2022. "UN report details summary executions of civilians by Russian troops in northern Ukraine." www.ohchr.org/en/press-releases/2022/12/un-report-details-summary-executions-civilians-russian-troops-northern.

Williams, Lauren. 2022. "Bucha: Capturing the horror." *The Interpreter*, April 14. www.lowyinstitute.org/the-interpreter/bucha-capturing-horror

Index

About the Editors and Contributors

Editors

Kateřina Turková is a researcher and associate lecturer at the Faculty of Social Sciences of Charles University in Prague, Czech Republic. She was a researcher at the Central European Digital Media Observatory (CEDMO), an international multidisciplinary project supported by the European Commission. She is part of the research team Resilient Media for Democracy in the Digital Age (ReMeD), responding to the European Commission's Horizon call. She also participated in several projects supported by the Technology Agency of the Czech Republic. In her academic research, she focuses on issues associated with social media, sport, and quantitative research.

Veronika Macková is an academic researcher at the Faculty of Social Sciences, Charles University in Prague. She worked as a journalist at Czech Television, which is why she mainly teaches practical journalism-oriented courses. Her areas of research interest include sports journalism and AI journalism. In her publications, she focuses mainly on Para sports and athletes with a disability. She was a researcher at the Central European Digital Media Observatory (CEDMO), and currently, she takes part in Resilient Media for Democracy in the Digital Age (ReMeD). She also participated in several projects supported by the Technology Agency of the Czech Republic.

Contributors

Ana Azurmendi is Associate Dean of Research and Full Professor of Constitutional Law at the University of Navarra, where she has been teaching media law since 1991. Her research focuses on media law; in particular, media for democracy, freedom of expression, digital rights, public broadcasting, and copyright. She has been involved in the promotion of freedom of information and the legal protection of journalists in México through the ONGs Derecho de la Información and Art. 19 Freedom of Expression. Her second area of political work has been the audiovisual sector, where she has participated in regional and national commissions for the reform of audiovisual laws.

Alina Bârgăoanu is a Romanian communication scholar at the College of Communication and Public Relations, National University of Political Studies and Public Administration, Bucharest. She is a member of the "Communication & Health Literacy" working group, European Code Against Cancer, and a member of EDMO and of EDMO's task force on the war in Ukraine. She was a Marcin Król Fellow at Visegrad Insight and a visiting fellow at Minda de Gunzburg Center for European Studies at Harvard University. She is a media commentator and columnist on topics related to influence operation, anti-Western propaganda, resilience, and the information ecosystem.

Iuliana Călin is a teaching assistant at the College of Communication and Public Relations, National University of Political Studies and Public Administration (SNSPA), Bucharest. She has a PhD in communication sciences with a thesis tackling online disinformation. She is a member of the Center for EU Communication Studies, SNSPA. She has participated in projects meant to build societal resilience against disinformation and regulate the use of AI in the university.

Flavia Durach is an associate professor at the National University for Political Studies and Public Administration, Bucharest, and is Head of Digital Communication and Emerging Media Department. In 2024, she acted as a rapporteur for OID, which aimed to offer policymakers a research-based assessment of the global information and communication space and how it impacts democracy. Her research interests include the study of media effects, with an emphasis on online disinformation, strategic communication, the role of digital platforms, and EU attitudes. She is the author/editor/contributor of volumes published by prestigious publishing houses and the author of numerous scientific articles on the aforementioned topics.

Eva Fialová has experience in the information technology law, especially in the area of algorithms and autonomous systems application and data protection. She is the author of *Contactless Chips and Privacy Protection*, and coauthor of *Profiling and Automated Decision Making (Not Only) in the Light of Human Rights and Fundamental Freedoms* and *Protection of Personality, Privacy and Personal Data*, as well as the author of scientific articles concerning various aspects of modern technologies and the law. Eva Fialová works at the Institute of State and Law of the Academy of Sciences of the Czech Republic.

Ľuboš Greguš is an assistant professor at the Faculty of Mass Media Communication University of SS Cyril and Methodius in Trnava, Slovakia. In his research, he focuses mainly on electronic and traditional media news, with particular emphasis on television and the online environment. He also examines the audience of news content and its needs. His research focuses primarily on specifying the quality of news articles and the ability of recipients to understand and interpret the news. Ľuboš Greguš has been working for three years on the foreign news desk at the Slovak national television broadcaster TA3

Zuzana Jarolímková is a PhD student in media and communication studies at the Faculty of Social Sciences, Charles University. Her research focuses on photojournalism in wartime and how news photography shapes the memory of wars. Outside academia, she is a photojournalist for the national public service broadcaster Czech Radio's news website iROZHLAS.cz.

Victoria Nainová is a researcher and ISCJ Centre for Doctoral Studies coordinator at the Faculty of Social Sciences, Charles University. Her research covers the use of digital media by minorities and children, primarily focusing on integration, digital divide, and social identity. During her studies, she has been a member of research teams of several grant projects in the fields of media studies and journalism supported by the Technology Agency of the Czech Republic and the Primus Research Program of Charles University. She is currently a team member in the ReMeD research project.

Alice Němcová Tejkalová is Head of Journalism Department. She used to be the Dean of the Faculty of Social Sciences at Charles University, the Director of the Institute of Communication Studies and Journalism, a member of the Rector's Collegium, and a TV sports journalist. Her primary interests are in journalism studies (principal investigator of the Czech branch of worldwide research "Worlds of Journalism Study" and regional co-coordinator) and sports journalism. She is an investigator of Horizon Europe grant ReMeD. She is the author of numerous research publications. Her work and projects she participated in were awarded at the national and international levels.

María Fernanda Novoa-Jaso is an Assistant Professor in the Department of Public Communication at the University of Navarra, Spain, where she teaches International Communication, Public Opinion, and Sociology. She has been a visiting fellow at the Reuters Institute for the Study of Journalism and the Institute for Ethics in AI (University of Oxford). Her research is focused on international audiences, journalistic roles, misinformation, and social representations in popular culture.

Jana Radošinská is Vice Dean for Scientific Research and Foreign Relations at the Faculty of Mass Media Communication University of SS Cyril and Methodius in Trnava, Slovakia. She is interested in media culture, globalized film production, mainstream journalism, and specific media industries and entertainment forms. She has published several books on media industries (film, television, music, digital games) and their synergies. Her scholarly expertise also involves superhero films, digital games, and entertainment hybrids presented within globalized cinema, as well as new perspectives of understanding media audiences.

Barbara Ravbar is a PhD candidate at the Faculty of Social Sciences, Charles University, with various research interests such as gender studies, human rights, popular culture, social media, identity, disinformation, and consumer studies. She works as a researcher at the National Institute for Research on Socioeconomic Impacts of Diseases and Systemic Risks, where she studies the effects of COVID-19 on the media environment. She is a member of the International Association for Media and Communication Research, and the European Communication Research and Education Association. Her career prior to academia was in journalism, where she has experience in national, agency, and commercial media. In her journalistic career, she has been awarded a prize for a multimedia project about Syrian refugees (2017) and nominated for the Eighth Annual Award for journalistic work that promotes the values of education (2021).

Ethan Shattock is Lecturer in Law at Queens University, Belfast School of Law. His work broadly covers the links between law, technology, and human rights. He focuses on the regulation of harmful online communications (such as disinformation and hate speech) and the associated legal responsibilities for online platforms to moderate such communications. Ethan Shattock is also interested in the right to freedom of expression and the right to free elections as protected under European human rights law.

Anna Shavit holds a PhD in political science and works as an assistant professor at the Department of Marketing Communication and PR at Charles University, Prague. Her research areas are political marketing (focusing on relations to political parties, citizen participation, and democratic process), government communication (covering mainly the Czech environment), and election campaigns (professionalization of campaigns, role of political consultants, etc.). She also works as a campaign strategist and has extensive experience with many campaigns in the Czech Republic and Slovakia. She is currently a team member in the ReMeD research project.

Barbora Součková is a PhD student in media and communication studies at the Faculty of Social Sciences, Charles University, with main research interests in visual studies, war photojournalism, and gender studies. Her academic experience includes participation in Worlds of Journalism Study. Besides that, she works as a journalist and presenter for the public service Czech Radio's channel Radio Wave.

Nicole Stremlau is Head of Comparative Media Law and Policy program at the University of Oxford, and a research professor in the humanities at the University of Johannesburg. Her research focuses on media and governance, particularly in areas of conflict and insecurity. Her recent projects examine, among others, the role of new media in political participation and governance and how governments engage citizens and communicate law-making processes. Her research was profiled by the National Endowment for Democracy highlighting ten of the most significant academics who have contributed to empirical understandings of the relationship between media and governance.

Loredana Vladu is Associate Professor and Head of the Communication Department at the College of Communication and Public Relations, National University of Political Studies and Public Administration, Bucharest. She focuses on disinformation studies, having authored key publications and led projects to enhance media literacy and combat disinformation. Her research delves into the communicational aspects of sociopolitical issues, particularly within the EU context. Loredana Vladu coordinates the Center for EU Communication Studies, where she pioneers initiatives to address disinformation permeability and societal resilience during crises. She can be contacted at loredana.vladu@comunicare.ro.

www.ingramcontent.com/pod-product-compliance
Ingram Content Group UK Ltd.
Pitfield, Milton Keynes, MK11 3LW, UK
UKHW020215290926
15470UKWH00001B/201

9 781666 972085